PAID

THE DEFINITIVE PICTORIAL CHRONICLE OF
WORLD WAR II

Daily Mail

THE DEFINITIVE PICTORIAL CHRONICLE OF

WORLD WAR II

Eric Good • Michael Wilkinson • James Alexander • Duncan Hill

Research Alice Hill

Trans
Atlantic
Press

This edition published by Transatlantic Press in 2011

Transatlantic Press
38 Copthorne Road
Croxley Green
WD3 4 AQ
United Kingdom

A catalogue record for this book is available
from the British Library.

ISBN: 978-1-907176-20-3
Printed in China

Contents

Introduction

A mere 20 years after the Treaty of Versailles had, supposedly, drawn a line under 'the war to end all wars', the world was consumed by an even bloodier global conflagration. The 1919 treaty imposed swingeing terms on vanquished Germany, leaving it emasculated and humiliated; a nation seething with discontent, an economy crippled by hyper-inflation. Adolf Hitler, an Iron Cross-winning soldier in the 1914-18 conflict, was among the embittered. He blamed the Jews for all ills, and brought his warped views on racial purity into the political mainstream when his Nazi Party gained power in 1933.

Hitler dreamed of a glorious, 1000-year Reich. Territorial gains in Austria and Czechoslovakia were never going to sate his militaristic desires, a forlorn hope Britain and France still cleaved to at the beginning of 1939. Winston Churchill, then on the political sidelines, was one of the few siren voices warning of the Nazi threat. When Germany turned its expansionist gaze on Poland on 1 September 1939, war was inevitable. A vindicated Churchill emerged from his 'wilderness years' to head the Coalition Government. His stirring speeches helped boost morale, even as the German Army cut a swathe across Western Europe, with Britain the final prize. The situation became even more perilous as Mussolini's Italy weighed in on the Axis side just as the Battle of Britain was about to begin in the summer of 1940.

America played a pivotal role. Its Lend-Lease arrangement kept the Allies well supplied; in the Atlantic Charter Churchill and US President Franklin Roosevelt expressed their shared principles and goals, which could only be implemented 'after the final destruction of the Nazi tyranny'; Roosevelt fully backed the Manhattan Project, America's atomic weapons programme; and following the attack on Pearl Harbor in December 1941, the Axis now had to contend with the mighty US military machine.

The Allies prevailed, and the 'broad, sunlit uplands' of victory and freedom became a reality after six years of bloodshed. The battle was won first in Europe, when the full horrors of the Nazi death camps were revealed; then in Japan, after President Truman sanctioned the use of the atomic bomb on Hiroshima and Nagasaki. The obliteration of those cities helped make this the first war to claim more civilian than servicemen's lives, over 50 million fatalities in total.

The Definitive Pictorial Chronicle of World War II uses contemporaneous reports and photographs from the *Daily Mail* archives, including many eyewitness accounts, to show how the conflict developed, describing the key battles, tactical decisions and turning points that settled the outcome.

THE DEFINITIVE PICTORIAL CHRONICLE OF

WORLD WAR II

Chapter One

The Road to War

During the 1930s it was becoming increasingly obvious that the League of Nations was effectively toothless, unable to enforce its authority when challenged by a powerful state. The first challenge had come in the Far East rather than in Europe. Japan, a country which had been closed to outsiders and virtually unknown until 1853, was undergoing an extraordinary industrial transformation. The country's population was increasing, however, and it had limited natural resources. The Japanese elite were casting envious eyes on China, the country's near neighbour, where there was enormous potential, both in terms of untapped natural wealth and sheer space. Japan attacked and conquered the northern Chinese province of Manchuria, renaming it Manchukuo, in 1931. This was exactly the kind of situation which had been anticipated when the League of Nations had been established, and China appealed to the League, which stated that Japan was the aggressor – but that was all it did; there was no further action.

This response did not escape the attention of other ambitious states. Four years later, Benito Mussolini, the Fascist dictator of Italy, had become intent on reviving the imperial past of Ancient Rome. He attacked the African kingdom of Abyssinia (now Ethiopia). The Abyssinians were helpless against the machinery of modern warfare – heavy artillery, poison gas and air power were all used by the Italians – and again, the League did nothing to prevent any of it. Italy annexed Abyssinia with impunity.

The next test for the League, which further exposed its lack of resolve, was the harrowing civil war in Spain. General Franco and his army attacked the Republican government, and was fully supported by both Hitler and Mussolini in doing so. Britain and France refused to become involved, though many international volunteers flocked to Spain to aid the Republicans. There were many appalling incidents, but one of the most ominous was the total destruction of the town of Guernica by German bombers in 1937. Many people later saw this as a precursor, a rehearsal for the air raids which were to become so significant a few years later. Franco captured Madrid in 1939, becoming the dictator of yet another right-wing one-party European state. The Spanish Civil War did not just demonstrate the impotence of the League of Nations and the lack of unity among the democratic states, however; it also gave the aggressive Fascist states a common cause around which to unite. Hitler and Mussolini signed a treaty early in November 1936 which became known as the Rome–Berlin Axis. Japan signed a similar treaty of co-operation with Germany later the very same month.

The Treaty of Versailles, the controversial peace settlement drawn up at the end of the First World War, imposed certain conditions on Germany. Hitler had already defied its terms in 1934, when he started to rearm the country, but his increasing demands from 1936 onwards were an even more obvious contravention of its terms. He reoccupied the Rhineland, which had been established as a demilitarised zone, in blatant defiance of the Treaty. He seemed to have been testing the other European countries, and the League of Nations too (though that was hardly necessary). The German officers who were involved carried sealed orders which they were supposed to open if they met any resistance – and these orders instructed them to withdraw should that happen. This may have been the final point at which Hitler could have been stopped without actual war breaking out. Yet again, however, there was no firm response from the League and Hitler, emboldened by the inactivity, began to build a line of fortifications along the French and Belgian borders.

Austria was the next country to attract his attention. The Treaty of Versailles had decreed that Austria and Germany should never be united. Austria was, however, in chaos – much of it caused by Austrian Nazis – and Hitler used this as a pretext for sending the German army into the country. They marched into Vienna and Austria became part of the Third Reich on 13 March, 1938. Hitler, an Austrian himself, returned in triumph to the capital where he had lived in poverty before the First World War.

Czechoslovakia was a democratic country which had been created by the Versailles Treaty and it, too, attracted Hitler's attention. Some three million Germans lived in Czechoslovakia, mainly in the Sudetenland, and Hitler insisted that the region should, accordingly, be absorbed into the Reich.

The rise of Hitler

The end of the First World War had not really brought about any improvement in the level of tension between nations; it had simply changed the nature of the grievances and added some new ones. After the war, hopes for future peace in the world had been enshrined in the League of Nations, created to provide for a policy of 'Collective Security', but there were some doubts about how effective it would be, doubts which were to be fully vindicated.

Adolf Hitler had first come to public attention in 1923 when he made an unconstitutional attempt to seize power in Bavaria, known as the 'Munich Putsch'. It failed and he was sent to prison for nine months as a consequence. While imprisoned, he used the time to write *Mein Kampf* (My Struggle), which became his political programme. He claimed that Germany had not really been defeated as such in 1918, and that both the apparent defeat and the post-war settlement had been a betrayal, for which he blamed the Jews. One of the consequences of the Munich Putsch was that Hitler was now determined to seek power by legitimate means, as far as that was possible. Following his release in 1924, he reorganized his political party, creating what was in effect a private army. This paramilitary organization was known as the SA (Sturmabteilung), and by 1927 there were over 30,000 people in it. They were the 'Brownshirts', who intimidated their opponents and instigated violent conflicts with both Communists and Jews. In the meantime, the economic situation went from bad to worse.

Above: Nazi supporters line the streets of Weimar during Hitler's visit to the town in July 1936.

Left: Crowds fawn upon Hitler as he attends the May 1934 Labour Day celebrations in Berlin's Lustgarten.

Below left: A group of German officers wearing full military uniform.

Opposite above: Upon becoming Chancellor, Hitler set about consolidating his power. He had his closest rivals murdered on the 'Night of the Long Knives' in July 1934.

Opposite middle: German troops in Berlin swear an oath of allegiance to Adolf Hitler.

Opposite below: Hitler addresses a crowd of Hitler Youth at the annual Nazi Party Congress in Nuremberg.

The Great Depression

In October 1929, a contagious outbreak of panic selling on the New York Stock Exchange – which had previously been booming – resulted in the Wall Street Crash. This financial disaster wiped millions of dollars off the value of shares and reverberated on the global economy as a whole, ushering in the Great Depression. The economic collapse had an enormous impact throughout Europe, but was most severe in Germany, where the government was completely dependent on American finance. The value of the mark fell swiftly and catastrophically, unemployment soared and, not surprisingly, discontent spread. In this atmosphere the more moderate and democratic political parties were unable to provide any solutions to the problems besetting the nation. People began to turn to the extreme parties of the right and left in increasing numbers, and unrest and violent street fighting became more common.

Above: **Chancellor Hitler (right), as commander-in-chief of the German Army, watched the manoeuvres of the Sixth Army Corps near Munster in September 1935. He was accompanied by General von Blomberg, the German War Minister (left), and Artillery-General Baron von Fritsch (back to camera).**

Left: **Hitler poses for a photograph with a Polish delegation led by Poland's Foreign Minister, Colonel Joseph Beck. One of Hitler's first foreign policy achievements as Chancellor was to conclude a Non-Aggression Pact with neighbouring Poland.**

Below left: **German soldiers marching at a military parade in Berlin in 1935.**

Opposite above: **In June 1935 Hitler was among the mourners at the funeral of 60 victims of the explosion in the munitions factory at Reinsdorf, near Wittenberg. After the service he personally expressed his sympathy with the relatives of the victims. He was accompanied by General Goering, Dr. Goebbels and other Nazi chiefs.**

Opposite below: **Hitler shakes the hand of one of 'Hitler's Maids', the women's branch of the Labour Service, who were included in the great parade of nearly 40,000 Labour Service men before the Chancellor on the Zeppelin Meadow at Nuremberg, where the Nazi Party Congress was in progress. Five hundred of the young women joined in the choral singing and took part in the neo-pagan 'Hour of Dedication'.**

Nazi popularity grows

There were only 12 National Socialist members in the Reichstag, the German parliament, by the start of 1930. However, as the Great Depression set in, support for the Nazis skyrocketed. They won 107 seats in the elections of autumn 1930, becoming the second-strongest political party in the Reichstag. Hitler stood for the presidency of Germany in 1932 and won more than 13 million votes, placing him a close second behind Paul von Hindenburg, the great general of the First World War. Parliamentary elections that year saw the Nazis becoming the largest single party in the Reichstag.

Alarmed at the rapid rise of Hitler and his party, a group of Conservative politicians persuaded President Hindenburg to appoint Hitler as Chancellor. They hoped that they could control Hitler by bringing him into the establishment and separating him from his party.

The Führer

However, the Nazis continued to expand their influence. Chancellor Hitler blamed the Communists for an arson attack on the Reichstag building in February 1933. This certainly boosted support for the Nazi party in the March 1933 elections, and allowed them to achieve an overall majority in parliament.

Hitler used his small majority to pass a law giving him power as Chancellor to govern without the consent of the Reichstag. President Hindenburg died in August 1934 and Hitler seized the opportunity to combine the two offices of the Chancellor and the President in one new role. He was now in control of the armed forces and called himself by the title 'Führer', the leader of all the German people. All German servicemen had to swear an oath of personal loyalty to him.

Appeasement

While he consolidated his power inside Germany, Hitler moved cautiously in his foreign policy. He signed a non-aggression pact with Poland and agreed to negotiate with European powers over disarmament. However, from 1934 he secretly began rearming Germany so that it would become strong enough to achieve his main foreign policy goal: the reversal of the Treaty of Versailles.

As the 1930s progressed, the German military grew stronger and the international situation became ever more favourable. The failure of the League of Nations to tackle both Japanese aggression in Manchuria in 1931 and Italian aggression in Abyssinia in 1935 made it obvious that the organization would not seriously challenge Hitler's attempts to reverse the Treaty of Versailles. The ineffectiveness of the League revealed that the Great Powers were distracted and indifferent. The United States, Britain and France were still grappling with the Great Depression and Stalin was busy purging and collectivizing in the Soviet Union.

Above: Hitler salutes the thousands of German singers from inside and outside the Reich's borders as they marched past when the song festivals at Breslau were closed on August 1, 1937.

Left: Chancellor Hitler (centre) and members of the Reichstag giving the Nazi salute beneath the Nazi eagle as the National hymn is played. Next to him (left) are Herr Rudolf Hess, Hitler's Deputy, and Baron von Neurath, the German Foreign Minister. A repeated demand for the return of Germany's colonies, a pledge of safety for France and Belgium and the scrapping of two more clauses of the mutilated Versailles Treaty were the main points of Chancellor Hitler's anxiously awaited speech to the Reichstag in the Kroll Opera House, Berlin, in January 1937, the fourth anniversary of the Nazi regime. A considerable portion of his words were devoted to answering Anthony Eden's recent speech in which he appealed to Germany. Immediately afterwards the Reichstag gave the Chancellor full powers for another four years.

Reoccupying the Rhine

In 1936, Hitler decided to test the waters and send troops into the Rhineland, which had been established as a demilitarized zone under the terms of the treaty. His officers had been instructed to withdraw should they encounter any resistance. However, there was no response from the Great Powers, and an emboldened Hitler began building a line of fortifications along the French and Belgian borders.

Austria was the next country to attract his attention. The Treaty of Versailles had decreed that Austria and Germany should never be united. Austria was, however, in chaos – much of it caused by Austrian Nazis – and Hitler used this as a pretext for sending the German army into the country. On March 13, 1938, his troops marched into Vienna and Austria was integrated into the Reich. Hitler, himself an Austrian, returned in triumph to the capital where he had lived in poverty before the First World War.

Next on Hitler's agenda was Czechoslovakia, a democratic country that had been created by the Versailles Treaty. Some three million Germans lived in Czechoslovakia, mainly in a region along the German border called the Sudetenland. Hitler insisted that this region should be absorbed into the Reich.

Above: **The Chancellor receives M. François-Poncet, French Ambassador to Germany along with ambassadors from several other countries at the Deutschen Hotel, Nuremberg on German Party Day in September 1937.**

Right: **Hitler and Chamberlain meet at Bad Godesberg in Germany on September 23, 1938, where Hitler detailed his demands for the Sudetenland. Chamberlain spent the week convincing the Czechoslovak government to agree the terms before signing the Agreement with Hitler in Munich a week later.**

Far right: **Neville Chamberlain returns home waving a 'piece of paper' signed by Hitler promising a peaceful resolution to European disputes in future. Chamberlain declared that he had returned bringing 'peace with honour, peace for our time.'**

The Munich Agreement

These demands caused concern in London, but Britain was in no position to challenge Germany in Central Europe. The British military was greatly overstretched across the vast Empire and the public had no appetite for a new European conflict. Instead, the British Prime Minister, Neville Chamberlain went to Germany to negotiate with Hitler. At their meeting in Munich on September 29, 1938, Hitler and Chamberlain agreed that the Sudetenland should join Germany, but that this would be Hitler's last territorial demand in Europe. Chamberlain returned, claiming he had secured 'peace for our time', but his critics labelled this as 'appeasement'.

In March 1939, under the pretext of unrest in Slovakia, Germany occupied the rest of Czechoslovakia. The Munich Agreement was in tatters and the British public were outraged. Hitherto, many people had believed that Hitler's demands had been reasonable, but overt aggression in Czechoslovakia was a step too far, and the public called for firm action. In response, the British government issued guarantees to protect Poland, Romania and Greece against German aggression.

Right: American President Franklin Delano Roosevelt pictured in his home in Hyde Park, New York in 1938. The United States stayed out of European disputes while it tried to rebuild its battered economy in the 1930s.

Middle right: Joseph Stalin, leader of the Soviet Union, pictured at a conference in January 1938. In the late 1930s, Stalin was preoccupied with industrial development, agricultural collectivization and purging Russian society of 'saboteurs'.

Below: Hitler's position was further strengthened in May 1939 when he signed an alliance, 'The Pact of Steel' with Mussolini.

Opposite above: Hitler salutes as he walks through a sea of flowers in the Sudetenland, October 3, 1938.

Opposite below left: Hitler congratulates his Foreign Minister, Joachim von Ribbentrop, upon his return from signing the Nazi-Soviet Pact in Moscow.

Opposite below right: Hitler follows his army into Linz, Austria to oversee the 'Anschluss', the Union of Austria and Germany, in March 1938.

Occupation of Czechoslovakia

Hitler's plans to make Germany the ruling power of Europe started with pulling in the ethnic German peoples that lived in the nearby states of Austria, Bohemia, Moravia and Czechoslovakia; with the people came their territory. After moving first on Austria in March 1938, Hitler's ultimatum regarding the other Sudeten territories led to their annexation under the Munich Agreement negotiated with Britain and France in September 1938.

In March 1939, events reached their inevitable conclusion: however willing and able to resist Nazi aggression, Czechoslovakia would not go to war without support from Britain and France who maintained their course of appeasement. Hitler forced a bloodless surrender by Czechoslovakia and brought some of its territories under control as German Protectorates. The rest of the country was gradually broken up, with Hungary and Poland both acquiring territory. As with all his treaties and agreements, Munich was a device to buy time and to allay the suspicions of his opponents.

Although the break-up of Czechoslovakia was achieved by political means, a government in exile was formed and many Czechs fled to serve with Allied forces; an active resistance was maintained through the war, notably assassinating Reinard Heydrich, Himmler's deputy and at the time the Protector of Bohemia and Moravia.

Below right: **A local girl in the newly-freed Sudeten areas fraternises with German soldiers after troops occupied the No.2 zone of the Czech Sudetenland in October 1938, in accordance with the recently agreed Four Power Pact.**

Below: **The inhabitants give a hearty welcome to German troops at Kleinphilipsreuth.**

APRIL 1, 1939

British pledge to Poland is without reserve

The pledge: ... In the event of any action which clearly threatened Polish independence, and which the Polish Government accordingly considered it vital to resist with their national forces, His Majesty's Government would feel themselves bound at once to lend the Polish Government all support in their power. - The Premier in the House yesterday.

Britain has offered Poland a mutual anti-aggression pact to which other Powers will be invited to subscribe. It is hoped that Col. Beck, Polish Foreign Minister, will sign it when he comes to London next week. The pledge given by the Prime Minister in the House of Commons yesterday to support Poland if she is attacked was purely to cover an interim period following rumours - which have not been confirmed - of German troop movements.

Apparently the Cabinet thought that the situation in Eastern Europe was sufficiently urgent to justify a unilateral declaration by the British Government. Ministers were also becoming acutely aware of the necessity to give the country some idea of their intentions.

The pledge given by the Prime Minister goes far beyond any commitment entered into by Britain since the end of the Great War. It is meant to form the basis of a strong anti-aggression front, by which it is hoped to preserve peace.

The Prime Minister's pledge to Poland is without reservation. Contrary to assertions made in London yesterday, there are no British conditions regarding Danzig or the Polish Corridor.

Above: Crestfallen men and women watched the Germans troops enter Prague on March 17, 1939.

Left: An elderly lady in Friedland presented German soldiers with flowers after General Von Book's troops crossed the Czech frontier at Rumburg and Friedland.

Britain prepares

In response to the threat from Germany, Britain began to speed up programmes of rearmament and civil defence. By late March the British government had come to believe that Hitler's next claims would be made against Poland, and promised to protect Poland from German aggression. In actual fact there was no way in which Britain could really help Poland, but the government did think that fear of Russia would contain German ambitions, a belief which was widely held. It was also a completely incorrect belief, which was revealed in September 1939.

Right, below left, below right: Major General Sir John Brown, Deputy Director-General of the Territorial Army and Lady Londonderry, chairman of the Women's Legion Mechanical Transport Service, and delegates from the Women's Emergency Service and the V.A.D. Council met at the War Office in May 1938. Their aim was to plan the creation of a women's section of the Territorial Army to undertake certain kinds of work, which would release men for more active military duties.

Conscription to-day

Compulsory military service affecting the majority of Britain's men under 25 will be announced in the House of Commons by the Prime Minister this afternoon. Precise details of the scheme envisaged by the Government will be approved by the Cabinet this morning, together with a long statement in which Mr. Chamberlain will explain this historic decision to the nation. In this statement the Premier will indicate plans for a compulsory national register affecting all classes. The Prime Minister will lay particular stress on the fact that the developments in the international situation have made this departure from the voluntary system a vital necessity.

The general opinion in the lobbies of the House of Commons last night was that the compulsory scheme will, in the first instance, apply to all men between the ages of 18 and 25. It is estimated that in this case at least 750,000 men will be affected immediately the necessary Bill has been passed. The Bill will probably be presented early next week.

The Nazi-Soviet Pact

The British government began preparing for a war during 1939 by speeding up programmes of rearmament and civil defence. However, the government's inherent anti-Communism meant that it was slow to develop ties with the Soviet Union, which was vital if Germany was to be threatened with a two-front war. Given the violent ideological differences between the Soviet Union and the Nazis, the British believed that Stalin would inevitably support a war against Hitler and did very little to strengthen relations. The announcement on August 23 that Germany and the Soviet Union had signed a non-aggression pact came as a complete surprise to London. The pact was expedient; Hitler avoided a two-front war and Stalin avoided a war he was not yet ready to fight. A secret clause of the pact also promised Stalin a free hand in the Baltic states and in eastern Poland. On September 1, 1939, with his Eastern Front secure, Hitler risked war in the West by invading Poland.

Above: **Grouped around President Roosevelt in the historic East Room at the White House, Washington, are the plenipotentiaries and other Canadian and British officials who signed the Reciprocal Trade Agreements between Great Britain, Canada and the United States on November 11, 1938.**
L to r in front: A.E. Overton, Second Permanent Secretary of the British Board of Trade; Sir Ronald Lindsay, British Ambassador to the United States; President Roosevelt; MacKenzie King, Premier of Canada; and Secretary of State Mr. Cordell Hull.
L to r standing: Mr. Francis S. Sayre of the United States State Department; Dr. O.D. Skelton, Canada's Under Secretary of State; Charles Barnes of the Trade Agreement Division of the United States State Department; and Sir Herbert Marler, Canadian Minister.

Below right: **Neville Chamberlain, the Prime Minister, walking with Sir Horace Wilson, Chief Industrial Advisor to the Government in St. James's Park on August 31, 1939, just before they went to the House of Commons for the debate on the international situation.**

Below: **Even before war was declared, the evacuation of children and vulnerable adults had begun. These mothers are locked behind the platform gates at Waterloo Station, waving tearful farewells to their children boarding trains to safe areas.**

German invasion of Poland

In the early hours of September 1, 1939, German troops crossed the border into Polish territory, triggering the largest war the world has ever seen. The Polish army, consisting mainly of cavalry divisions, was no match for the modern, mechanized German army. The Luftwaffe quickly won air superiority over the smaller Polish air force and began pummelling Polish cities. As Poland met its fate, frantic debates ensued in London and Paris over how to respond. By evening, the decision was made to issue an ultimatum demanding that Hitler withdraw promptly from Poland or face war.

The British and French Ambassadors handed the text of their ultimatums to the German foreign minister, Ribbentrop, who agreed to pass them on to Hitler. The British and French ultimatums expired at 11 a.m. and 5 p.m. on Sunday September 3 respectively. Neither country heard back from Hitler and consequently a state of war ensued.

Above: Hitler observes the destruction of Warsaw from a hill overlooking the city.

Below: Hitler addresses the Reichstag in the Kroll Opera House on the day of the invasion of Poland. In the speech he blamed Poland for starting the war by firing upon German territory that morning. He warned that 'whoever departs from the rules of humane warfare can only expect that we shall do the same'.

Left: Polish troops wait for the Germans to arrive in Warsaw after the city's capitulation.

Below left: Poles march through Warsaw on their way to dig trenches for the defence of the city.

Below right: Polish POWs line up for food in German prison camps.

Stalin invades Poland

The Polish commander, Marshal Smigly-Rydz, hoped in vain that Polish defences could hold out until Britain and France attacked in the west. However, his men were sitting ducks for Germany's 'Stuka' dive-bombers, and Polish cavalrymen were gunned down with ease as they futilely tried to take on German tank units.

On September 17, Stalin moved his troops into eastern Poland to fulfil the secret clause of the Nazi-Soviet Pact. He disguised his land grab as a mission to liberate Ukrainians and White Russians from Polish domination. The Red Army encountered little resistance from the Poles who were completely tied up on the Western Front. On September 28, Ribbentrop met with his Soviet counterpart Vyacheslav Molotov to sign the German-Soviet Boundary and Friendship Treaty, which officially carved the spoils of Poland between them. There was some resentment among Germans that the Soviets were to be handed territory that had been won by the Wehrmacht, especially as Stalin waited more than two weeks before declaring war.

Above left: A German cavalry detachment advancing in Poland on September 3, 1939.

Middle left: The *Daily Mail* front page on September 6, 1939.

Below left: Hitler, accompanied by the designer Dr. Forsche, was at the car factory in Fallensleben in May 1938, which had been designed to turn out six million 'people's cars' at £79 each. Hitler told his audience at the foundation stone ceremony that the car could be bought on an instalment plan for between nine and ten shillings per week.

The fall of Warsaw

The Polish capital, Warsaw, held out for several weeks against the Wehrmacht, which feared that street fighting would be too costly. Instead, the German army besieged the city and then bombed it into submission. The devastating attacks resulted in thousands of civilian deaths and the destruction of the city. The troops defending Warsaw surrendered on September 27 in order to relieve the suffering of the city's civilian population, but the German occupation that followed was to make their lives much worse. Politicians, academics, soldiers and ordinary civilians were massacred as the Nazis immediately set about destroying any potential opposition. The Germans began to ethnically cleanse Poland by expelling the 'subhuman' Poles from their homes and sending German families to replace them. Exceptions were made for those who were deemed sufficiently Aryan and agreed to be 'Germanized'.

Polish Jews were singled out for the harshest treatment; they were subjected to barbaric attacks and forced to move to ghettos, cut off from the outside world. However, this was only to be a temporary arrangement, and Poland's Jewish population was to suffer even further when the Nazis decided upon their 'Final Solution'.

Above left: **Polish soldiers captured by German troops being escorted through a town in Polish Silesia in September 1939.**

Left: On September 28, 1939, Russian and German officers met at Bialystock to discuss the demarcation of Poland.

Below left: **Polish refugees stream out of Warsaw to escape the relentless bombardment.**

War declared

As dawn broke on September 1, 1939, the German Luftwaffe began to strike strategic targets within Poland, with Stuka dive-bombers instilling terror in the civilian population and wiping out the Polish air force in a matter of hours. Simultaneously, nine armoured Panzer Divisions poured across the frontier. Britain's first reaction was to suggest a conference with Germany, but then presented an ultimatum when this was met with no response. This expired at 11a.m on September 3 and 15 minutes later Britain declared war with Germany, closely supported by France, Australia and New Zealand.

Left: On September 2, people gathered in the streets around the Houses of Parliament to hear news of Prime Minister Chamberlain's speech to the Commons in which he was expected to deliver an ultimatum to Germany to withdraw from Polish territory. When he failed to do so the derision from MPs forced the Cabinet into late-night talks, from which emerged a resolve to demand the withdrawal at 9.00 a.m. the following day, with an 11.00 a.m. deadline for compliance.

Above and below: The Town Clerk reads a Royal Proclamation from the steps of the Mansion House, calling on all men up to the age of 36 to register for military service. The call up for men was already well underway by the time Britain declared war on Germany.

War 11am., September 3, 1939

Great Britain and France are at war with Germany. We now fight against the blackest tyranny that has ever held men in bondage. We fight to defend, and to restore, freedom and justice on earth.

Let us face the truth. This was inevitable whether it began with Austria, Sudetenland, Bohemia, or Danzig. If it had not come over Danzig it would have come later upon some other issue. It became inevitable from the day Hitler seized power in Germany and began his criminal career by enslaving his own people. For his one aim since then has been gradually to enslave all others by the methods of brute force.

Once more Britain, her Empire and her friends are engaged in a conflict to uphold Right against Might.

If the democracies had flinched now, they would have been compelled to abdicate for ever their title to be called the champions of liberty. The fate of these small nations who have already lost their rights would have been theirs in turn.

This was the dominant thought in the inspiring message broadcast by the King to his people last night. We go to war because we must. In His Majesty's words: 'For the sake of all that we ourselves hold dear, and of the world's order and peace, it is unthinkable that we should refuse to meet the challenge.'

Above left: Crowds read the new warning orders posted outside the Paris Town Halls on September 2, 1939.

Above middle: The *Daily Mail* front page the day after war was declared.

Below left: Many German and Czech refugees were among the crowds that gathered at Downing Street to hear the inevitable announcement as Prime Minister Neville Chamberlain declared, 'This country is at war with Germany'.

Right: Part of a newspaper page from Sunday September 3, 1939.

'Phoney War'

For the first few months, there seemed to be little change. In Britain, rationing began. A night-time blackout was introduced and children were evacuated from cities to the country – both measures designed to protect the country from German air raids, which were not to happen for another nine months. There were, however, some raids on shipping by German submarines. A large French army and a much smaller British Expeditionary Force maintained defensive positions in Northern France, preparing for the possibility of invasion. However, as the months passed, it seemed increasingly unlikely that Hitler would strike in western Europe, and talk of a 'phoney war' spread. Further to the east, though, the situation was different. During the period of the phoney war in the west, bitter fighting continued in Poland, Lithuania, Latvia and Estonia.

Left: The trellis-work of tape on this shop window was designed to minimise flying glass in the event of a nearby explosion.

Below left: The British public were quick to support the government's declaration of war against the Nazi regime, and signs such as this one became commonplace.

Below right: Americans holidaying or living in Britain gather at the United States Lines in Haymarket on September 4, to book their passage home.

Above: As it became clear that war was a likely consequence of Germany's refusal to withdraw from Poland, people gathered at Downing Street. Here police hold back the crowd on the morning of September 3.

Below left: Soon after the declaration of war an air-raid warning sounded and people rushed for shelter.

Below right: On the same day that the Americans started leaving, the German Embassy in Carlton Terrace moved out.

Top: Signposts and street names were removed across Britain in case they assisted invading German troops.

Middle: Bacon, butter and sugar were the first products to be rationed, quickly followed by other foodstuffs and household goods. More than once during the war, attacks on merchant shipping would bring Britain dangerously close to running out of essential supplies.

Below left: Treasures from the National Gallery were evacuated to a disused slate mine in North Wales.

Below right: In the early weeks of the war this garage proprietor ensured the petrol supplies were safe from the bombing with a liberal stacking of sandbags.

Left: One of the first steps taken when war was declared was to fill and surround your house with sandbags, in the event of attack.

Middle: Part of the preparations for the impending air raids on London involved the protection of various statues and other monuments. Eros in Piccadilly Circus was boarded up, having been first surrounded by sandbags.

Below: Troops marching into Piccadilly Circus, London, in 1939. Little funds had been made available for the military during the 1920s and 1930s and rearmament and civil defence programmes had to be rapidly stepped up after the Sudetenland crisis in 1938.

Hitler's threat

In Britain, measures were put into effect to combat the expected onslaught from the sky: gas masks were issued, people dug shelters in their gardens and blacked out light from their homes. Places of public entertainment were closed, large gatherings were outlawed and rationing began early in 1940. As a harsh winter progressed, though, people began to wonder if such hardships were necessary and whether Hitler's ambitions might not be confined to Eastern Europe. However, an awareness remained that the rapid fall of Poland meant that German troops could be quickly redeployed for an attack in the west.

Above right: Iron railings were removed from many public places such as parks, gardens and squares in order to be resmelted for use in munitions, and private owners were encouraged to do the same. There were some objections, notably from several Lords, and usually in defence of 'historically important' railings. Some were preserved, but most of London's parks and squares were stripped of theirs, and it was a similar story in many cities across Britain. These railings are being removed in Manchester.

Below left: The civilian war effort was stepped up, with increased productivity in all kinds of industries. Non-essential goods and services were reduced whilst recycling of various materials, particularly paper and metal, to be used mainly in the manufacture of munitions was increased. Here, a pair of Boy Scouts collect waste paper.

Below right: Children in Croydon are encouraged to help in the recycling effort, receiving donkey rides in return for collecting paper.

Compulsory gas masks

Gas masks were designed to protect the public in the event of a poison attack and it was actually an offence not to carry one. Babies were issued with complete suits and Mickey Mouse designs were provided for children. Mussolini had used chemical weapons when he attacked Ethiopia in 1935 so everyone's fears were fully justified. Leaflets advised the public how to recognize the signs of gas by the smell of pear drops, geraniums or musty hay and the tops of pillar-boxes had been painted with a special paint that changed colour if exposed to gas. Wardens used hand rattles to alert everyone in the event of a gas attack.

Top: A young couple walk hand in hand down a London street in the first month of the war.

Above and above left: Some 38 million gas masks had been issued in the lead up to war, and came in a variety of sizes and styles to ensure that everyone could be protected in the event of a poison gas attack.

Left: In the early days of the 'Phoney War' people were very lax about carrying them and many ended up at lost property offices such as this one in Baker Street.

Braced for attack

Whilst Poland was still under attack, British troops began to land in France, but the Allies were unable to mobilise quickly and efficiently enough to be able to prevent the fall of Poland and were expecting instead to fight a defensive campaign. There was little activity in the west as the Germans remained behind their Siegfried Line and the French watched from the Maginot Line, with most of the British forces being concentrated on the Belgian border. Meanwhile, at home, Britain braced herself against a possible attack on the mainland.

Above right: A view of the Houses of Parliament seen through barbed-wire defences.

Right: Shop displays continued to be lit at night, but they were noticeably dimmer

Below left: Troopers from the London Irish Regiment at training with rifles and fixed bayonets in October 1940. Despite the failure of Hitler's invasions plans for September, there remained the fear of an enemy landing.

Below right: A shop in Manchester after taping up its windows was in the process of constructing an air raid shelter.

Left: The statue of King Charles I, just across from Trafalgar Square is given full protection as the lions quietly stand guard.

Below right: Sandbags being filled in Hampstead. They were used to protect buildings across the country.

Below left: Concrete obstructions such as these were positioned in some open areas to prevent the landing of enemy aircraft.

Evacuating the cities

As the most likely targets of German bombing raids, London and other major British industrial cities began to see the mass evacuation of schoolchildren to rural areas from September 1939. For many children it would be the first time they had been separated from their families, and would certainly be the first time that most would spend Christmas in unfamiliar surroundings.

Above: A group of young children sheltering during an air raid at a school on the south coast; teachers used songs and comics to entertain them.

Above right: Carrying their gas masks in cases and wearing luggage labels to help identify them, this group of children from the Hugh Myddelton School in Clerkenwell were part of the first wave of evacuees who left London on the day Hitler invaded Poland, 1st September, 1939.

Below right: Children at Maryville Road School in Leyton escorted down to the school air raid shelter for safety. Initially, the new start of term had been delayed by many weeks, as schools could not reopen until they had their own air raid shelter. Schools were only allowed to teach the number of children for which the shelter could provide safety, often resulting in a part-time shift system with many limited to half a day's schooling.

Seeking safety

In the first weeks of the war nearly four million people moved from evacuation to reception areas. These included pregnant women, mothers of pre-school children and disabled people, as well as school-age children. Throughout the war, evacuation schemes continued, with peak numbers related directly to the severity of the bombing. After the 'phoney war' of the first year, many children returned home, only to be re-evacuated when the Blitz began. Even before then, some children, evacuated to the south coast of England, had to be relocated when the area suffered attacks during the summer of 1940.

School-age children were evacuated without their parents. They were required to report to their school with only a change of clothes, basic toilet essentials, a packed lunch and, of course, a gas mask. At the school they were tagged with luggage labels, a precaution against children becoming lost but especially important for the youngest, who may not have known their address. Accompanied by teachers and helpers, the children were taken by buses and trains to the reception areas. Trips were as long as twelve hours; many children arrived exhausted by the journey, upset at leaving their parents and fearful of what life would be like in their new home.

Above right: Initially, those who had been evacuated to coastal areas were able to enjoy their freedom playing on the beaches but this luxury was limited as gradually coastlines were covered in barbed wire to protect the public from mines.

Middle right: A group of British children wave goodbye to their families as they wait to board a train.

Below right: Even prior to the declaration of war, children began to be evacuated from areas most at risk of bombing. Schoolchildren such as these in Edgware were ferried by buses to railway stations.

"The children have all behaved marvellously"

The greatest organised movement of a human population in the world's history started yesterday. As if by some quiet smooth-working machine, nearly 1,000,000 children, mothers, blind and maimed people were taken from danger to safety. In three days - perhaps less - 3,000,000 will have made the journey across the invisible frontier. Thousands of households all over Britain yesterday welcomed small strangers who were to be for a time members of the family.

Most homes in the evacuated areas were adapting themselves bravely to a sadder change which had robbed them of their children. London has lost much of its laughter. Nearly half of the 3,000,000 are being evacuated from the Greater London area. The rest are from the naval and shipping areas and the industrial districts of the Midlands, North, and Scotland.

Everywhere the task of moving this enormous number of children was carried out with great ease, owing to the thorough preparation and the co-operation of officials, parents, and children. And officials everywhere said "the children behaved simply marvellously."

Town meets country

Evacuation was the major impact of the war on many children's lives. Often the clash of cultures between children from the city and their hosts in the countryside was a source of problems for all concerned. Children from the poorest areas in the major cities frequently lived in deprived conditions, often without access to running water. Consequently, they were often unwashed and prone to minor infections such as scabies and impetigo. While this shocked many host families, most were understanding and worked hard to accept the evacuees into their homes. Sometimes the difference in standards was the other way round and children with baths and electric lights at home found themselves staying in farm labourers' cottages without running water or electricity.

Above: Robert Yoghill and William Williams from Islington soon had to learn new skills at Eileen Hocking's family farm in Cornwall. For many children, evacuation meant a completely new culture and way of life. Some children who lived in squalid conditions in inner cities were suddenly exposed to all that the countryside had to offer, while others moved from advantaged homes to remote farms with no running water or electricity. It was obviously an experience that had a huge impact on them and often caused major problems for the children and their host families.

Below left: Two youngsters on their way from London to Devon.

Below right: A young evacuee headed for Yorkshire says goodbye to her mother and baby sister who remain in London.

Opposite: Children greeted by a train driver as they await evacuation.

Recruiting a fighting force

Following the declaration of war there was an immediate need to extend the numbers of men in the armed services. In addition to regular soldiers, members of territorial reserve forces, volunteers and those who were conscripted prepared to be called up to serve as required. A Conscription Bill had been passed in May 1939, and soon afterwards all young men under 21 were registered. The following year, some 30,000 more were signed up.

Above left: Charles Remnant calls for volunteers to join the 'Citizen's Army' at a meeting held on Tooting Bec Common.

Middle left: Soon after the evacuation from Dunkirk, on June 22, 1940, 30,000 men registered for military service at labour exchanges throughout the country.

Below: The first batch of men aged 22, but not yet 23, report at various military centres for training, 15th January, 1940.

Defenders of the home front

Although its appeasement strategy prevailed until Germany's invasion of Poland, Britain had been preparing for possible war. As refugees from Nazi oppression steadily arrived on Britain's shores, the consequences of invasion could be seen immediately in Poland, where resistance failed under German tactics. Churchill proposed the formation of a defence force of 500,000 volunteers not deemed fit for military service but still able to fight. On 14th May 1940, Anthony Eden, Secretary of State for War broadcast to the nation inviting men to sign up for the Local Defence Volunteers. The bland acronym LDV and the problems of training and equipment held back its success. Churchill turned the situation around by renaming it the Home Guard in July. The Battle of Britain and the threatened German invasion made the Home Guard one more demand among many for training and equipment; the return from Dunkirk of thousands of troops minus their weapons made those combatants a priority and the role of the Home Guard was seen as secondary support. However by 1943, even though the threat of invasion had largely subsided, the Home Guard was more of a force to be reckoned with, numbering 1.5m armed and trained, with a plan of defence – from standing look-out for German paratroop attacks, to guerrilla warfare. The Home Guard was stood down in December 1944 finally disbanding in December 1945.

SEPTEMBER 12, 1939

Britain's troops in action on western front - official

British troops have landed in France and are in action alongside the French Army. They have taken part in the advances into German territory. This news was released dramatically at 9.35 p.m. yesterday by the Ministry of Information.

The transport of the B.E.F. has taken several days, and has been carried out successfully without the loss of a single life.

The despatch of the troops was carried out with the greatest secrecy, so as to reduce to a minimum the danger of attack by submarines or aircraft. A tremendous ovation was given by the French populace when the first soldier marched ashore - and the scenes recalled those of 1914. No details of the units or their positions in France can be given.

Above: **Local Defence Volunteers (LDV) on parade.** The LDV was set up as Germany unleashed its blitzkrieg in Europe. In July 1940 the LDV changed its name to the Home Guard, which later became affectionately known as 'Dad's Army'. Many of those who joined up were older but had seen action in the Great War.

Middle: **Local Defence Volunteers march at a parade ground in Balham.** They are weaponless but some have LDV armbands and soldiers' caps.

Below: **The Citizen's Army hold their first parade on Tooting Bec Common,** dressed in civilian clothes and 'armed' with sticks and umbrellas. It was intended as a defence force in the event of a German invasion.

The Altmark Incident

Although both the Allied and German forces were initially reluctant to make an offensive move on land, at sea it was a different story. On September 4, the British liner Athenia was sunk by a German U-boat, and a further ten ships would be lost in the first week of British involvement, prompting Chamberlain to restore Churchill to the post of First Lord of the Admiralty, an office he had held 25 years previously. The German Battleship *Graf Spee* had claimed a number of British vessels in 1939, the prisoners from which were then transported on a supply ship, the Altmark. In early 1940, contravening international law as the Altmark was in neutral Norwegian waters, the ship was intercepted by the British destroyer Cossack, boarded, and the prisoners rescued.

Below left and right: The RAF played its part in the Altmark incident by locating and identifying the ship. These pilots study maps of the area before embarking on reconnaissance missions.

Bottom: Trenches along the Harbour of Schevengue. in Holland in November 1939.

War in Scandinavia

At the end of 1939, the Red Army invaded neutral Finland because the Finnish government had refused to accept Stalin's territorial demands. Helsinki was badly damaged by Soviet bombing raids, but the winter snow came to the aid of the Finns. Finnish soldiers used guerrilla tactics to slow and reverse the Soviet advance during December and January. The Soviets struck back with a major offensive in February, forcing the Finnish government to accept a punitive peace agreement.

On April 9, 1940, Hitler launched simultaneous attacks against major ports in Denmark and Norway. There were some contingents from Britain and its Allies already in Norway, and these were rapidly deployed in defence. But the German command of the air – and a general lack of reinforcements, despite strong naval support – meant that the defenders were quickly forced to withdraw. There was one possible bright spot, though: the Allies had managed to inflict significant losses on the German fleet in the Norwegian campaign.

Graf Spee

The Admiral Graf Spee was one of the most famous German naval warships of World War II, along with the Bismarck. Her size was limited to that of a cruiser by the Treaty of Versailles, but she was much more heavily armed than a cruiser due to innovative weight-saving techniques employed in her construction.

She was sent to the Atlantic Ocean as a commerce raider in 1939, where she sank nine Allied merchant ships. Numerous British hunting groups were assigned to find her, with three British ships finally tracking her down in December 1939. The Battle of the River Plate ensued, during which the Graf Spee was damaged. She docked for repairs in the neutral port of Montevideo, but was forced by international law to leave within 72 hours. Faced with what he believed to be overwhelming odds, the captain scuttled his ship rather than risk the lives of his crew

Above: The passing of the German rocket battleship the Admiral Graf Spee in flames seven miles off the Uruguayan coast near Montevideo. The battleship was still flaming when these pictures were sent to London on December 19, 1939

Middle: The burial service of the German sailors who died in the Graf Spee. German seamen carried the coffins of their fallen comrades to the cemetery at Montevideo.

Below: To the rousing strains of 'Rule Britannia', played by the ship's band, and the roaring cheers of the crowd, H.M.S. Exeter, triumphant and battle-scarred, glides into Devonport dockyard. The gallant 8,390-tons cruiser that bore the brunt of the River Plate battle, with 64 of her crew killed in action, came home with Winston Churchill there to give the crew a special welcome.

DECEMBER 18, 1939

Graf Spee blown up by her crew

Admiral Graf Spee, 10,000- tons pocket battleship and pride of Hitler's fleet, was blown up and sunk by her own crew five miles off shore in the mouth of the River Plate at 10.55, G.M.T., last night. The German Legation in Montevideo announced that Captain Langsdorff went down with his ship.

This morning, however, his fate was in doubt. According to some sources, he was picked up after the sinking and is on his way to Buenos Aires.

Before leaving Montevideo harbour he sent a long letter to the German Minister protesting bitterly against the Uruguayan Government's refusal to allow more time for repairs to his ship. The letter declared that it was impossible to effect the repairs within 72 hours. The only course left in view of his responsibility for the lives of a thousand men was to blow up his ship.

A series of explosions shattered the Graf Spee and she was ablaze from end to end before the waters closed over her. Her control tower and superstructure are still showing.

A quarter-of-a-million people crowded the rooftops and quays of Montevideo when she weighed anchor and slipped out of harbour to meet her fate at 9.0 p.m.

The 'Phoney War' ends

The 'phoney war' came to an abrupt end on April 9,1940 when Hitler invaded Denmark and Norway, swiftly followed by attacks on the Low Countries and then France. This blitzkrieg or 'lightning war' saw the defeat of Allied troops. At Trondheim in Norway, 2,000 German soldiers trained in winter warfare forced the withdrawal of a 13,000-strong Allied force. But, perhaps most famously, the blitzkrieg caused the evacuation of troops of the British Expeditionary Force and their allies from the beaches of Dunkirk in northern France. Following the German occupation of most of Holland, Belgium and Luxembourg, and a large part of France, British and French troops were pushed into a small pocket on the coast around Dunkirk. Operation Dynamo, as the rescue mission was codenamed, was expected at best to rescue 50,000 troops – in the event 338, 226 men were saved.

Above: Throughout the war uniformed servicemen would become a common sight in Britain, whether they were waiting to be shipped to foreign fronts, home on leave or permanently stationed here, as many RAF crews were. However, this private, George Pinnock of the Highland Light Infantry, was granted just 72 hours leave from his regiment in order to marry his fiancée, Miss Joan Cox, and he would see her just once more before the war was over.

Right: Station staff from Waterloo entertain the troops in the YMCA canteen.

Below: American stars who 'live over here' broadcast from an R.A.F. aerodrome on Sunday night as a gesture of gratitude to our airmen.

Bottom: BEF troops add their own talents to the open air concert.

Entertaining the troops

The Entertainments National Service Association, or ENSA was a government sponsored organisation set up in 1939 by West End actor, writer and producer Basil Dean who made his headquarters in the Drury Lane Theatre. Dean had experience with the Navy, Army and Air Force Institute's (NAAFI) predecessor, Expeditionary Forces Canteen (EFC) that offered comfort and entertainment to Allied Forces in World War I. When war was declared all the theatres and music halls closed; entertainers found themselves unemployed and not necessarily suited to military service. ENSA was able to employ renowned stars and pier-end entertainers alike and send them out to cheer the troops. Gracie Fields, Noel Coward and Tommy Trinder and hundreds of others performed at home and abroad. George Formby, who had a huge following, landed with the first wave of the Normandy invasion, giving an impromptu performance to US troops hours later. An ENSA entourage of 144 artistes landed in France 8 days after D-Day. Humour and music were the principle morale boosters of World War II; radio shows that particularly targeted factory workers and service personnel offered both – led by the BBC Home Service's ITMA (It's That Man Again) and music programmes such as Workers' Playtime which from 1941 broadcast live from un-named factory locations 'somewhere in Britain'.

Rationing comes into force

The first food rationing came into effect in January 1940 and included items such as milk, meat, sugar and butter. Other items were also often in short supply. As the war progressed, other foods such as tinned fruit were included under the 'points' system which at least allowed people to purchase luxury items occasionally. Shoppers had to register with a particular shop and could only buy rationed goods from there.

Above: Queuing came to be a necessary part of shopping during the war. A long queue had formed outside a fish shop in Hammersmith with the customers needing to bring their own paper to wrap purchases.

Above right: All those with a surname beginning with 'A' were called to the Fulham office to register for new ration books.

Below right: As the war progressed, the age for conscription would be widened to include men aged up to 50. In 1941 the call up was also extended to single women between the ages of 20 and 30. Most conscripted men were sent into the army and by June 1941 over two million were in the service.

Bottom: A scene at Upton Park where West Ham United played Leicester City showing the usual football fans watching the game – in Army uniform, on the day before war was declared.

The west falls

Just before dawn on May 10, 1939 the German assault on western Europe finally began. In a swift and comprehensive move, soon to be widely known as blitzkreig, German paratroopers and bombers successfully struck at positions in Holland, Belgium and Luxembourg, facilitating rapid infantry assaults deep into these countries. In response, the Allies committed a large part of their forces to Belgium.

The Germans advanced at speed through the Low Countries, aiming to cut the Allied forces in two and push many of their troops towards the coast. At the same time armoured Panzer divisions broke through the French lines at Sedan. They stormed across northern France, heading towards the Channel coast within a matter of days. There was comparative chaos in the Allied forces; the speed and scope of the assault had stunned everyone. Their troops in the north, now successfully caught in the German pincer movement, began to retreat towards the Channel ports, notably to a perimeter around Dunkirk.

Above: **German paratroopers, May 1940.**

Left: **Paris experiences its first air raid, September 1939. There was relatively little aerial bombardment of the city in comparison with other European capitals.**

Below: **Reservists dig air-raid shelters in Paris in September 1939.**

B.E.F. may yet win out

THE B.E.F., with their French allies in Northern France, continuing their withdrawal to a defence line covering the coast, are fighting the greatest rearguard battle in history.

But to-night, though the German pincers flung across Flanders have closed in still further on our forces, there is hope in official circles in Paris that the bulk of the B.E.F. may yet win safely through to their coastal objectives. There are indications that the German assault, by its very ferocity, is tiring.

Attacking on both flanks of the Allies, the Germans are sacrificing thousands of men and large quantities of material for every section of territory they take in their furious, unrelenting drive towards the 60 miles of coast between Calais and Nieuport.

Dunkirk is still in our hands, after being battered by bombs all day. Ships of French Navy are using their guns to smash up German forces trying to push along the coast and are shielding the landing of supplies.

Above: French soldiers return from manning border posts.

Left: French tanks on manoeuvres in January 1940. This period was known as the 'Phoney War' because both sides had declared a state of war existed, but neither side had launched an attack.

The fall of France

Hitler launched the expected attack on France in May after rapidly neutralising the Low Countries. By 14th May the British Expeditionary force sent to reinforce Belgium and northern France was engaged by German armour of Army Group B that had overrun French and Belgian forward positions. This move was a feint; the main attack was carried out by German Army Group A, pushing through the Ardennes to bypass the heavily defended Maginot Line in a rapid advance that enabled them to reach the Channel coast south of the retreating BEF by 21st May, surrounding nearly 400,000 British and other Allied Forces who fell back on Dunkirk. The rapid collapse of the combined Allied defence is attributed to the massive bombardment by the Luftwaffe that cleared the way for the swiftly-moving armour which cut through the demoralised and less-well equipped Allies. Individual German commanders, particularly Heinz Guderian commanding XIXth Army Corps and his colleague Erwin Rommel, seized their advantage, ignoring orders from their superiors.

Churchill visiting the French government in Paris on 16th May found them already admitting defeat – their forces fully committed and no reserve for a counter-attack. By 14th June, Paris was taken and on the 22nd France capitulated, signing an Armistice at Compiègne in the very railway carriage where Germany formalised its ignominious surrender in 1918.

Inset: French troops take aim at German positions from the first-floor windows of a ruined house in a village near the Belgian border. The French military censor forbade the publication of the name of the village.

Below: More troops rush up a rickety stairway to man the first-floor windows, while their commanding officer issues orders from a niche in the wall in the right of the picture.

Germans advance south of Paris

While German troops were goose-stepping down the Champs Elysées yesterday the bulk of the German Army was streaming to the south. To-night the German forces are twenty miles beyond Paris, their mechanised forces rushing in lines east and west of the capital. They are moving forward in an attempt to prevent the French forming and maintaining a continuous line, and to cut off the Maginot Line from its supplies. And as the tanks and motorised columns sweep on, they create new difficulties for the French defenders. The roads are choked with a phalanx of refugees, whose vehicles move in a serried mass, often for many miles, at a rate of about one to three miles an hour.

The German advance has been so rapid that it has been impossible for the French to evacuate towns in any proper order or supply means of transport.

The French have difficulty in rushing up reinforcements as a stream of refugees pour down every road southwards. The French, the military spokesman stated, have been fighting a continuous battle, while the Germans have been throwing two or three series of reinforcements against them.

One question asked by the French public is: "What will America do?" There is still hope that the miracle of American intervention may happen which will save the situation.

Above: With fierce fighting occurring on the other side of the building, French troops run from house to house to take up more positions in a desperate attempt to stem the German advance until reinforcements arrived.

Left: French soldiers march towards the front line. Germany unexpectedly invaded France through the dense forest of the Ardennes region of Belgium, and in doing so, circumvented France's heavily defended 'Maginot Line' fortifications along the German border.

Dunkirk

On 21st May the British Expeditionary Force, who were being pushed back across France, counter-attacked at Arras, south of Dunkirk, but they were unable to hold out against the Panzer Divisions. They risked being cut off by others who had circumvented them via Amiens and Abbeville and were taking control of Channel ports such as Boulogne and Calais. Dunkirk appeared to be the only viable point from which to evacuate the troops by sea, and British, French and some Belgian soldiers began to amass on the beaches there. The tanks pursuing them held off for long enough for the Allies to be able to strengthen their defences on the ground, but the beaches were to come under attack from the Luftwaffe throughout the evacuation, which began on 26th May. Three days later, the operation, codenamed Dynamo, was announced to the British public, and a number of civilian vessels became involved in the rescue. By 4th June, almost 40,000 troops had been ferried to the English South Coast from Dunkirk, with still more being rescued from other parts of the coastline. In terms of lives saved the mission was a resounding success and it would allow the Allied troops to fight another day, but Britain had been forced to abandon much of its equipment, as well as control of the Channel coast. As men returned from Dunkirk, women and children were eager to greet them, offering food and handshakes. Many of the men had waited for hours and even days before being rescued and were given a hero's welcome as the trains passed through.

JUNE 5, 1940

Dunkirk: the end

Dunkirk has fallen. The last Allied land and naval forces were withdrawn in the early hours of yesterday. This, the end of one of the most terrible, yet glorious, chapters in the history of the British Army, was announced by the War Office and the French G.H.Q. and Admiralty last night.

The port has been made unusable to the enemy. More than 300,000 men have been saved - 335,000 was the figure given by Mr Churchill in the Commons last night - and it had not been thought possible to save more than a third of this number.

As the last embarkation was made the Germans had brought their machine-guns and artillery right up to the shore. The men of the heroic rearguard, who had withdrawn from the town, ceaselessly attacked and counter-attacking, fighting house to house, stepped to safety under a hail of German bullets and shells, as well as bombs from the air.

The last man to leave was Admiral Abrial, commanding the French Forces, the man who organised Dunkirk as an entrenched camp and the man most responsible for the magnificent defensive plan which enabled so many to escape. He left the port at 7 o'clock in the morning, and before embarking personally supervised the destruction of the port facilities. Last night he was in London with two other French admirals and three French generals.

Above: **Columns of Allied soldiers await evacuation at Dunkirk.**

Middle left: **The returning troops in their trains were often met by welcoming children; most soldiers had no contact with home for some time and were desperate to get news to their loved ones that they had survived. Frequently a short message with a name and address would be handed into the crowd in the hope that news would get through.**

Below left: **One of the many ships involved in the evacuation at Dunkirk sets off for Britain. The plumes of smoke beyond are testimony to the constant bombardment endured by the Allied forces throughout the operation.**

Below right: **Towards the end of summer 1940 the first German aircraft began to reach British shores. A flaming barrage balloon plummets earthwards near Dover Castle, having been shot down by a German plane.**

A new Prime Minister

The spring 1940 blitzkrieg had significant effects, not only in continental Europe but also in Britain, where there was a profound political shift. Chamberlain resigned his premiership when he failed to prevent the German occupation of Norway, Denmark, Holland, Belgium and Luxembourg. On May 10, Winston Churchill (below) took over as Prime Minister at the head of a coalition government. In addition to being Prime Minister, Churchill appointed himself Minister of Defence, giving him control of Britain's armed forces.

The Vichy government

Hitler had now succeeded in gaining control of the Channel coast, and the rest of France was soon to fall. The German army entered Paris some ten days later, on June 14 – just a month after the initial attacks on the country. Italy entered the war in support of Hitler, and by June 22, with all of northern France occupied by German troops and columns advancing southwards towards the border with Spain, the French Premier, Marshal Pétain, agreed to an armistice with Hitler. Under its conditions, France had to disarm and was to be divided into two basic sections. The northern zone and the northern and western coasts were under direct German control, but the southern part of the country would be governed by a collaborationist government led by Pétain and based at the spa town of Vichy. By the end of June the British-owned Channel Islands, so close to France, had also fallen to Germany.

Above left: **By June 1940 the British Government recognised General de Gaulle as the 'leader of free Frenchmen wherever they may be, who rally to him to support the allied cause'. The General saluted as he arrived at his London headquarters after this official recognition.**

Above middle: **Prime Minister Neville Chamberlain waves cheerfully as he takes his morning walk on his 71st birthday. He was soon to be replaced by Winston Churchill.**

Right: **A hospital in Hertfordshire was the destination for some of the soldiers wounded at Dunkirk.**

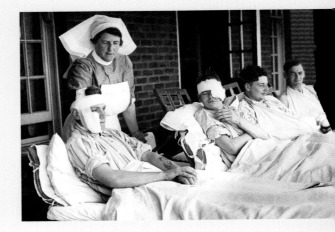

Chapter Two

The Battle of Britain

Most of Western Europe was now under Hitler's control, but Britain remained a serious obstacle to his ambitions. He set his sights on invading the country, and developed a plan called Operation Sea Lion. In order for this to be successful, however, the Germans had to effectively control the Channel and subdue Britain's south coast. As a result, attacks were initiated, both on the sea and from the air. Shipping convoys were the first victims, and then, by August 1940, attacks began on the vital airfields of southern England. This was the start of the Battle of Britain.

The RAF was heavily outnumbered by the German Luftwaffe. Initially, there were heavy losses, but the RAF had some advantages, notably ground radar, and began to regain control of the skies over Britain in late August. The Germans, who had been incurring increasing losses themselves, changed their strategy – moving from fighter attacks on airfields to bomber raids on the factories and docks of London, marking the beginning of the Blitz. One unintentional result of this was that it allowed time for repairs to the airfields, which had been almost destroyed, and there was some opportunity for the RAF to regroup.

The Luftwaffe began to lose many more aircraft – and pilots – than the RAF, and it was becoming obvious to the Germans that their estimates of British losses were inaccurate, not to say wildly over-optimistic. They had underestimated Fighter Command in every way, and the invasion of Britain was called off in September.

THE BATTLE OF BRITAIN   55

'We shall defend our island'

By the time Winston Churchill stepped into the position of Prime Minister on May 10, 1940, Germany had occupied Norway and Denmark, invaded the Netherlands and was well on the way to turning back the British Expeditionary Force in France; soon it would bring France to submission. The gravity of the British situation was brought home in the incredible rescue, 'Operation Dynamo', of over 330,000 Allied troops in the evacuation from Dunkirk during the nine days from May 26 to June 4.

The success of this operation camouflaged the real losses to the British Army and the Royal Air Force in France but the resolve of Fighter Command's Air Chief Marshal Hugh Dowding, ensured that Britain retained a reserve of fighter aircraft, even though the Hurricane squadrons in France lost 200 machines – a significant proportion of the RAF total fighter strength. At this low point in Britain's fortunes, Churchill electrified and boosted the nation with his speech to the Commons on 4 June: 'We shall defend our island, whatever the cost may be. We shall fight on the beaches, we shall fight on the landing grounds, we shall fight in the fields and in the streets, we shall fight in the hills; we shall never surrender.'

Top: An aircrew pose in front of their badly damaged Avro Anson bomber, hit by anti-aircraft fire on a reconnaissance mission. Despite wing and engine damage, shell-splintered fuselage and shot-out tyres they managed to return home without injury.

Above: The Luftwaffe's proven fighter plane at the start of the war was the Messerschmitt Bf 109. It became the most produced fighter aircraft in history with a total of 33,984 built until production stopped in April 1945. The RAF's Spitfire was a good match in many respects, but performance was still dictated by the pilot's skill, knowledge of his own plane and the key strengths and weaknesses of the machine he was fighting against.

Right: Inside an Observer Corps control room, 'plotters' move counters across an area map tracking incoming information from clusters of observation posts. 'Tellers' overlooking the plotters are responsible for liaising with fellow control rooms and local defence organisations as well as their contact at Fighter Command HQ at Bentley Priory.

Above: Rapid rearming and refuelling were critical for the RAF, which flew many more sorties in France and during the Battle of Britain than its German opponents. A Spitfire at this time carried 300 rounds of ammunition for each of its 8 Browning .303 machine guns housed in the wings. The thin wing profile made rearming more laborious than the Hurricane. The Messerschmitt Bf 109 carried more ammunition for its machine guns; RAF pilots had to count every burst in seconds, having less than 20 seconds total supply.

Left: Pilots of 501 Squadron, the first Auxiliary Fighter Squadron to join the Advanced Air Striking Force (AASF) in France, unwind after their latest dogfight in the middle of May. In the foreground is future RAF Ace, Flt Sergeant 'Ginger' Lacey.

Below left: Members of the Women's Auxiliary Air Force (WAAFs) manoeuvre an anti-aircraft barrage balloon into position. Tethered balloons had been used in WWI as observation platforms for artillery aiming, giving rise to the expression 'the balloon goes up'. The aerodynamic shape was developed to keep them more manageable in the wind. By the middle of 1940, there were about 1,400 deployed around the country, a third of them assigned to London. Their purpose was to inhibit dive bombing and force aircraft to fly within the height range of anti-aircraft guns which were not agile enough to engage diving or low-flying aircraft. The combined effect forced enemy bombers to keep above both balloons and anti-aircraft shells, thus decreasing their bombing accuracy.

Below right: The vital job of spotting aircraft was a 24-hour task, with observers staring into the sky for long hours, day and night. Special spotter chairs were made for the purpose, seen here being used during the day in France; they were also used by night-time searchlight crews.

Goering's four-day promise

Hitler and his blitzkrieg commanders were understandably confident about their war machine but Nazi hubris bred false assumptions that would lead to Germany's unexpected defeat in the Battle of Britain. The Luftwaffe had dominated the skies of Western Europe during the blitzkrieg; its task now was to crush the RAF and disable its aircraft production. Field Marshal Hermann Goering, the Luftwaffe commander, boasted that the RAF would be broken in four days and its production capability wiped out in four weeks. However, the RAF were not to succumb to Goering's plan; the Battle of Britain was to have four clear phases and on June 18, Churchill predicted Britain's struggle for survival with his famous 'Finest Hour' speech.

Above: **RAF pilots sleep and play games in their rest room at their base 'somewhere in Scotland'.**

Below left: **Fighter pilots leap into action and rush to their planes after a warning from HQ that an unidentified plane had been spotted by the Observer Corps.**

JUNE 11, 1940

Italy: hostilities open

Hostilities between Italy and the Allies began at midnight. New York reports that Italian troops invaded the French Riviera at 6.30 last night were emphatically denied by a Government spokesman in Rome.

Signor Mussolini has chosen the crucial hour in the great battle for France to take his momentous step, but Britain and France have long been prepared to meet such a situation. It can be assumed that Britain will quickly take the offensive at sea. Her naval dispositions in the Mediterranean and other preparations have been made with the object of aiming swift and heavy blows at Italy.

A few days ago the British Government, in agreement with the French, decided to impose the full force of contraband control on all Italian ships. Italian shipping at Malta was seized early this morning. All Italians on the island were rounded up.

Rome radio announced that Signor Mussolini will be Supreme Commander of Italian armed forces, "although the King of Italy still remains the nominal chief." Marshal Badoglio has been made Commander-in-Chief of the Army.

Mr. Churchill will make a statement on the new situation to-day.

Above left: The overwhelming speed of the German war machine as it moved west, and Prime Minister Chamberlain's general failure to effect any resistance, frustrated Winston Churchill. In the years before the war, Churchill was critical of Chamberlain's lack of preparation against the obvious rearming of Germany by Hitler's Nazis. On May 10, Chamberlain resigned and recommended Churchill as the man to head an all-party war government. He accepted the invitation from George VI and immediately stepped into the role, much to the relief of the nation. On May 13, his first great speech to Parliament sounded around the nation with the immortal words "I have nothing to offer but blood, toil, tears and sweat."

Above right: In April 1940 Winston Churchill paid a visit to one of Britain's dockyards, the primary targets for Luftwaffe bombers. Addressing the assembled workers, he questioned, 'Are we downhearted?' to be greeted with a resounding, 'No!' This was a catchphrase from a song that was used throughout the Battle of Britain and the Blitz.

Above middle: Adolf Hitler in conference with Reichsmarschall Hermann Goering (2nd left), commander of the Luftwaffe. Hitler made him personally responsible for defeating the RAF prior to Operation Sealion, the planned invasion of Britain in September 1940.

The Battle of Dover Straits

The first phase of the German offensive, dubbed 'Kanalkampf' (translated 'Channel battles'), targeted Britain's shipping and coastal defences to bring home the country's vulnerability, isolation and dependence on sea transport. Traditional shipping routes made extensive use of the English Channel and the North Sea, placing convoys of ships within striking distance of German fighters and bombers, as well as heavy coastal guns sited close by in France.

During the summer in 1940, the Channel witnessed endless land and sea battles. The Germans had long-range guns sited on the French coast with the shellfire sometimes reaching Dover. Small barrage balloons known as kite balloons would be raised over convoys to try to avoid dive-bombers or low-flying swoops. The supplies the convoys brought in from abroad were vital to Britain and were often subject to attacks from mines and U-boats as well.

Below: Semaphore being used to guide a merchant ship through a known minefield.

Above left: At the outbreak of war, Britain was still very much a maritime nation; as an island it was dependent on the merchant navy for trade and transport of bulk goods. Furthermore the Royal Navy was the Senior Service of Britain's military might and an industry in itself. Germany opened its hostilities with aerial and submarine attacks on Britain's shipping; immediately, defensive tactics had to be put in place in British waters. Here a convoy sails along the east coast.

Below left: HMS Green Fly was a trawler converted to naval use as an escort vessel and lookout for German E boats; its armament was one four-inch gun and two machine guns housed in sponsons either side of the bridge. Its rudimentary anti-submarine equipment would have been little use against hunting pairs of submarines. In this dramatic photograph, shells burst near the convoy as it sails along the Channel; they have been fired from long-range German guns located on the French coast.

The Battle of Britain

The Prime Minister gave the House of Commons last night 'some indication of the solid, practical grounds upon which we are basing our invincible resolve to continue the war.'

The professional advisers of the three Services, he said, unitedly advised that we should do it and that there were good and reasonable hopes of final victory.

In this island there were now over 1,250,000 men under arms, backed by 500,000 Local Defence Volunteers. We might expect very large additions to our weapons in the near future. And, 'after all we have a Navy, which some people seem to forget.' Our fighter air strength is stronger at present in relation to Germany's than it had ever been.

'The Battle of Britain' said Mr. Churchill, 'is about to begin. On this battle depends the survival of Christian civilisation. I look forward confidently to the exploits of our fighter pilots, who will have the glory of saving their native land and our island home from the most deadly of all attacks.

'There remains the danger of the bombing attacks, which will certainly be made very soon upon us by the bomber forces of the enemy. It is quite true that these forces are superior in number to ours, but we have a very large bombing force also, which we shall use to strike at the military targets in Germany without intermission.

'What General Weygand called the Battle of France is over. The Battle of Britain is about to begin. On this battle depends the survival of Christian civilisation. Upon it depends our own British life and the long continuity of our institutions and our Empire. The whole fury and might of the enemy must very soon be turned upon us. Hitler knows he will have to break us in this island or lose the war. If we can stand up to him all Europe may be freed and the life of the world may move forward into broad, sunlit uplands. But if we fail, the whole world, including the United States and all that we have known and cared for, will sink into the abyss of a new dark age made more sinister and perhaps more prolonged by the lights of a perverted silence.

'Let us therefore brace ourselves to our duty and so bear ourselves that if the British Commonwealth and Empire last for a thousand years, men will still say, 'This was their finest hour'.'

Top: Views from the cliffs at Dover show a convoy under attack from the French coast.

Above: Puffs of smoke in the sky mark where anti-aircraft shells are bursting around the German planes which have just dropped bombs. On this occasion the bombers missed their targets making a hundred-foot-high waterspout.

Right: The Royal Naval Patrol Service was mobilised in August 1939 with its Central Depot based in Lowestoft. The depot became known as HMS Europa and provided the administrative headquarters for 6,000 vessels and 70,000 men. During World War I, it had been realised that small vessels were very useful for duties such as minesweeping and many fishing fleets had joined the Royal Naval Reserve. Their main role in the Second World War was anti-submarine work and minesweeping, initially around the British Isles. Their aim was to constantly minesweep the area to keep the shipping lanes clear, allowing the passage of convoys that were providing supplies.

Radar prototype

Early in this phase of the battle, Britain's Radio Direction Finding (RDF) Chain (a prototype radar developed as an early warning system in the 1930s), proved effective in anticipating Luftwaffe raids, scrambling the fighter squadrons of Coastal Command to meet the Luftwaffe before they reached their targets. However, the German raiders employed teasing tactics, feinting raids to spook RAF aircraft into the air, calculating their flying time and the need to return to base to refuel. These same tactics kept the civilian population on constant alert, fearful that an air raid was imminent.

Above: A typical suburban street devastated by bombing in the early hours of July 15, 1940 becomes a scene of extraordinary calm as workers repair a water main and the bomb damage to the road while ARP officers converse in the background. The close-packed terraces increased the efficiency of the bombs, while fire from incendiaries could quickly spread from house to house. From September 7, the Luftwaffe moved their main attention from the RAF airfields to a campaign of terror delivered from the air; this marked the beginning of the Blitz and the final phase of the Battle of Britain.

Middle: Under attack from British fighters, the laden German bombers had to jettison their bombs or find an available target quickly and hope to escape. The power of the ordnance is visible in this enormous crater.

Above and right: Vapour trails of fighter aircraft engaged in aerial combat.

JUNE 20, 1940

Massed bombing begins

Hitler last night launched his greatest air attack of the war on Britain. Swarms of raiders swooped on the east coast of Scotland, on Yorkshire and on its coast on Co. Durham, down to Lincolnshire and as far south as towns on the south-east coast. While wave upon wave of German bombers were launching their attack, Hamburg and Bremen radio went off the air, indicating the presence of British 'planes.

The alarms in Yorkshire were over a wide area. Some unidentified 'planes were reported flying high. Heavy explosions were heard some distance from a Lincolnshire coast town.

Earlier there had been considerable air activity and large numbers of British 'planes were heard flying out over the sea. After the alarms British fighters were heard also going out to sea.

Numbers of people were caught in the streets in the coast towns. Many were returning from cinemas. An unconfirmed report states that one raider crashed into the sea off a coast town after being engaged by A.A. guns.

Right: The wreckage of a German plane lies in a farmer's field having been shot down in a dogfight. The pilot survived the crash and was immediately captured.

Middle right: Although the south-east was most heavily targeted by the Luftwaffe, fighter patrols engaged German aircraft all over Britain. This reconnaissance plane was brought down in Scotland.

Below right: This German plane crashed nose-first into a field near the coast of north-east England.

Below: An RAF corporal inspects bullet holes in the tail of a German plane on a reconnaisance flight shot down near Dalkeith, Scotland.

Eagle attack

On August 12, the pace and spread of German attacks stepped up as Goering set in motion preparations for a September invasion of the British Isles, code-named 'Operation Sealion'. This phase of the Battle was called 'Adlerangriff' or 'Eagle Attack' and was launched with massed attacks by hundreds of bombers and fighters on August 13, 'Adlertag' ('Eagle Day'). By mid-August fine weather meant the Luftwaffe had clear skies for their daylight raids and a series of attacks were raised on Britain's RDF Chain with the intention of permanently disabling it. The speed with which the RDF was restored caused the Luftwaffe to draw incorrect conclusions about the robustness of the system; if they had persevered with their plan Britain would have been much more vulnerable. In fact the Luftwaffe failed to destroy the RAF's fleet on the ground and although the Messerschmitt Bf109 was superior to the RAF's main defensive aircraft, the Hurricane and its glamorous cousin the Supermarine Spitfire, the Luftwaffe was unable to get the better of Fighter Command in the air, paying a heavy price in machines and pilots. August 15 brought serious losses to the Luftwaffe – they named it 'Black Thursday'; and on August 18 – 'the Hardest Day' – losses on both sides were equally high.

Above: British airmen, hard at work between missions, preparing ground for an airbase.

Inset: Warships of the Royal Navy plough through choppy seas, their guns at the ready. In July 1940, Allied shipping losses in British waters peaked at 67 vessels sunk, nearly 200,000 combined tonnage. The great ships of the Royal Navy were called south from Scapa Flow in anticipation of the imminent German invasion.

Left: A shell is loaded into an anti-aircraft, or ack-ack, gun. These weapons played an important part in defending British airfields and other important installations.

Above left: Pilots of the West Lancashire RAF Squadron race to their waiting aircraft after they receive the call to 'action stations'; their mascot, Joker, joins in the spirit of the scramble.

Middle left: Winston Churchill visits Ramsgate, one of the most heavily bombed areas of Britain during the Battle of Britain in 1940.

Below: A row of British Spitfire fighter planes prepare for take-off.

Heavy German losses

The summer of 1940 was balmy, with many days of sunshine. Aircrews fighting for their life one moment could be recuperating at the margins of their grassy runways soon after, ready at an instant to return to battle. However, the weather wasn't good the whole time. At the beginning of August, Eagle Day - the day the Luftwaffe began its real assault on the RAF - was quite seriously delayed by bad flying conditions, finally launching in earnest on August 13, after low cloud cleared in the early afternoon. Confusion in the German command made the planned attack less effective; the Luftwaffe were surprised by the firm resolve and force of the defending RAF who lost 13 aircraft in the air compared with 47 German planes.

Luftwaffe target airfields

The next phase of the battle, which began on August 24 concentrated on the destruction of RAF airfields. Although the Luftwaffe killed many ground personnel and damaged airfields with monotonous regularity, they still did not succeed in destroying Fighter Command's defensive capability. Much of this failure must be attributed to the tactical skills of Fighter Command who had to calculate their response to German raids with the greatest care: scrambling squadrons too soon might lead to their running out of fuel just as German raiders were approaching their targets. Luftwaffe Command knew that RDF would alert Fighter Command and often set traps for the hard-pressed RAF, which quickly realised the cat-and-mouse element to German attacks and that responding too soon or too late or with too few or too many aircraft could have disastrous results. Dowding's conservative approach, emulated by Air Vice Marshal Keith Park, in charge of 11 Group, kept up a continuous response to Luftwaffe attack, despite the exhaustion of pilots and the loss of aircraft.

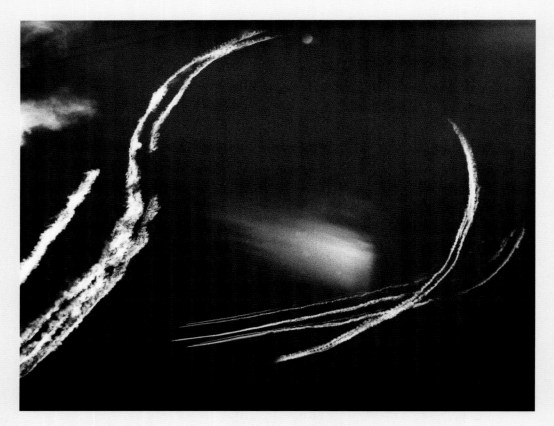

Above: **A formation of Spitfires dives into battle leaving trails of vapour.**

Below: **A squadron of Hurricane fighters flies in close formation. Along with the Spitfire this aircraft was the best defence Britain had against the Luftwaffe.**

Above: A night-fighter crew get a last-minute weather briefing. The Bristol Blenheims that proved so vulnerable over daytime France suited night patrol well: in the night raid on London, June 18 1940, Blenheims accounted for five German bombers. In July, 600 Squadron, based at RAF Manston, had some of its Mk IFs equipped with AI Mk III radar. With this radar equipment, a Blenheim from the Fighter Interception Unit (FIU) at RAF Ford achieved the first success on the night of July 2-3 1940, accounting for a Dornier Do 17 bomber. More successes confirmed the Blenheim's invaluable role.

Top: A Spitfire goes in for the kill. Already crippled and trailing smoke, this Heinkel 111 is seconds away from ditching in the Channel. This photograph shows how close RAF fighters had to get to their

targets to make their ammunition effective. Their relatively light machine guns were eventually upgraded to include heavier 20mm cannon.

Top right: Hurricanes speed on their way to intercept enemy aircraft on July 29. Three planes are in the classic V formation. The others are adopting the increasingly favoured 'finger four', which paired planes as two couples. With the lead pilot in attack, his wingman would keep a lookout for attacking aircraft from above and from the direction of the sun.

Right: The wreckage of a German plane engulfed in flames, shot down as it headed home after a bombing raid.

'The few'

"The gratitude of every home in our Island, in our Empire, and indeed throughout the world, except in the abodes of the guilty, goes out to the British airmen who, undaunted by odds, unwearied in their constant challenge and mortal danger, are turning the tide of the World War by their prowess and by their devotion. Never in the field of human conflict was so much owed by so many to so few. All hearts go out to the fighter pilots, whose brilliant actions we see with our own eyes day after day; but we must never forget that all the time, night after night, month after month, our bomber squadrons travel far into Germany, find their targets in the darkness by the highest navigational skill, aim their attacks, often under the heaviest fire, often with serious loss, with deliberate careful discrimination, and inflict shattering blows upon the whole of the technical and war-making structure of the Nazi power. On no part of the Royal Air Force does the weight of the war fall more heavily than on the daylight bombers, who will play an invaluable part in the case of invasion and whose unflinching zeal it has been necessary in the meanwhile on numerous occasions to restrain."

Prime Minister Winson Churchill's speech to the House of Commons on August 1940

Top: Hawker Hurricane aircraft in flight. By the start of the Battle of Britain, the RAF had a total of 2,309 of these aircraft in 32 squadrons. They were ultimately responsible for taking out more Luftwaffe planes than any other forms of defence.

Above: A German plane plummets to the ground over Sussex in August 1940.

Right: German bombers attacking over Britain.

JULY 26, 1940

RAF in greatest air battle

The Air Ministry announced at 2.30 a.m. to-day that 20 German raiders were shot down yesterday. Eleven were bombers and nine fighters. Five of our fighters were lost, but the pilots of two are safe. Yesterday's "kill" by the R.A.F. is the third biggest since Hitler's air war began.

By Daily Mail Correspondent on the South-East coast:

For hours to-day, from afternoon into evening, I watched scores of British fighters and masses of German raiders battling madly above the Channel. The onslaught, the most serious seen off our coasts, began with a raid on a convoy of more than 20 small cargo ships. Again and again the raiders were driven off. New squadrons returned to the attack. At least 200 'planes were engaged.

It was long before Spitfires and A.A. gunners cleared the skies, but at last, after bitter fighting, it was done. Sometimes during the air battle 'planes "fought it out" a few feet above the roof-tops of the houses along the coast.

The sky was darkened by clouds of 'planes. Everywhere I looked there was a duel. The battle opened with a sudden dive-bombing attack by more than 20 German 'planes which dropped almost vertically from the clouds on to the moving ships.

Above: Badly shot up on August 12, this Bf 109 crash-landed in a Kent cornfield, almost intact. The wounded pilot managed to get out of the plane but covered no more than 50 yards before he was captured by a sergeant of the Royal Engineers.

Left: Whilst anti-aircraft gunners, such as these Bren gunners, kept a watchful eye on the skies over Britain, many civilians played an important role as roof spotters, providing early warnings to the public and to colleagues at factories, other workplaces and institutions.

Non-stop production lines

The Minister of Aircraft Production was in charge of the Ministry of Aircraft Production, one of the specialised supply ministries set up by the British Government during World War II. As the name suggests, it was responsible for aircraft production for the British forces; primarily the Royal Air Force, but also the Fleet Air Arm. The department was formed in 1940 by Winston Churchill in response to the production problems that winning the Battle of Britain posed. The first minister was Lord Beaverbrook and under his control the Ministry presided over an enormous increase in British aircraft production. Lord Beaverbrook, pushed for aircraft production to have priority over virtually all other types of munitions production for raw materials. In 1940 Britain produced in excess of 15,000 aircraft, 4,000 more than Germany.

Above: A production line for the Miles Master, one of the RAF training aircraft.

Below: A Spitfire production line. Whilst the Hurricane was more numerous, and accounted for more German losses than the Spitfire, the speed and agility of the Spitfire made it a formidable fighter plane.

Above: The limitations of the Bristol Blenheim led to the development of the Beaufort, which entered service with a Coastal Command squadron in 1940. Just over 2,000 were built with the bulk of production at Blackburn's Yorkshire works. The light bomber was intended to carry torpedoes to be used against the German navy and in aerial mine-laying as well as short-range. From July 1940 to the end of the year, Bomber Command lost nearly 330 aircraft and over 1,400 aircrew killed, missing or PoW.

Left: The Spitfire, designed by R. J. Mitchell and powered by a single Rolls-Royce engine, could fly at high or low altitudes, was able to evade most enemy fighters and also performed valuable reconnaissance work. During the war 'Spitfire Funds' were set up, when groups would fundraise for a Spitfire to be manufactured. This was combined with public collections of donated metal such as aluminium pans. By the close of the war 20,351 planes had been produced for the RAF.

Luftwaffe change tactics

At the beginning of September 1940, RAF Fighter Command was at breaking point: the RAF had lost 300 pilots in August alone, and had only been able to replace 260 of them; in the 14 days leading up to September 4, 295 RAF fighters were destroyed, with 171 badly damaged; and in 11 Group, which bore the brunt of Luftwaffe raids, 6 out of 7 sector stations were almost out of action. Nevertheless, despite being on the brink of collapse, Fighter Command had succeeded in convincing the Luftwaffe that its strategy to destroy British fighter capability had failed. Alongside this state of affairs, in late August, German bombers had dropped bombs on civilians in London; in response, Bomber Command launched a night raid on Berlin on August 25. Inexplicably, this enraged Hitler who had given strict instructions that the Luftwaffe should not bomb civilian targets unless he specifically ordered it and led to a change in the German's line of attack when, on September 4, his response was the escalated bombing of British cities. Just at the point where Fighter Command was on its knees with a shortage of planes and pilots, as well as its airfields being at breaking point, the Luftwaffe halted their effective strategy for a change in tactics.

Above left: Workmen carry a section of fuselage belonging to a downed German bomber. They are adding the latest wreckage to a scrap heap covering 20 acres, stacked high with recovered debris, which was then recycled into British aircraft and weapon production.

Left: Mechanics strip down a German aircraft..

Above: Locals survey the wreckage from a German plane that had fallen into a Kent garden in August 1940.

London's first air raid

AUGUST 16, 1940

German dive-bombers swooped on Croydon Aerodrome last evening in the first bombing raid in the London area. One bomb hit an aerodrome building and there were some casualties, but there was little damage in the town. At least one 'plane, swooping over the streets, machine-gunned groups of civilians, but there were no serious casualties.

It was London's first real air raid, and the fifth alarm of the war. Sirens were sounded all over London, the alarm lasting for only a few minutes.

Heinkel twin-engined bombers, escorted by Messerschmitt fighters, came over and divided into two sections to attack. They were met by terrific anti-aircraft gun barrage, and fighters went up to intercept them.

At least three Germans were brought down over and around Croydon, and others were destroyed on their way home. One came down in a wood and was burned out. One of the crew, caught in a tree by his parachute ropes, shook hands with his captors when released.

Several 'planes swooped to within a few hundred feet of the streets and machine-gunned civilians. A Mr. Green and his wife and children were machine-gunned as they ran to their garden shelter, but none was hit. Mrs. Green had her baby in her arms.

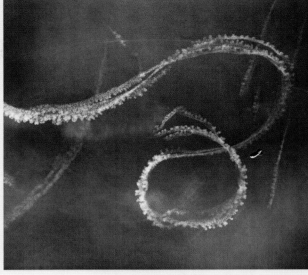

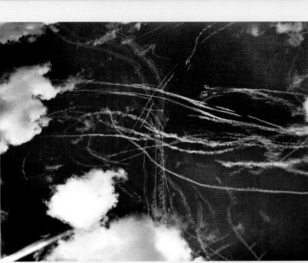

Above and below right: Daytime dogfights marked by vapour trails as British fighters engage the Luftwaffe during the Blitz.

Hill aerodrome on August 31, 1940. Located in Kent, the airfield was a favourite target for the Luftwaffe. Between August 18, 1940 and January 7, 1941, the aerodrome was attacked twelve times. On August 18th, KG 76, a Luftwaffe bomber unit, sent in a high level and low level attack with Dornier Do 17s and Junkers Ju 88s, but the main damage was the cratering of the landing ground. In the second of two attacks on August 30, a small formation of less than a dozen bombers at low level reduced Biggin Hill to a shambles with 1,000 lb. bombs. Workshops, stores, barracks, WAAF quarters and a hangar were wrecked, and 39 were killed. The next day, a high level attack did further extensive damage, including a direct hit on the Ops block. After the attacks, the airfield was quickly returned to operational status and continued to operate throughout the Battle.

Above: Weary and unshaven airmen of 32 Squadron share a joke at Biggin

Far left: Squadron Leader Douglas Bader, one of the most remarkable RAF pilots of the Battle of Britain, having lost both of his legs in a crash in 1931. His artificial limbs proved no hindrance, and he was regarded as a particularly skilful pilot.

Left: Bader, having just received the DSO pictured with Pilot Officer W.L. Knight (right) and Flight Lieutenant G.E. Ball.

Below: Bader (centre) surrounded by fellow officers and crew. In 1941 he had to bail out over German-occupied France and was placed in a prisoner-of-war camp. After repeated attempts to escape he was sent to Colditz and finally freed by the U S Army in April 1945. Despite his request, he was not able to fight in the remainder of the war.

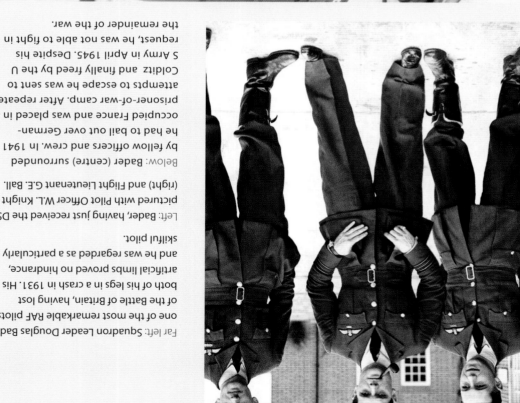

Hitler abandons 'Operation Sealion'

On September 7, the new German approach ushered in the fourth and final phase of the Battle of Britain with the beginning of the Blitz as 950 German aircraft attacked London in the first and last massed daylight raid on the capital; 300 civilians were killed and 1,300 seriously wounded. For the next 57 consecutive days, London was remorselessly bombed in night raids. Fighter Command was amazed at this development, which perversely saved it from destruction, allowing its forces to recuperate and airfields to be restored. It was a terrible price for Londoners to pay, the death toll rose to 2,000 by September 10. September 15 marked the heaviest bombardment of the capital so far – but at a cost to the Luftwaffe of 56 planes. This date, originally designated as the launch for 'Operation Sealion', would prove a turning point in the Battle of Britain, as the German High Command realised that their invasion of Britain would be at an unsustainable cost. Thus, September 15 became Battle of Britain Day. On September 17, Hitler abandoned 'Operation Sealion' but not until October 29 could Britain breathe a little easier as the stream of German raiding aircraft subsided.

Above left: Shipping and submarine movements are tracked in the control room of RAF Coastal Command, which provided aerial protection of Allied shipping from both the Luftwaffe and German U-boats. It received much less glory than its Fighter and Bomber Command cousins. In the first phase of the Battle of Britain, the so-called 'Kanalkampf', from July 10 to August 11, Luftwaffe attacks focused on shipping in the English Channel and the North Sea.

Below left: Women of the Auxiliary Territorial Service (ATS) on observation duty at an anti-aircraft battery. Although they didn't handle the armament they were trained to use the rangefinders and accurately identify enemy aircraft.

Above: Members of the Women's Auxiliary Air Force (WAAF) in training. Although women did not fly combat missions, the contribution of women in the auxiliary services was invaluable. The WAAF staffed radar stations whilst, amongst other duties, the women in the ATS manned anti-aircraft guns, and those of the Air Transport Auxiliary flew missions delivering new aircraft.

Defending the shores

At the start of the Battle of Britain, Fighter Command was outnumbered four to one by the Luftwaffe and faced a better-equipped German force that was battle-hardened and had superior aerial tactics. Both sides revealed, in almost equal measure, gaps in their knowledge and understanding of the opposition. The Germans generally under-estimated Britain's will to defend its shores and over-estimated the RAF's defensive capability. Additionally, German intelligence was inferior to British, which began to experience the benefit of ULTRA – the British code name for the breaking of the German Enigma encoding system. On its part, RAF Fighter Command over-estimated Luftwaffe strength and will, but it is easy to understand why this happened, when the attrition of aircraft continued for so long. In reality, however, the Luftwaffe was also close to exhaustion by September 1940.

Above left: New Zealander Alan 'Al' Deere was one of the RAF's most intrepid pilots and at the end of the Battle had risen to the rank of Flight Lieutenant with DFC and Bar. His many brushes with death and lucky escapes while shooting down 17 German aircraft, were recorded in his 'Nine Lives' autobiography. He retired in 1977 with the rank of Air Commodore.

Below left: Amongst the most outstanding RAF pilots during the Battle of Britain was James 'Ginger' Lacey, who shot down more German planes than any other pilot, with a total of eighteen.

Below: A large part of the life of a fighter plane crew was spent waiting to be called up for action. Ways of passing this time would include sleeping, listening to the gramophone or radio or on this occasion, a game of chess.

Above: A bomber crew rest on a tender of bombs. These were soon to be loaded onto the aircraft behind, to be dropped over Germany.

Far left: This young pilot wears a very non-regulation Mae West decorated with a caricature of the star herself, displaying the pneumatic talent that led to the nickname for the RAF standard issue flotation aid.

Left: A glimpse of the spartan interior of the Spitfire cockpit. The steering column or joystick incorporated a red firing button. A gun sight is ranged in the pilot's forward vision. Pilots had to learn how best to fire the Spitfire's machine guns - housed in the wings, they affected the aircraft's balance and it was essential that the pilot set up the plane correctly and held the joystick with both hands while firing.

Top: Scrambling RAF pilots launched to reinforce already engaged squardrons in the south east in September 1940. From the expression on their faces it's hard to believe they were on their way to an experience which would terrify normal people.

Above: The last moments of this crippled Heinkel are captured by the camera after being shot down by a Hurricane.

Left: Two barrage balloons brought down on September 1, 1940, after being shot by Messerschmitt 109s. One of the Messerschmitts was eventually brought down by rifle fire from the balloon crew afterwards. The barrage defences were raised into the air to deter low-flying bombers.

Above: On September 2, night attacks by 120 Luftwaffe bombers were followed by dawn raids, with continual attacks by hundreds of enemy bombers with fighter escorts, in waves throughout the day. Many bombs found their targets, making Eastchurch airfield in Kent non-operational. Despite their losses, such as this downed Bf 109, the German attrition was steadily weakening Fighter Command who had flown 700 sorties that day alone.

Left: Each one of the pilots pictured here had been decorated for his actions in France or the Battle of Britain. They had just returned from a sortie over German-occupied France.

Counting the cost

The milestone date for the end of the Battle of Britain – October 29– was arbitrary to some extent as Britain would continue to experience the German Blitz until the early summer of 1941. Nevertheless, at this point in the war, it was possible to begin counting the cost of this decisive battle: during the Battle of Britain from July 10 to October 31, Britain lost 1,065 aircraft (including 1,004 fighters) and 544 pilots; German losses numbered 1,922 aircraft (including 879 fighters, 80 Stukas and 881 bombers). British civilian losses in the Blitz that ended in May 1941 soared to over 40,000 killed and 50,000 injured. German Luftwaffe losses from August 1940 until March 1941 were nearly 3,000 aircraft lost and 3,363 aircrew killed, with 2,117 wounded and 2,641 taken prisoner.

Below: As this picture shows, RAF pilots needed considerable stamina: sorties might begin at dawn with an adrenalin-fuelled run to their aircraft, laden down with their flying equipment. At the peak of the Battle, they would continue flying sorties as long as they could keep awake and had an airworthy machine. They were known to bale out of a doomed plane, be picked up and then immediately return to combat. Many in their crippled aircraft preferred to glide to earth in forced landings, especially when over the Channel.

Above: Only one member of the four-man crew of this Heinkel bomber survived when it was brought down on a night mission at the beginning of September.

Above: The kills tally on this shot-down Bf 109 gives an indication of RAF losses and the performance of the German fighter plane. In the early days of the war the Bf 109 clearly had an advantage over the British machines, especially the many outdated craft that were deployed in France.

London's First Air Raid

German dive-bombers swooped on Croydon Aerodrome last evening in the first bombing raid in the London area. One bomb hit an aerodrome building and there were some casualties, but there was little damage in the town. At least one 'plane, swooping over the streets, machine-gunned groups of civilians, but there were no serious casualties.

It was London's first real air raid, and the fifth alarm of the war. Sirens were sounded all over London, the alarm lasting for only a few minutes.

Heinkel twin-engined bombers, escorted by Messerschmitt fighters, came over and divided into two sections to attack. They were met by terrific anti-aircraft gun barrage, and fighters went up to intercept them.

At least three Germans were brought down over and around Croydon, and others were destroyed on their way home. One came down in a wood and was burned out. One of the crew, caught in a tree by his parachute ropes, shook hands with his captors when released.

Several 'planes swooped to within a few hundred feet of the streets and machine-gunned civilians. A Mr. Green and his wife and children were machine-gunned as they ran to their garden shelter, but none was hit. Mrs. Green had her baby in her arms.

Top: Battle of Britain aircraft flew at great height with unpressurised cabins. From 16,000 feet oxygen was required to maintain consciousness, the cockpit would become very cold and ice could impair the mechanics and cloud the plexiglass. To combat the intense cold, the parachute manufacturer Leslie Irvin devised the characteristic airman's jacket from very supple sheepskin, tailored to give maximum warmth whilst allowing freedom to move. The aircrew also wore fleece-lined boots and gloves.

Above: The stove in this airmen's mess provides the warming focal point for the pilots. Their inertia belies the squadron's energy - they had a tally of 60 Luftwaffe kills by the end of 1940.

RAF offensive

The Battle of Britain, Hitler's attempt to gain mastery of the British skies, might have failed but the Blitz continued to be a potent and almost crushing strategy. However, the RAF, freed from the pressure of massed daytime raids and the need to engage hundreds of Luftwaffe fighters could now move onto the offensive and began regular sweeps over occupied France, harrassing German troops and destroying their defensive positions.

Above left: The symbol of the Spitfire and the bravery of its pilots gained the backing of the entire nation; Beaverbrook's Spitfire Fund led to organisations of all sizes raising money to 'buy' Spitfires, which entered service with appropriate names. Here 19-year-old Nora Margaret Fish hands over a Spitfire named 'Counter Attack' on behalf of the NAAFI canteen workers who raised the funds. The Kennel Club was responsible for 'The Dog Fighter' and Marks & Spencer, 'The Marksman'.

Middle left: Crew of the Fleet Air Arm go over charts in their mess. The Royal Navy had its own aircraft at the beginning of the century but merged with the Royal Flying Corps to form the RAF in 1918. The Navy continued to fly ship-based aircraft as tactical weapons but the great changes in warfare slowly forced the imperial powers to recognise the importance of air power and the Fleet Air Arm was formed under admiralty control in 1939. By the end of the War, aircraft carriers became the capital ships in the navies of the world and the Fleet Air Arm operated nearly 4,000 aircraft from 59 carriers.

Below left: Hurricanes patrol the skies. RDF provided efficient screening for the massed Luftwaffe attacks of the Battle of Britain but German planes learned to fly under the radar and the RAF daylight patrols were the only sure way to intercept attacking and reconnaissance aircraft.

Daylight attacks by the Luftwaffe more or less ended on October 29, 1940 but were substituted with devastating night raids. The Hurricane received further adaptations to make it effective by day and by night as an interceptor. As can be seen in this formation of 87 Squadron, parading its brand-new Mark IIC aircraft donated by the people of the United Provinces of India, the colour scheme of the aircraft has been darkened considerably while its armament now boasts four wing-mounted 20mm cannon.

SEPTEMBER 20, 1940

Hitler to turn east for winter campaign

From various sources, wide apart, come signs that invasion of Britain is no longer the first item on Hitler's agenda. Signs accumulate that the Axis Powers have decided to shift the war's centre of gravity from the West to the Near East, from the English Channel to the Mediterranean.

Gales having scattered Hitler's armada and the R.A.F. having smashed his invasion ports, it would seem that he has rolled up the map of Western Europe for the time being and is concentrating his attention on a winter campaign in the Mediterranean in general and the Eastern Mediterranean in particular.

Three moves point to that conclusion:

- The Italian advance along the Egyptian coast, sixty miles toward Mersa Matruh and Alexandria.
- Ribbentrop's call on Mussolini in Rome.
- The visit of General Franco's envoy, Senor Suner, to Hitler is to be followed, it is reported, by a visit to Rome.

Alexander Clifford, cabling from Cairo, says that he learns from several neutral sources that Ribbentrop has been sent to Rome to give Mussolini instructions for the winter blitzkrieg in the Middle East.

Mussolini was in a position to tell Ribbentrop, when he received him yesterday, that he had completed the preliminary phase essential for any blow at Egypt.

The super Supermarine Spitfire

The Spitfire came through the Battle of Britain with flying colours, proving itself not just to be a sleek, high-speed fighter, but an efficient killing machine, thanks to continuing improvements: finally its carburettor was adapted to enable a dive as steep as the Bf 109 and the limited machine guns were beefed up with wing-mounted cannon. Further developments were made to the Rolls-Royce Merlin engine and improved propellers stepped up the plane's performance. The next generation was equipped with new wing-mounted cannon with a cowling covering adaptations for deployment in north Africa's Western Desert.

Above left: The Mark XII version of the Spitfire took to the air in April 1942, equipped with the much more powerful Griffon engine and a strengthened airframe to take advantage of the extra horsepower. Only 100 went into production as a speed advantage at lower altitudes compromised performance at high altitudes. In effect it was a prototype for the much more successful Mk XIV that entered service in January 1943, with dramatic improvements to its climb rate and top speed.

Above: The latest Spitfire, equipped with two wing-mounted 20mm cannon, practises aerial tactics on this RAF trainer during exercises. The veteran pilots and Fighter Command reckoned that a pilot needed a year of flying to be sufficiently trained to meet the Luftwaffe challenge. During the Battle, novices were filling the ranks of their lost and wounded seniors, leading to increased casualties.

Left: Spitfire pilots in their Scottish base await the controller's call to scramble in April 1941.

Left: Winston Churchill caught in a quiet moment. His ironic look, cigar in hand and his iconic black felt Bowker hat and stick laid on the table make him seem very human. Yet if the RAF were 'the Few' he was 'the One'.

Left: This shot-down Messerschmitt Bf 109 went on display to raise money for the Croydon Spitfire Fund; a high proportion of the estimated 1,500 'Presentation Spitfires' were funded in this way. Those who couldn't afford money donated their pots and pans as raw materials for manufacturing.

Below: Winston Churchill receives a rapturous welcome in Sheffield as people crowd his open car to greet him. The nation was in no doubt that Churchill's indomitable leadership brought them through the Battle of Britain and that his objective was unchanged from his first speech to Parliament as Prime Minister: total victory over the Nazi regime, 'Victory at all costs'.

Chapter Three

Blitz on Britain
Sept 1940 - May 1941

Even though the invasion of Britain was called off, Germany continued to bomb Britain's cities in the hope of breaking civilian morale. The Blitz began in September 1940 with attacks on London. Civilian targets were struck across the city from the docklands in the east to Buckingham Palace in the west. Londoners were especially vulnerable because few people had space for air-raid shelters. Consequently many people crammed into underground Tube stations. These undoubtedly saved many lives, but were not without risk. On October 14, 1940, sixty-four people were killed at Balham Tube station when a bomb hit a water main, flooding the station.

Britain had been prepared for such an aerial bombardment since the beginning of the war, and many targets had been anticipated. The country had made provision for air raids: blackout conditions were imposed at night, air-raid shelters had been built, and there had even been a mass issue of gas masks, on the assumption that Hitler might make use of chemical weapons. Although poison gas was never used in the Blitz, casualties were high as densely populated areas were subjected to sustained bombardment. Though a lot of children had been evacuated to the countryside from the cities at the start of the war, most of them had returned during the period of the 'phoney war', and many of them died.

Left: A new view of St Paul's is revealed from Queen Victoria Street after vast bombing damage and subsequent demolition.

Terrorising civilians

On September 7, 1940, the Blitz began in earnest. Throughout the Battle of Britain many south-east towns, including the capital itself, had suffered bombing from German aircraft as the Luftwaffe attempted to destroy ground air defences as well as the RAF. During this period there were also glimpses of the use of aerial terror tactics on the civilian population as bombs were dropped on non-military targets or machine gunners strafed public areas. In September, with the failure of 'Operation Sealion', these tactics became German policy.

Left: **London's Regent Street badly damaged following a night of heavy bombing.**

Below: **A row of taxis destroyed in London's Leicester Square.**

Top: On the fifth night of the Blitz, East Enders used Liverpool Street and aother underground stations to try and escape the bombing raids

Left: Seemingly undeterred, these workers bombed out of their office building continue their jobs in the street, protected only by their steel helmets.

Above: Burlington Arcade also suffered damage. Although bombing began in the docklands, the carnage soon spread across the city.

First strikes

London was the focus for most Blitz attacks. At first, the Germans mounted sorties day and night but losses were large and after a week the Luftwaffe switched most of their operations to take place under cover of darkness.

Left: Urban bombing destroyed hundreds of homes and businesses, leaving many civilians homeless and shops and services wiped out. However, people had little choice but to adjust to these challenging circumstances and most did so well. Provisions were made for the homeless, with buildings such as schools being used as temporary accomodation.

Below: A British soldier, heavily laden with equipment, pauses for a mug of tea at a London station.

Left: Temporary Post Offices were designed to be portable and could be erected swiftly in order to replace Post Offices which had been damaged by bombing.

Below: Women and children queue for food at a communal cooking centre set up by the London Council.

Bottom: This street fruit seller boasts that his oranges have come through Musso's (Mussolini's) 'Lake' – a nickname for the Mediterranean. He also has bananas for sale – a rarity during the war, especially by the time of the Blitz.

55-day onslaught

The first raid hit London during the daylight hours of a beautiful, sunny September day. Hundreds of incendiary bombs were dropped on the dock area and the fires they started provided a guide and target for the night-time raiders. All night the Luftwaffe bombed the East End and by morning there were 430 civilians dead, 1600 injured and thousands made homeless. The raids on London continued for the next 55 days, although after the first week most raids took place at night as the Germans found their losses too great with daylight raids.

Above and middle left: Both John Lewis and Peter Robinson's department stores were completely gutted by fire after a night raid. The Inner Temple library, County Hall and several other major shops were also bombed that night.

Below left: A tramcar destroyed during a daylight raid in Blackfriars Road.

Below: Firemen play their hoses on the National Bank in Oxford Street, hit during an early Blitz raid.

Left and far left: Police were often first on the scene, taking charge, directing people to safety and co-ordinating rescue services. After a daylight raid, a policeman had to climb up to check whether gas was leaking from this street lamp. Fires and gas explosions after bomb attacks were a constant hazard and the Civil Defence along with members of the general public needed to be continually vigilant.

Below: Every night London's Underground Stations were crowded with people seeking shelter. Many of them arrived early in the evening with their bedding, prepared to settle down for a night's sleep on the platforms. Some came from the suburbs and outlying districts.

The King and Queen stay at home

Lowering public morale was a key aim in the German High Command's bombing strategy and it proved to be a frightening experience for many, and affected everyone's life. Nevertheless, while every member of the population was touched in some way, they did not become demoralised. In fact, the constant attacks seemed to provoke the reverse effect to that intended – the sense of a nation pulling together, for bombs did not discriminate, no one, not even the King and Queen who remained in Buckingham Palace for the duration of the war, was spared the effects or the fear.

Above: A crater just outside the gates of Buckingham Palace was one of five, all caused by bombs dropped near to each other in September 1940.

Above right: Workmen labour to repair one of the areas of damage.

Right: Winston Churchill joined King George VI and Queen Elizabeth to inspect some damage in the grounds. The culprit was a time bomb dropped by a German raider. The area affected was part of the building adapted to provide a swimming pool for Princess Elizabeth and Princess Margaret.

Above left: A policeman shows off some of the wreckage caused by the bomb that destroyed the Palace's North Lodge.

Above right and inset: Following a night of heavy bombing the Queen toured the East End, visiting the site of a bombed hospital and speaking to local families.

Below left: The North Lodge, next to Constitution Hill, received a direct hit in a raid in March 1941. A policeman died when one of the stone pillars fell on him.

SEPTEMBER 12, 1940

Buckingham Palace hit by bomb

Buckingham Palace has now shared with Britain's humblest homes the fury of the Nazi raiders. Yesterday I walked round the gardens with Sir Alan Lascelles, the King's Assistant Private Secretary, and saw the effects of a time bomb which landed 6ft. from the Palace.

It exploded early on Tuesday - during another raid - wrecked part of the Princesses' swimming pool and smashed nearly every window in the north wing, including the windows of the royal suite.

The King and Queen spent the week-end at Windsor, but when the King returned to London yesterday he, the Queen, and Mr. Churchill, who lunched at the Palace, inspected the crater and also the damaged part of the Palace.

No one was hurt. Members of the household had been moved to another part of the Palace when the bomb was discovered near the Belgian Suite.

250-pounder

The windows of the King's and Queen's bedrooms and dressing-rooms; the Queen's bow-windowed sitting-room and the King's little balconied work-room were blown out. Showers of soot, glass and masonry poured into these rooms, covering the floors with thick dust and chipping walls and doors. The bomb - believed to be a 250-pounder - buried itself 10ft. deep, forcing up stone slabs on the terrace.

It demolished one wall of a Georgian-period building which was converted into a swimming pool about two years ago. This had previously been a conservatory.

The explosion broke in pieces some of the huge columns of the building. Masonry, weighing many tons, was flung into the air. Some of it was hurled over roofs and landed in the quadrangle. An underground shelter underneath the pool was also damaged.

Heavy casualties

Casualties in London for September and October were high – 13,000 killed and 20,000 injured. However, the availability of deep shelters in the Underground system helped reduce the numbers. Tube stations became the preferred shelters for Londoners, although initially the authorities were averse to the system being used for this purpose, believing it would seriously compromise the Underground's ability to function. There were also fears that the population would develop a 'deep shelter mentality', making it difficult to carry on as normally as possible. Public demand, and the clear evidence that the city and its people could still function, changed the government's mind.

Above: **Thurston's, home of billiards, and the Automobile Association's HQ, that stand side-by-side in Leicester Square, were damaged when a bomb dropped on the area in October 1940.**

Above left: **A downed fighter-bomber lies almost intact in this London street.**

Left: **Even the humblest of buildings needed protection!**

Builders recalled from army

In October 1940, the government decided to release 5,000 building workers from the armed forces to try to repair the bomb damage. By this time 76,000 homes had either been destroyed or were uninhabitable. 250,000 people had been made homeless (albeit some only temporarily) and local authorities had only been able to rehouse 7,000. They had provided Rest Centres but these were severely overcrowded.

Left: Despite losing the complete wall of one side of this house, the interior remains largely intact – even the miror on the wall survived.

Below: Families gather in the street as they sit surrounded by whatever they can salvage.

Bottom: The Wolverhampton Auxiliary Fire Service demonstrates the power of one hundred hoses blasting water simultaneously

Auxiliary Fire Service

The Auxiliary Fire Service was initiated to support the existing fire services during the extensive bombing campaigns. The service consisted of 60,000 members who would work a rota of 48 hours on, 24 hours off, which left many fighting for 40 hours at a time while bombing raids continued. The death and injury rate was extremely high. At times pumps were brought in from neighbouring areas but hose couplings did not always match other authorities' hydrants, which highlighted the need for standardisation in the future. A favourite German tactic was to send down incendiary devices and then attack the water mains to limit the supply of water to the fires.

Above right: **Fire crews clearing up after fighting blazes all night.**

Below and below right: **Captured German airmen escorted through a London station in October 1940; they would be taken by rail to a Prisoner of War camp.**

The homeless

During the closing months of 1940, life for most Londoners became a relentless routine of going into shelters as dusk fell, sleeping or dozing through the night, listening to the raids outside and emerging in the morning to see the extent of the damage. Days were spent at work, or clearing up the remains of bombed homes and workplaces, or trying to look after a family at home. Those made homeless tried to carry on their lives in temporary accommodation in public buildings such as church halls and schools.

Top: A family occupy themselves as they wait for the removal van that would transport their belongings salvaged from their bombed-out home.

Above: A London family hitches a ride on the tailboard of the removal van taking their belongings to a place of safety.

Left: A child at play on a home-made cart calmly reads the danger notice.

Coventry blitzed

A devastating attack on the ancient cathedral city of Coventry on November 14, 1940 was the first major raid on a town or city outside London. It marked a change in the tactics of the German High Command; not only were there to be attacks on the symbolic heart of the nation, but the destruction was to be spread throughout the country. The attack on Coventry was carried out by a squad of 500 bombers which dropped 500 tonnes of high explosives and 36,000 incendiaries in an attempt to set the city ablaze. The strategy was largely successful and although firecrews and emergency services worked tirelessly, by the morning Coventry's mediaeval cathedral was almost entirely reduced to rubble, along with around 50,000 buildings. A death toll of 568 civilians was reported.

Top: Coventry city centre was almost completely destroyed by fires started by night-time bombing. Although London was perhaps the most heavily and regularly bombed British city, others such as Coventry, Birmingham, Manchester, Liverpool, Bristol and Southampton also suffered from devastating air raids.

Above: Smouldering ruins, including a burnt-out bus, in a Coventry street after the November raid. It is notable that most of the damage in the majority of air raids was caused, not by the impact of high explosive devices, but by the fires they started or incendiary bombs dropped with the specific objective of starting fires.

Left: Coventry's main shopping area still smoulders the following day, after the previous night's 13-hour raid, which saw the Luftwaffe fly sortie after sortie to bomb the ancient city.

Above top: Pedestrians pick their way through the smouldering debris of Coventry city centre as they resume their daily lives.

Above middle: Only the chimney stacks are left standing in what was once a busy shopping street in the centre of Coventry.

Above: Rescue workers bring out a Mr Newman from a bombed building after he was buried under debris for 14 hours. Apart from suffering from shock, he was unharmed.

Left: Just over a week after the attack on Coventry, Birmingham was bombed relentlessly in an attack which lasted some eleven hours. The following morning, firemen continued to deal with a blaze at a Birmingham factory.

NOVEMBER 16, 1940

Spirit of the people is unconquerable

A pall of smoke hung over many areas of Coventry to-day. Two thousand high-explosive and thousands of incendiary bombs were rained indiscriminately on the city last night in a dusk-till-dawn air raid. Main streets were reduced to acres of rubble, and famous public buildings, cinemas, shops, houses, were obliterated.

A thousand people were killed and injured and thousands more found themselves without homes. Yet the spirit of the people is unconquerable.

Only a shell of walls remains of Coventry's famous cathedral.

Churches, public baths, clubs, cinemas, hotels, and hundreds of shops and business premises have been damaged. In the suburbs hundreds of houses have been demolished and thousands of people made homeless.

Early to-day men, women, and children trudged out into the countryside carrying all the belongings they had been able to salvage, pushing perambulators, carts, and bicycles laden with their possessions, hoping to find country billets before to-night's black-out.

Many had only a blanket or two and a pillow. As evening

approached people in the bombed suburbs were loading up cars with mattresses and bedding. But many private cars were seen approaching Coventry too - all of them loaded with food and other supplies.

The attack lasted eleven hours. It is estimated here that at least 100 'planes, arriving in waves, took part. The first raiders to arrive dropped incendiary bombs, and many fires were started. As the intensity of the attack grew, the din became terrific.

Above right: An anti-aircraft battery at work during a raid on the north of England.

Left: A few days after the bombing of Coventry, King George visited the city with the Minister for Home Security, Herbert Morrison.

New roles for women

Prior to the start of the Second World War, most women were at home without any paid employment. In January 1940, Churchill asked women to help with the war effort which usually meant working in the munitions factories. In December 1941, women aged 20 to 30, with no specific responsibilities in the home were conscripted to either the forces or industry. As with men the age of conscription was gradually raised and even those needed in the home often took on part-time work. The roles undertaken varied from factory work, food production, and fulfilling tasks normally carried out by the men who had been called up.

Top: **Princess Elizabeth made her first broadcast in 1940. It was a task that her father hated, due to a stammer, so the BBC used to record his voice in small sections at a time. Elizabeth, however, embraced the challenge and would record her speeches live.**

Above: **Volunteer ambulance women at their station in north-west London preparing for a practice run.**

Left: **A team of five female demolition workers take a break after pulling down a bridge over the LNER line in Wembley.**

Targeting industrial cities

Many cities and towns throughout Britain were targeted as important industrial centres where the weapons of war were produced, from small ordnance to tanks and anti-aircraft guns. Many coastal areas were home to major naval ports building both war and merchant ships, often at the rate of one per week. Hardly a town of any size escaped aerial assault throughout the war. Many, like Liverpool, Manchester, Bristol, Birmingham and Southampton suffered nights of severe bombing. During November and December 1940 each of these cities was prey to a favoured German tactic of a heavy raid one night followed by a further heavy raid either the following night or very soon after.

Liverpool was constantly under attack. It was the most important port outside London and as a result of raids on the London docks, became even more essential. A vital route for military equipment and supplies, it was also home to many munitions factories. Liverpool and Birkenhead were attacked on December 20 and 21, resulting in 365 people losing their lives. Forty-two were killed after bombing attacks on two air raid shelters and another 42 were killed after railway arches being used as unofficial air raid shelters were hit. 1,399 children were evacuated out of the city. Between August 1940 and January 1942, a total of 4,000 people were killed and 3,500 seriously injured.

Above left: A child, a nun and a parishioner pray amongst the bombed-out wreckage of a London church.

Right and inset right: Damage to Liverpool's buildings after the pre-Christmas raid.

Above left: This bus was damaged by the falling masonry during a bombing raid.

Middle left: Salvation Army workers were on hand to provide tea to victims of bomb damage. It was up to the occupants to salvage as much as they could from their homes.

Below left: A Dornier which had just machine-gunned streets in a coastal town was finally brought down on a beach. South-east England was known as 'Hellfire Corner' when it initially suffered from daily attacks. Eventually the Germans changed tactics and focused their bombing raids on major cities.

Below: The city of Sheffield suffered from a severe attack on December 12 1940 which destroyed thirty-one tramcars and damaged nearly all the remaining stock. Sheffield United's Bramall Lane stand was also hit during the raid.

The second Fire of London

At the very end of the year, London was hit by one of the most devastating raids of the war. It was Sunday night, December 29, and the Thames was at its lowest ebb. High explosive parachute mines severed the water mains at the beginning of the raid, during which more than 10,000 incendiary bombs were dropped on the City of London. The result was the second Fire of London. Twenty thousand firefighters, assisted by countless soldiers, using 2,300 pumps to take water directly from the river, fought to control the blaze which threatened to turn the City into one huge conflagration.

Above left: On the Monday morning, clerks were helped by soldiers to salvage books from their offices. Much time was subsequently spent reconstituting records.

Below left: St Paul's Cathedral standing defiantly amongst the surrounding mayhem. Although St. Paul's was bombed during the war, it remained relatively intact. This image taken from the roof of the *Daily Mail* building by photographer Herbert Mason was to become one of the most enduring and iconic images of the Blitz.

Inset: As daylight arrived on December 30, firefighters in some areas continued the struggle for control.

Above Left: The Pioneer Corps clear up around Tower Hill after the raid – the Tower of London can be seen in the background.

Below left: Taken a week after the Fire of London, the buildings around St Paul's are still smouldering.

Below right: London's firefighters try to prevent the spread of the fire beneath St Paul's Cathedral.

Avoiding 'deep shelter mentality'

In London, Blitz casualties were high, with 13,000 killed and 20,000 injured during September and October alone. However, the availability of deep shelters in the London Underground system kept numbers lower than might have been expected. The London Underground provided a haven for many Londoners, though some concerns were raised about a small minority of people who became too frightened to return above ground and adopted a subterranean existence throughout much of the Blitz.

Left: Adapted from the Borough tube, this was the largest air-raid shelter in Britain. It was able to hold 11,000 people and had eight entrances.

Below: By January 1941, bunks had been installed on Underground platforms and passengers waited for the last train while others settled down to sleep. The deep tunnels of the Underground offered a safe haven, but even they were not entirely bombproof. In one of the worst incidents of the war 110 people were killed while sheltering in, or travelling through, Bank tube station when it received a direct hit.

Opposite: Families sheltering at Piccadilly Circus Underground station during an air raid.

Legacy of the bombing

Following the Fire of London raid, the capital suffered almost nightly bombing until May 1941. During the night of May 11 over 500 Luftwaffe planes dropped hundreds of high explosive bombs and tens of thousands of incendiary devices. Many important London landmarks were damaged that night, including the chamber of the House of Commons and Big Ben. This was the last great bombing raid on London, but one of the legacies of the months of sustained bombing, was the fear of the attackers returning.

Left: The Lord Mayor of London spent New Year's Day 1941 inspecting the damage in Aldermanbury.

Below: The Guildhall suffered severe damage during the raid. Here, wreckage of the roof beams lies in the Banqueting Hall. It was to take years of careful restoration work post-war to return the building to its former glory.

Left: The scene at St Bride's Street in London after a raid. The majority of the people were on their way to work and would need to salvage what they could from the premises and find alternative places to work.

Below left: A quick and effective method for the police to give the 'All Clear'.

Below right: The Pioneer Corps was formed to help with clearance and salvage operations with the workers largely drawn from the unemployed. The Salvation Army was again on hand to provide food and drink for them.

Right: An area close to St Paul's was closed to the public and used to store materials needed to make buildings safe and subsequently rebuild them.

Below: The blast at Grose's sports shop, New Bridge Street had forced several bicycles into the air leaving them strangely suspended from the wreckage.

Bottom: The Duke of Kent (centre) inspecting bomb damage. He was an RAF pilot and was killed later in the war.

Unloaded - and ran

In one of their most vicious and indiscriminate attacks on London, the German Air Force on Saturday night were forced by R.A.F. night fighters to pay a staggering toll out of all proportion to the military damage they inflicted. At the rate of six a minute during the height of the attack 29 of the raiders were shot to pieces by our avenging night fighters, and four more were brought down by A.A. gunfire.

It was a perfect full moon night for accurate bombing of important objectives, but the Luftwaffe unloaded their fire-bombs and high explosives over London as indiscriminately as if they were bombing through thick clouds.

In such conditions a force half the size of that sent over by the Luftwaffe - estimated to be between 300 and 400 aircraft - should have been able to strike telling blows.

It is clear, therefore, that either Hitler ordered his airmen to unload their bombs on London without bothering to pick out targets, or the increasing deadliness of our night fighters is having its effect on the morale of the Nazi airmen, causing them to unload and get away home as quickly as possible.

In the first ten nights of May, 124 German night raiders have been destroyed - 34 more than the previous record of 90 for the whole of April. They represent at least 500 trained German pilots and air crews - an average of 50 a night.

Below left: Hatfield House in Hertfordshire was taken over by the government and used as a military hospital.

Below right and bottom: Hospitals were frequently a target during the bombing raids. In the clear-up operations, everything possible would be rescued, cleaned and reused.

MAY 12, 1941

German communiqué

The German communiqué on the raid says: "In successive waves German planes dropped high-explosive bombs of all calibres and tens of thousands of incendiary bombs on London during the whole of the night. "Large fires in the Thames Loop, particularly in the Commercial and Millwall Docks, as well as between Waterloo Bridge and the Victoria Docks, testified to the effectiveness of the attack."

Above left: A new type of bunk for the home-based Anderson shelters was initially designed and made by a London policeman. The Ministry of Home Security then adopted and used the idea.

Middle left: A soldier is greeted by his delighted family as he begins ten days' leave.

Below left: : A hairdresser's in the West End of London after a raid sports the legend 'Business as Usual'.

Above: Servicemen drinking tea outside a mobile canteen in a blitzed area of Manchester.

Middle left: Lever Brothers were instrumental in providing hot baths along with free towels and soap for homeless children.

Below left: All factories and institutions had their own roof spotters, usually members of staff who did an extra shift. The roof spotter's job was to act as an early warning to those inside the building of the approach of a raid. Here, the roof spotter works on while West Ham play Chelsea in December 1940 at the height of the Blitz.

Below: Herbert Morrison's appeal for hundreds of fire-spotters to guard buildings in towns all over the country met with wide response. The Boy Scouts Association arranged for squads of Scouts to act as spotters in their own districts. This spotter has seen an incendiary with the alarm sounded on a dustbin lid by his comrade.

Plymouth hit hard again

Food convoys were rushed to Plymouth yesterday and emergency centres set up to feed the city's homeless after German bombers had heavily raided the town for the second night running. It was Plymouth's worst raid yet. Rescue work went on through the yesterday. Last night it was feared that the death toll would be heavy.

A large number were killed in public shelters which received a direct hit. Some dead were recovered yesterday. An elderly man who was rescued after being buried for seven hours in the ruins of a shelter sang 'Tipperary' while his rescuers were taking him to hospital.

One heavy bomb fell in a square and devastated buildings and badly damaged a school where 9d dinners have been served regularly since the big blitz of a month ago. When those in charge arrived yesterday to find the building bombed, they at once set out to clear the debris and install new equipment. At midday they were able to serve 350 dinners to bombed-out people.

One Remains...

The raiders poured thousands of incendiaries on the city. A great number of houses and other premises were alight at one time over a wide area. In some streets few buildings now remain intact. In one the only building still standing is a cinema - itself badly damaged. The devastated area is large, and some streets yesterday were closed to pedestrians as well as to traffic.

In part of the town a shopping centre, churches and hospitals were wrecked. A post office, three cinemas, a library, a number of public-houses, two-stores, and a large draper's shop are among the buildings destroyed.

More than 100 planes were engaged in the raid, which lasted several hours. They faced a tremendous barrage.

Indiscriminate

In the later stages they bombed indiscriminately, but early on they followed a set plan. Waves of bombers followed each other with time-table precision and took full advantage of knowledge gained by those preceding them.

One complete terrace of houses was bombed. The occupants escaped with their lives but they lost their furniture. Seventy pianos were destroyed in one building that was set alight.

Above right: Sailors help with the clear-up after three successive nights of raids in April 1941. As home to Devonport, Britain's major naval base, Plymouth was a prime Luftwaffe target as German High Command sought to gain domination in the Atlantic. As a consequence, the city was hit by almost 60 air raids.

Below right: The Dean of St Peter's Church in Plymouth reflects on the ruins of the bombed-out church.

Above left: Some residents in Plymouth remained undaunted as they gathered round a salvaged piano for a song; they had been bombed for three nights in succession.

Below left: The Old Gaiety Theatre in Manchester received damage to the outside of the building during an air raid in June 1941.

Above: Hull was subject to constant bombing during May 1941 and the city continued to be attacked during the following summer months. During one raid in July 1941, extensive damage was caused in New Bridge Road, a residential district.

Abbey and Parliament bombed

The Houses of Parliament, with Big Ben and Westminster Hall, and Westminster Abbey and the British Museum, were among the buildings damaged by bombs in what the German High Command yesterday claimed to be a "reprisal raid on military targets in London."

Big Ben, with its face scarred and blackened, having been hit by a high explosive, continued to show the time, though the apparatus which broadcasts the chimes to the world was for a time out of order.

The Debating Chamber of the Commons - the cradle of democracy - was wrecked and it is feared that it cannot be used again until it is rebuilt. The Speaker's Chair and the Government front benches are now merely charred wood.

High-explosive bombs and incendiaries fell on the Houses of Parliament, and soon flames were seen licking round Big Ben's Tower. They spread shortly afterwards to the Abbey. One explosive fell into the centre of the Chamber, and in a short time fire had destroyed the contents.

In the House of Lords, Captain E. L. H. Elliott, resident superintendent, two policemen and a custodian were killed. Other members of the staff, who worked through the night putting out the flames and salvaging valuable records and relics, had remarkable escapes when the bombs fell.

Bombs smashed the roof of the famous Members' Lobby, which had already been damaged in previous raids, and was shored up by elaborate scaffolding. Doors were torn off and windows smashed.

What is considered the most magnificent roof in the world, that of Westminster Hall, with its soaring arches and sweeping beams of oak, was pierced by bombs, and damage was done to the interior. The hall last night was inches deep in water.

Above left: Richard the Lionheart managed to survive an attack on the Houses of Parliament although his sword was not so lucky.

Below left: The Bank tube station was the site of the largest bomb crater in London, caused by a direct hit on January 11, 1941, killing over fifty people. A temporary bridge was built over the damage.

Opposite: During a twelve-hour raid by 413 aircraft in December, bombs hit the Houses of Parliament, causing damage to Cloister Court. The Members' Cloakroom is to the left of the guard.

MAY 16, 1941

The Old Bailey hit

London, who cannot lose her courage, cannot, alas, save her treasures. Recent raids have scarred her streets and destroyed her rich heritage of the years.

St. Clement Danes - little island church of the Strand - stands now a tragic shell. The bells of St. Clement's, known to every boy and girl, are believed to have been cracked by the heat and damaged beyond repair. The roof has gone. The walls alone remain. So passes one more Wren masterpiece.

St. James's Palace has been hit. In the south wing of Friary Court - scene of the changing of the guard - a bomb landed on a building used as offices. The State Apartments of the palace escaped.

Queen's Hall was burned out. Under the debris lie the organ and thousands of pounds worth of instruments belonging to the London Philharmonic Orchestra. The orchestra are trying to borrow enough new ones for their Whitsun season of "Proms" at the London Coliseum. Mr. Cedric Sharpe's £600 cello was damaged almost beyond repair. Two harps, the complete percussion equipment, and 60 per cent. of the strings were destroyed.

The Archbishop of Canterbury, Dr. Lang, was spending the night in Lambeth Palace when a basket of incendiaries fell. Thousands of books in the ecclesiastical library were destroyed.

At the Old Bailey, damaged for the third time, Court No. 2 is a ruin and the other three courts have gaping holes and splintered wood-work. The great Marble-Hall is littered with masonry, but on the dome the gilded figure of sightless Justice still stands with arms outstretched.

Above left: A man surveys the debris after eight churches designed by Christopher Wren, the Old Bailey and three hospitals were set on fire and the Guildhall was badly damaged.

Below left: A bomb dropped in April 1941 causes a crater in the north transept of St Paul's.

Left: Capturing the humour of ordinary people, the notice painted on the side of this shelter suggests, perhaps ironically, that a night sheltering in an air raid is as entertaining as an evening in the music hall.

Middle: A messenger puzzles out where to redirect his packages as the businesses to which he is delivering have been re-homed following the destruction of their original premises in one of the worst raids of the Blitz.

Below: A family removing articles from their wrecked house.

Biggest London raid

It had been a fantastic night. London was bathed in the golden glow of the full moon. Soon the mingled incendiaries and explosives turned parts of the city into an inferno. Rolling billows of smoke blotted out the moonlit sky.

Some commercial buildings were hit. But once more it was the houses of the people, rich and poor, that suffered most.

Over all was the roar of the guns, the whistle and crump of bombs, and the crackle of the fighters machine-guns high in the sky. Five hospitals were hit and there were casualties at three of them. One was a children's hospital.

At one hospital four wards were demolished, and twelve people, including a night sister and a woman dispenser, were killed. A sister saw the bomb tear its way through her ward and then explode in the one beneath. She at once started rescuing 18 men patients who were buried under the debris. With the help of nurses, she got them all out except one, who was killed.

Nearby, an earlier bomb had hit an A.R.P. rescue party depot. Two men were killed and six injured. Those who escaped had just finished extricating their colleagues when the hospital was hit. They immediately ran to the spot and helped nurses who were struggling with huge pieces of masonry beneath which some of the patients were trapped.

Women left the shelter in a block of flats to help the men fire-watchers and to salvage furniture when the roof of the flats was set on fire by incendiary bombs. They formed human chains to pass buckets of water for the stirrup pumps.

There was heavy loss of life when a bomb crashed through the roof of a London hotel and exploded in the basement, in which many of the 140 guests and employees were sheltering.

There were other casualties at a shelter, a rest centre, and a warden's post and a street market, where people were trapped. A cinema and several churches were struck. A club and an A.T.S. post also received direct hits.

Left: Young women pick their way through the debris after the the last major, and most devastating raid on London.

Right: A postman tries to deliver letters in Watling Street, London.

Chapter Four

Working for the war effort

During the war, everyone in Britain, whether young or old, rich or poor, male or female, experienced at some stage, and to varying degrees, a life of unremitting toil, privation and loss. Complaints about conditions were frequently greeted with: 'Don't you know there's a war on!' The war effort required everyone's energy, through military service, paid employment, voluntary work or running a home. Through the effects of bombing, or the need to commandeer houses to accommodate military personnel or evacuees, some lost their homes and often their way of life. Everyone financed the war through their taxation and savings schemes which targeted everyone, even children. However, there was little to spend money on because there was insufficient spare manufacturing capacity in the country to produce luxury items, while imported goods and raw materials were seen to put the lives of merchant seamen at risk of attack from German battleships and U-boats.

Left: Unfazed by their masculine work clothes, these sledgehammer-wielding women pose with their tools – visibly proud of their contribution being equal to that of men.

Top: Inspecting shells at a Royal Ordnance factory. Quality control was very important in order to prevent the military being put at risk from its own equipment.

Above left: Men at work in the torpedo workroom.

Above right: Shells arriving in the shell-inspecting shop at an ordnance factory.

Left: Inspection was carried out at all stages of production. Here the casings for naval shells are checked.

Munitions

Once the government had established a military force, its next priority was to organise the production of the munitions with which that force could fight the war. Factory space, a labour force and raw materials were needed to produce weapons in large quantities. Some raw materials were imported but many were provided by 'salvaging' or recycling items already in the country. Teams of women and children, organised by the Women's Voluntary Service (WVS), toured from house to house, collecting metal in the form of tin baths, saucepans and old tin cans. Additionally, they collected scrap rubber, rags, waste paper and old animal bones, all of which had some use in the production of weaponry.

Above right: **Thousands of empty cartridge cases ready for filling.**

Below right: **Every torpedo was 'tried out' and 'passed under working condition' before being dispatched to a Royal Navy ship.**

Below: **A factory inspecting room which was 'working at emergency pressure, day and night, to produce small arms, spare parts and tools.' Britain had not spent money on armaments in the years after the First World War and consequently, when war broke out again, it was a race to provide the equipment the military needed.**

Above: A production method new to Britain, but widely used in the USA, enabled the production of warships and merchant ships to be speeded up. The various parts of the ship were constructed at inland factories and then assembled on the slipway of the shipyard. This ship frame, photographed in September 1942, was one of the first built by this method.

Middle left: A newly built 8000-ton warship is pulled by tugs into the fitting-out basin for the final touches before it assumes active service.

Left: Workers constructing a bulkhead for a merchant ship (in background). Britain's merchant fleet was vital in keeping the country supplied with food and raw materials. At this stage of the war, 1942, Britain was launching a 10,000-ton merchant ship every three weeks; this yard had the target of constructing 16 ships in the year.

Ship building

Right: This warship gliding down the slipway was a product of Britain's one-a-week ship construction programme. As soon as it cleared the slipway, the workers would start preparing the berth for the keel-plate of the next ship.

Below: Britain produced military hardware, like these tanks, not only for itself but also for allies such as Russia.

Bottom: Shells being readied for transfer to the filling shops. Often ordnance produced in factories inside towns and cities were sent out of town to be filled with explosives. This reduced the risk of loss of life from explosions, caused either by enemy bombing or by accident.

AIRCRAFT

Opposite: A production line for the Blenheim bomber, 'whose speed and range', it was claimed, had 'outclassed anything the Germans have'. This was just one of the several aircraft factories around Britain producing fighter and bomber planes.

Above: Men stacking pure ingots of aluminium to dispatch to the Aircraft Presses. The thousands of tons of aluminium pans that housewives gave up to the Ministry of Aircraft Production made first-rate Spitfires. Smelting factories where saucepans, preserving pans and kettles were turned into ingots for the plane factories worked at full pressure.

Left: Anti-aircraft guns on the production line in a Midlands factory.

Coal supplies

Coal was the most essential fuel during the war. It powered the electricity stations, was needed for the production of gas, was required for smelting metal for munitions and was the chief source of domestic heating. Ensuring supplies of coal throughout the war was always a problem. With around three million working men in the forces, it was important to have enough labour to produce the weapons they needed. Men not eligible for active duty were redirected into war work; both men and women were conscripted into war work. The most notable of these were the 'Bevin Boys' – from December 1943 one in ten of newly conscripted men were selected by ballot to work in the coal mines. Other workers, such as farmers and train drivers, came under an Essential Work Order and were not required to undertake military service as their skills and experience were vital to keeping the country running smoothly. They could not be sacked and were not permitted to move to another job.

Top: Keeping coal supplies close to where they would be used helped avoid congestion on the rail network at peak times of demand. Here Marylebone Borough Council store coal for the winter at a bomb-damage site in Baker Street.

Middle left: This notice informs residents that, due to a shortage of coal in southern England, the emergency coal dumps would be closed down.

Middle right: Vehicle fuel was reserved for the military and other transport necessary to the war effort. It was only available to members of the public for 'essential' journeys – a doctor doing his rounds in a rural area, for example. Most cars were out of action for the duration of the war.

Left: Coal dumps ran a cash-and-carry scheme whereby local people could visit, pay for coal and take it away with them.

Queues for everything

As everything was in short supply, people spent hours queuing for food and goods. The government controlled prices in an attempt to avoid profiteering. Some shopkeepers kept unrationed items 'under the counter' to sell only to regular customers. There was also a black market, which was illegal and often involved those who had been on the wrong side of the law before the war.

Above: In July 1942, a queue forms outside a sweet shop near Leicester Square, London, as people try to stock up before sweets are rationed.

Middle: Queuing for tomatoes at a Birmingham greengrocer's soon after VE Day; a time when most people felt something should be done about the endless queuing.

Middle inset: The war brought horses back to Britain's roads in increasing numbers – for all manner of jobs but mainly transporting goods.

Left: 'First day of petrol rationing and this was the scene on a by-pass road near London which is usually crowded with speeding cars. People ambled pleasantly on horseback or bicycled happily by, but for the greater part of the day there was not a car to be seen.'

Dig for victory

By the end of the war Britain looked very different. Six years of war had scarred many of its most beautiful buildings and the landscape had changed as more and more of its acreage had been brought into production. People too looked different; many were worn out after years of hard work and worry and were dressed in either uniform or old and worn or 'utility' style clothing. Life seemed dull and dreary, with shortages of even the most basic household items and a diet that was nutritionally sound but very limited in range and variety.

Above left: **Soldiers help gather the harvest in 1941. After the retreat from Dunkirk, there was little active fighting to be done, as Britain gathered its forces for an invasion of Hitler's 'Fortress Europe'.**

Above: **Westminster City Council put galvanised bins at street corners. Notices on the covers told housewives what they should put in the bins to help feed pigs and other livestock on farms.**

Left: **A farm about a quarter of an acre in extent, tucked away under the shadow of St Giles, Cripplegate, which was damaged in the 1940 air raids. Firemen from the station across the way made it, almost everything there, except the livestock, was provided by the Blitz. The bricks for the pigsties came from bombed buildings, as did the wood from which the fowl-houses and the "tomatory" were made. On it there were almost every vegetable known to gardeners, and six apple trees, reputed to be the only apple trees in the City.**

Britain needed to be able to produce as much food as possible and the 'Dig for Victory' campaign encouraged people to grow their own. Often this would provide the majority of a family's fresh fruit and vegetables.

Above: **Workers from Ilford shoulder their forks and march to their allotments.**

Top right: **Schoolchildren in Monmouthshire tend vegetables in the school garden.**

Middle right: **Maureen Copeland helps her dad prepare the soil on their plot on Clapham Common.**

Bottom right: **A worker tends crops within sight of the Albert Memorial in Kensington Gardens.**

Women at work

When the war started, there was a great demand for labour on all fronts. Pre-war, the workforce was largely male, but many of those men were required for the military. By 1940, Britain had three and a half million men in the armed forces. However, there was still a need to keep essential services, like power and transport, running and a need to produce the munitions necessary to fight the war. The war itself created a large number of new jobs, from ARP wardens and fire spotters to demolition crews. Other jobs, like those in the fire service, required an increase in numbers to deal with the effects of war on civilian life. Women were the only pool of labour from which to meet the shortfall caused by the loss of so many male workers. To this end, Winston Churchill, in January 1940, when still First Lord of the Admiralty, called for a million women to help with war work, principally in the production of munitions.

Right: **Two women model post office uniforms – the inclusion of a trousered uniform was hailed as a first.**

Below left: **Offering comfort and refreshments to children being evacuated by train.**

Below right: **Two women install a gas cooker. At the gas works, women took on a range of jobs, from installation and maintenance of appliances to heavy labouring jobs such as filling 100-ton coke sacks.**

Below middle: **Women sort parcels at Mount Pleasant Post Office, Christmas 1940.**

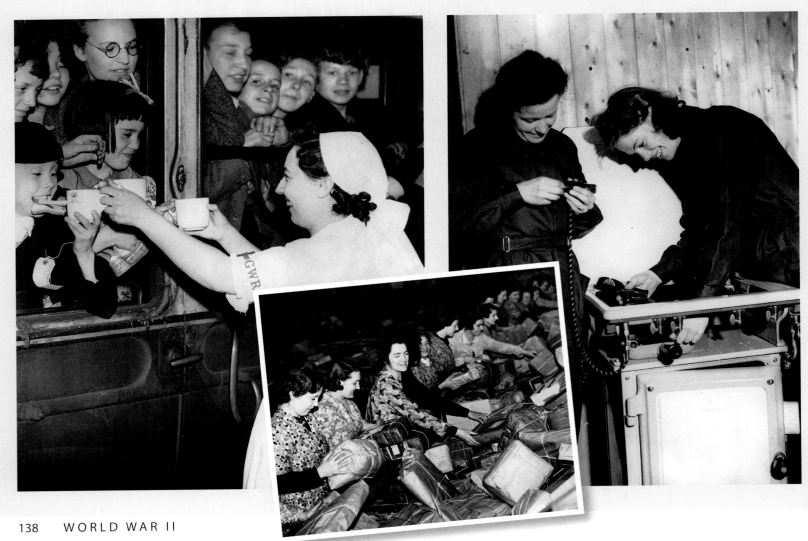

Top right: A uniformed postwoman collects letters and parcels from a London postbox.

Above left: Women delivering towels to City offices.

Left: A group of volunteer ambulance women prepare for a practice run from their station in north-west London.

Above: A postwoman delivers the Christmas mail. Women were employed to help with the increased mail. They were not given uniforms but wore their own clothes.

Women munitions workers

The production of munitions included not only the building of war machinery but also the manufacture of bombs, shells, mines and bullets used by those weapons. Hundreds of women were employed in producing the casings for these items, a task which involved working with smelting furnaces and hot metal. Once cast, the casings were sent to be filled in other factories, usually sited out of town because of the risk of explosion. In order to minimise this risk, women working with explosives wore a cloak and beret of undyed silk and rubber galoshes, and had to remove jewellery, corsets, hairpins or anything metal which might cause a spark.

Top: Manufacturing 'Sten' guns at the Royal Ordnance factory in Theale, Berkshire.

Above: Women checking cannon-shell bodies .

Left: One of ninety training at the Beaufoy Institute in Lambeth, this young woman is learning how to use measuring calipers. The women had all paid £1 2s 2d (about £1.11) for a twelve-week course.

Working all hours

Women who did 'go into the factories' or into any other work during the war found time short and their lives burdened. Women with a home to keep were hit particularly hard. Compulsory overtime meant working hours were long, with half-day working on Saturday. Shops were closed by the time work finished; the working housewife had to shop in her lunch hour. Queuing for everything took time and the lack of facilities for keeping food fresh meant shopping regularly. Sunday was often the only day off in which to do the household chores, usually without the benefit of any mechanical aids.

Nevertheless, despite the difficulties of managing a home, a family and a job in which the pay and conditions were often demoralisingly low, the women of Britain responded enthusiastically to the demands and problems created by the war. Absentee rates were lower than before the war and production rates were met in full, often by women working beyond their compulsory hours to get the job done.

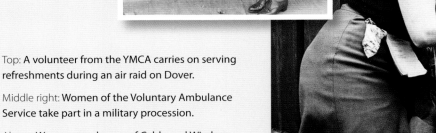

Top: A volunteer from the YMCA carries on serving refreshments during an air raid on Dover.

Middle right: Women of the Voluntary Ambulance Service take part in a military procession.

Above: Women employees of Cable and Wireless who were part of a new unit called 'Telecom' which was formed to aid communications.

Right: During a demonstration of ARP resources and procedures, a female ARP warden attends to a minor injury.

'Land Girls'

Food production was another area that needed to recruit a large workforce. The Women's Land Army, members of which were nicknamed 'Land Girls', formed the backbone of the body of women engaged in the cultivation of the land and rearing of meat. Many other women factory workers, along with schoolchildren, the forces and men in reserved occupations, helped out on the land by taking advantage of schemes that gave a holiday on a farm in return for a payment of several hours' labour.

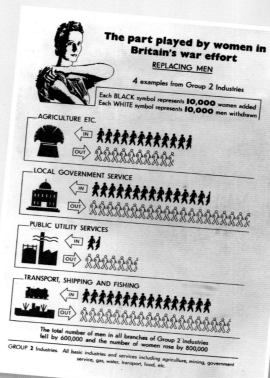

Above: A picturegraph distributed by the Ministry Of Information in 1944. The statistics show that more workers were needed on the land than before the war. This was because Britain had to produce more of its own food and, as a result, 200 per cent more land was brought into production.

Above right: Three women of the Women's Land Army ploughing reclaimed land on a farm in Bedford, with the aid of three tractors working in echelon.

Right: Land Girls gathering and stooking the sheaves on a farm in Buckinghamshire in the summer of 1944, by which time the WLA numbered 80,000.

Above left: In 1944, a Land Girl ploughs a field in southern England, wearing a tin helmet to protect her from the debris from flying bombs brought down by RAF fighters.

Above right: The Women's Land Army making hay on Arlington Manor Farm, Guildford, in the summer of 1942. The WLA was formed in response to the shortage of 100,000 farm labourers and the need for Britain to produce more of its food at home.

Left: Land Girls Margaret Gower and Mary Rigg (with 'Doodlebug' painted on her helmet) shelter from an overhead battle to bring down flying bombs.

Above: Daisy Beales, a farmer's daughter, clears land with a billhook.

Working conditions

Even though women in Britain daily proved their abilities as part of the workforce, they were paid considerably less than their male counterparts. The average woman's pay in 1943 was £3 2s 11d, just over 50 per cent of the £6 1s 4d that was the average male pay. Additionally, working conditions were often very basic. As munitions factories had generally been converted from peacetime production – not necessarily of munitions – or were hastily converted or constructed buildings, and as many of the machine tools were used for jobs for which they were not initially intended, safety was frequently a serious concern. Many factories were designed for men and far fewer workers than employed during the war, so that facilities like toilets and rest rooms were in short supply. Normal working hours were long and when there were calls for increased production, such as after the retreat from Dunkirk, the working day could be extended, so that women found themselves working from 8 a.m. to 7 p.m.

Above: Women in the "Pick and Shovel Brigade". At a new aerodrome somewhere in East Anglia about 100 women and girls are doing navvies' work with zest and enjoyment. Here they are laying pipes for drainage each side of the runway.

Left middle: These women, filling sandbags, were the first to be employed to clear air-raid debris and help make buildings safe.

Far left: Mrs Eilen Glassett, drilling wing spars for a Halifax bomber, had been a sales assistant in a womenswear shop in London's West End. Like many women she gave up her peacetime job to go into the factories.

Left: Miss Louisa Lines, aged 20, formerly a Yorkshire cotton machinist, painting along the scuppers of a nearly finished merchant ship. Women helped in the high speed ship production in British shipyards. Women were fast taking their places with the men in the yards, painting, plate marking, and generally carrying out tasks which, before the war, were considered hard even for the men.

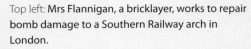

Top left: Mrs Flannigan, a bricklayer, works to repair bomb damage to a Southern Railway arch in London.

Above right: A woman works on making a shell casing at a factory in Southern England.

Above: In January 1941, Britain's first dustwomen assumed their roles in Ilford. The council employed 'eight comely dustbin-emptiers'.

Right: 'She-navvies' cheerfully wheel barrow loads of heavy stones at a railway goods yard. '

Chapter Five

A Global War

As the worst of the Blitz on Britain subsided in May 1941, most of the Luftwaffe was reassigned in readiness for the forthcoming attack on Russia to achieve 'Lebensraum' – living space – that would allow Germany to continue growing and gaining power. The invasion of Soviet territory by Germany and European Axis forces – Operation Barbarossa – began on June 22, 1941. The German army initially won several major victories, but were pushed back from Moscow and instead turned their attention to Leningrad, beginning a siege of the city in September 1941 that was to last for nearly two and a half years. By July 1942, Axis forces had also reached Stalingrad and a bitter battle for control of the city soon began. However, the Soviet counter-offensive trapped a large part of the German army around the city, leading to the first major German defeat of the war. By July 1943, the Soviets had launched substantial counter-offensives on several fronts, turning the course of the conflict on the Russian front in their favour.

In September 1940, while attention was on the conflict raging across Europe, Japan had taken the opportunity to invade French Indochina. This had led many Allied nations to freeze Japanese assets, while the United States – major supplier of oil to Japan – had reacted by putting an oil embargo in place. Japan immediately began planning an invasion of European colonies in the Far East to take what they wanted by force; the Japanese attack on Pearl Harbor in December 1941 was intended to put the US Naval Pacific fleet out of action so it could not be drawn into the conflict. As a result, the United States joined Britain and the other Allied nations to declare war on Japan; Germany retaliated by extending their declaration of war to include the United States. By mid 1942 the Japanese had swept across much of Burma, Malaya, the Dutch East Indies and Singapore and were soon moving on the Philippines, which they eventually captured in May 1942. Japan's next move was to launch an offensive against Midway Atoll in June 1942 in a another bid to destroy the US Navy, but this time the Japanese navy was roundly defeated. This Allied victory was quickly followed up on land as American, Australian and other Allied troops forced the Japanese army to withdraw at the Battle of Guadalcanal in September 1942; this marked a turning point for Allied troops in the Pacific, who from then on moved from defensive to offensive operations.

November 1941 saw the launch of Operation Crusader, a joint Anglo-American invasion of French North Africa, which briefly forced the German and Italian armies back and relieved the siege of Tobruk – bringing about the first defeat of Rommel's Afrika Korps. Although Axis forces quickly advanced again, they only reached as far as El Alamein, where they were halted by Allied troops in July 1942. The following month Axis troops again attacked El Alamein but were driven back by the Allies a second time, and – as well as relieving the siege on Malta – Allied forces then swept across Egypt and Libya. A joint Anglo-American force made a second invasion of French North Africa and this time the French colony chose to join the Allies, prompting Hitler to order the invasion of Vichy France in retaliation.

In northern Europe, Allied forces had carried out a disastrous raid on the French port of Dieppe in August 1942; the Germans knew about the forthcoming attack and it was called off only hours after it was launched – almost half the landing force had been killed, without any of the raid's key objectives having been achieved. The invasion of Sicily in July 1943 was much more successful: it indirectly led to the arrest of Mussolini by an Italian population out of patience with a series of Italian failures. By September 1943 the Allies occupied a portion of the Italian mainland and had achieved an armistice with Italy. Germany responded by seizing control of strategic Italian territory, which led to the battle of Monte Cassino and the Anzio landings in January 1944; by June, the Allies had reached Rome. In most theatres of war the tide had now turned in favour of the Allies and the scene was set for D-Day, on June 6, 1944.

Left: **In October 1942 aboard a US aircraft carrier in the Pacific, scout aircraft and dive-bombers, tightly packed together on deck, are re-fuelled and re-armed, ready for attack on the Japanese.**

Italy invades North Africa

As the Battle of Britain raged in the skies over the South Coast, Mussolini widened the offensive by launching a campaign in North Africa. Following an unsuccessful foray into British Somaliland in August, on the same day – September 13, 1940 – that Hitler was to abandon Operation Sea Lion, Italian forces launched an attack on Egypt from their colony of Libya, penetrating over 50 miles into Egypt and reaching Sidi Barrani by the 16th where the Italian advance halted. There was to be no further action until December, when General Wavell launched the first British offensive against the Italian forces on the 9th. Sidi Barrani was recaptured the following day, and by the end of the month British and Commonwealth troops had forced the Italians to retreat, driving them well back into Libya.

Above right: **Egyptian fighter pilots parade in front of their aircraft.**

Below right: **Maltese soldiers of the Royal Artillery, who volunteered for service in Egypt, practise running to their gun emplacements.**

Below: **Egyptian guards maintain defensive positions at strategic points such as bridges.**

Top: Hitler, Mussolini (left) and the Italian Foreign Minister, Count Galeazzo Clano (right) in the saloon car of Mussolini's armoured train during their meeting at the Brenner Pass in October 1940.

Above: In September 1940 South African troops attended a parade in East Africa during which the Governor of Kenya delivered a message from King George VI.

Right: Following Italy's declaration of war on Britain on June 10, 1940, anti-Italian sentiment grew in Britain during the summer; in some cases this resulted in attacks on Italians and their property, particularly their businesses. This man attempts to protect his shop with the message that his company is British.

Italy: Hostilities Open

Hostilities between Italy and the Allies began at midnight. New York reports that Italian troops invaded the French Riviera at 6.30 last night were emphatically denied by a Government spokesman in Rome.

Signor Mussolini has chosen the crucial hour in the great battle for France to take his momentous step, but Britain and France have long been prepared to meet such a situation. It can be assumed that Britain will quickly take the offensive at sea. Her naval dispositions in the Mediterranean and other preparations have been made with the object of aiming swift and heavy blows at Italy.

A few days ago the British Government, in agreement with the French, decided to impose the full force of contraband control on all Italian ships. Italian shipping at Malta was seized early this morning. All Italians on the island were rounded up.

Rome radio announced that Signor Mussolini will be Supreme Commander of Italian armed forces, "although the King of Italy still remains the nominal chief." Marshal Badoglio has been made Commander-in-Chief of the Army.

Mr. Churchill will make a statement on the new situation to-day.

Mercenaries Of Hitler

Which way will Italy march? Mussolini, in announcing his decision from the balcony of the Palazzo Venezia to a vast, excited crowd in the square below, implied that he desires to wage war only against Britain and France. Declaring that he did not wish to involve his other neighbours, he said: "Let Switzerland, Jugoslavia, Turkey, Egypt, and Greece take note of these words, for it will depend entirely on them if they are fully confirmed or not."

Mussolini gave as his excuse for entering the war what he described as the consistent refusal of Britain and France to discuss the revision of treaties. The real reason was given by M. Reynaud in a broadcast to the French nation last night.

"Why did Mussolini decide that blood must flow?" he asked. "When our Ambassador in Rome asked this question of Count Ciano this afternoon, the reply was: "Mussolini is only carrying out the plans which he has made with Hitler.""

Italy, in other words, now becomes an active instead of a passive ally of Hitler. Her declaration of war ends a period of uncertainty which has recently been intensified by relentless propaganda. Instead of accepting the Allies' offer to negotiate Mussolini has elected to make the people of Italy the mercenaries of Hitler.

The conflict extends further

By the spring of 1941 Romania, Hungary and Bulgaria had been forced to join the Axis (Germany and Italy) and, in April, an overwhelming attack began against Yugoslavia and Greece. Those British troops who had been in Greece, initially aiding Greek resistance to an Italian invasion, were evacuated to Crete, which in turn was invaded by German paratroopers and fell in May.

The Italian efforts in North Africa had been markedly unsuccessful but everything changed as Hitler intervened in the spring of 1941, in support of both his ally and his wider interests. By the end of April, the Afrika Korps, under the command of General Erwin Rommel, had driven the British out of Libya, back across Egypt and to within range of the Suez Canal.

Above left: Troops from the Australian and New Zealand Army Corps (ANZACS) wait on the quayside after arriving in Britain in June 1940.

Far left: The small town of Namsos, the base for Anglo-French forces in central Norway, after waves of Nazi bombers reduced the town's mainly wooden buildings to a mass of ruins following the landing by British naval forces on April 14, 1940.

Left: A German bomber shot down by the R.A.F. over Belgium in May 1940.

Crete Abandoned: 15,000 Men Safe

Fifteen thousand British and Empire troops have been evacuated from Crete after fighting for twelve days without rest. With the British and Greek comrades they left behind they fought - almost without air support - the fiercest campaign of the war against the pick of Germany's parachute troops and the full force of the Luftwaffe.

A high R.A.F. officer in Cairo last night estimated that 1,000 German aircraft took part in the attack. Hundreds were destroyed, including a high percentage of troop-carriers. Scores of dive-bombers are known to have been shot down by the Mediterranean Fleet, but the fighting between plane and warship was so fierce that the enemy losses could not be counted.

Above right: In June 1940, an anti-aircraft battery of the Royal Malta Artillery takes over a defence position in Egypt. The gunners were regular soldiers and volunteered for Foreign Service to assist the Allied and Empire War Effort.

Right: 500-pound bombs are hauled up in pairs to arm a squadron of RAF long-range bombers for another night raid over Germany in November 1940.

Below: The Australian Comforts Fund distributes tobacco rations to the Australian Imperial Force.

Desert War

At the start of 1941, Italian forces were pushed back across Libya by British and Australian troops; the Italians sustained major losses at the Battle of Beda Fomm, where hundreds of tanks were captured and around 130,000 Italians and Libyans were taken prisoner. However, Italy's fortunes changed dramatically as Hitler committed troops to support them. General Erwin Rommel's Afrika Korps arrived in Libya whilst many British troops were being redeployed to Greece in expectation of a German strike there. Rommel immediately began to fight back towards the Suez Canal and the oil fields of the Middle East, forcing the Allies back to Egypt in April. Conflict also occurred in Kenya, Somaliland and in Abyssinia throughout the year, with British and Commonwealth troops fighting alongside Haile Selassie's guerrillas. Abyssinia was reclaimed by the Allies with the surrender of 20,000 Italian troops in November.

Top right: German paratroopers were deployed in Crete with minimal equipment, as most of their supplies were dropped separately. This provided a two-fold advantage to the Allies, for the Germans were outgunned, and much of their kit was captured.

Above right: German paratroopers board transport planes in Greece bound for Crete, to where the remaining forces of the Greek and British armies had retreated.

Above: The Indian army faces the Italians in Eritrea in April 1941.

Below right: The Germans had taken control of Crete by the end of May 1941. Many of the Allied troops were evacuated, but about 18,000 were captured.

Bottom right: The Sudan Defence Force, pictured in December 1940, were a force of Sudanese with British and indigenous officers which swiftly expanded after the outbreak of the war.

Tobruk Falls

Tobruk has fallen. Australian troops entered the town at noon to-day - 30 hours after the attack started. All its defenders, perhaps 25,000 in all, have been taken prisoner and the remainder of the defences are in our hands.

Graziani has now lost two-thirds of the total Italian forces which were in Libya when the British drive started on December 9. Eleven divisions have been eliminated.

These astounding figures are not mere estimates, but exact statistics given me by G.H.Q. A final piece of good news I have just learned is that our casualties in this attack have been relatively small.

In the western sector of the outer defences the Italians are still holding out and putting up stiff resistance. They are being battered from the front by British armoured formations and from behind by Australian units, who are now swarming inside the perimeter.

The number of prisoners is going to be huge and the number of guns astonishing. The Italians had at Tobruk at least one complete division, with heavy additional artillery, and a large proportion of the permanent garrison of Cyrenaica. It is another terrific bag - perhaps as big as at Bardia, but they are better troops.

Swift hammer-blow

Do not imagine the Italians did not put up a resistance. That would be a poor compliment to the fighting spirit and capacities of our troops, who have had to win every yard of ground as they advanced. The fact that they advanced quickly does not mean it was easy for them. It means they did their job magnificently.

When the fighting was resumed at dawn our troops, having penetrated the defences eight miles, had three miles to go. The swift hammer-blow which opened the attack smashed through both rings of fortifications and paralysed the Italians' defence system.

Imperial infantry and tanks which had made a gap five miles wide in the enemy's first and second lines to-day spread over the whole area inside the defences. To the left and right they came up behind entrenched Italians, whose defences were all facing the wrong way. Gun emplacements and concrete pillboxes were stormed and captured from their blind sides.

The British attack, I learn, was launched round the entire perimeter of Tobruk. Australian troops co-operated with British county regiments and Free French units in storming the 25 miles of positions with equal fury.

The Italians could not tell where the real break-through was planned, so they could not rush reinforcements to stiffen the menaced sectors. They had to distribute their forces equally, and therefore thinly, round the whole defence line.

Top: British Infantry troops in Eritrea find good cover among the rocks for sniping.

Centre right: South Africans charge through an Italian smokescreen in Libya.

Above: Australian troops in the Libyan desert.

Right: Pipers lead a well-known Transvaal regiment through the streets of Addis Ababa on April 5, 1941, as the British enter the Ethiopian capital. Italian forces had abandoned the city the previous day.

Sinking of the Bismarck

There had been some dramatic successes for the Allies in the Atlantic. On May 7, 1941 a German weather ship was captured off Iceland. It was discovered to be carrying secret documents which concerned the German coding machine, Enigma. In a piece of spectacular good fortune, a captured U-boat was found in possession of an Enigma cipher machine – and code books – only two days later. This enabled the skilled British code-breakers, based at Bletchley Park, to break the German codes used to issue orders to the U-boat fleet.

Later the same month the German battleship Bismarck sailed from the Baltic to the Atlantic on a mission to attack the vital Atlantic convoys, on which she could have inflicted great damage – undoubtedly the greatest surface threat to their safety. As Bismarck passed through the Denmark Strait on May 24 she was intercepted by Britain's great battlecruiser HMS Hood. The ships opened fire. The Hood received a series of direct hits and sank within minutes with the loss of 1415 men; only three survived. This served to further demonstrate the danger the Bismarck represented, and efforts were redoubled. Once the Bismarck was out in the Atlantic she was pursued by British warships and rather elderly torpedo-carrying Swordfish planes. Her steering mechanism was finally disabled by repeated attacks, and the ship was located on May 27 by a group of British warships – HMS Rodney, King George V, Norfolk and Dorsetshire. Unable to defend herself effectively, Bismarck's guns were put out out of action one by one and she finally sank.

Below: Smoke from the sinking Bismarck can be seen on the horizon from HMS Dorsetshire.

Bottom left: Survivors from the German battleship 'Bismarck' swim towards the British naval vessel that rescued them.

Bottom right: H.M.S. Rodney during the battle with the Bismarck.

Roosevelt Frees Arms Flood

President Roosevelt signed the Lease-Lend (all-out aid to Britain) Bill at the White House late this afternoon within minutes of the House of Representatives giving it the overwhelming majority of 317 votes to 71 - reached after a debate of only two hours.

Less than a quarter of an hour after signing the President met reporters and, speaking slowly, declared: "Immediately after I signed the Bill, authorities of the Army and Navy considered a list of United States Army and Navy war material and approved it being sent overseas. "Part goes to Britain and part to Greece. What is involved must be kept secret for military reasons."

The President explained that the list of material to be sent to Britain immediately does not include merchant ships, but includes ships and bombers from the American Navy, and bombers, guns, and other material from the American Army.

Earlier the President conferred with Congressional leaders and announced that he intended to ask Congress for £1,750,000,000 to carry out the aid-Britain programme. He said: "The avalanche of planes, ships, tanks, and materials which will cross the Atlantic to Britain is now in motion. "We know fully Britain's needs. It is our task to meet them with all possible speed."

Urgent Action

President Roosevelt's next move will be a "Fireside Talk" next week to the nation to explain in detail the aid which the United States will give Britain.

He will point out the need for urgent action and make the nation conscious of the stake they have in the struggle.

An Administration source hinted that the planes and warships are already secretly assembled at east coast points ready to start for Britain as a spectacular gesture to hearten the democracies and chill the Axis. The planes are said to be Army Boeing bombers ("Flying Fortresses") and Navy patrol bombers for convoy-protection duties. The warships are either destroyers or torpedo-boats.

Food, particularly cheese, pork and wheat, is also believed to be assembled ready to be sent over the Atlantic.

When the overwhelming vote for the Bill was announced in the House of Representatives members climbed on to their seats cheering and waving wildly.

As the cheers quietened, Representative Sol Bloom, chairman of the House Foreign Relations Committee, declared: "This Bill is the voice of aroused America. It sounds a trumpet call of victory for free government everywhere. "By it the United States gives the lie to the cowardly and defeatist cry that Democracy is powerless in the face of aggression.

"We are now proving that Democracy can and will unite to carry into effect Lincoln's high resolve that government of the people, by the people, for the people shall not perish from the earth."

The sea – and supplies

It was vital that Britain should continue to be supplied by sea; the country's survival depended upon it. The essential supply convoys were under constant attack from both the Luftwaffe and U-boats, which were now able to operate from bases along the Atlantic coastline of France, much extending their range. Most of the supplies came from the United States, but their cost was beginning to prove prohibitive to Britain's straitened wartime economy. President Roosevelt was willing to give any support short of actual military involvement, despite the USA's reluctance to become involved in what was seen as an essentially European affair. Churchill appealed for help and Roosevelt persuaded Congress to pass the Lend-Lease Act. This allowed the United States to lend war materials to a country whose defence was seen as necessary for the ultimate safety of the USA. The relationship between Britain and the United States was strengthened further when Churchill and Roosevelt met in August 1941. They issued the 'Atlantic Charter', in which they stated their mutual reasons for resisting Nazi aggression.

Below: **A great merchant flotilla of British and Allied ships assembles near New York as they prepare to take war materiel to Britain under the Lend-Lease Act.**

Right: **President Roosevelt signs the Lend-Lease Act into law.**

U.S. To Protect British Ships

President Roosevelt to-night bluntly warned Germany and Italy that from now on their warships would enter at their peril American "defensive waters" - a phrase which covers the route to Iceland and wherever else American ships may ply in the cause of American defence.

The United States Navy and air patrols would protect all merchant ships - not only American ships but ships of any flag - engaged in commerce in these defensive waters. "Let that warning be clear," he said. "Orders which I have given as Commander-in-Chief of the United States Navy and Army are to carry out that policy - at once."

He had ordered the Navy to shoot first when Axis submarines, surface raiders, or aircraft were encountered in the areas which the United States considered vital to its defence.

Speaking to the whole world in a broadcast from the White House, the President said: "The sole responsibility rests upon Germany. There will be no shooting unless Germany continues to seek it."

Rattlesnakes

Reaffirming the United States historic policy of the freedom of the seas, the President described German submarines and raiders along this country's supply lines to opponents of the Axis as "rattlesnakes of the Atlantic" and as a "menace to the free pathways of the high seas."

"We have sought no shooting war with Hitler. We don't seek it now. But neither do we want peace so much that we are willing to pay for it by permitting him to attack our naval and merchant ships while they are on legitimate business."

Right: Supplies get through: crated cargo is handled by dockers at a British port.

Below: High above the North Atlantic a Coastal Command Anson on patrol circles his charges as another British convoy is safely nearing home during August 1940

Bottom: The Australian-built Warraways fighter reconnaissance aircraft on the assembly line, pictured in August 1941. Australia rapidly established an aircraft industry on a mass production basis.

Far left: Ground crew walk on the wing of a giant Stirling bomber as petrol is pumped aboard. They are pictured preparing the aircraft for a big night raid on the Ruhr and Rhineland on 12th October 1941. Bomb doors hang open at the bottom, ready to receive their load.

Left: Dr. Paul Joseph Goebbels, Hitler's Reich Minister of Public Enlightenment and Propaganda pictured in August 1941.

Lower left: Ground staff servicing and bombing up a Blenheim aircraft, making it ready for a sortie across the English Channel in June 1941. It was just one of the aircraft participating in the non-stop day and night attacks that RAF Bomber Command carried out over Northern France and Germany.

Below: Early in 1941 selected RAF aircrew personnel began to train in the U.S.A. after full co-operation was agreed with the U.S. Army Air Corps and the U.S. Naval Air Service. The RAF crews were then able to return to Britain to complete their operational training on the front line.

Soviets invasion of Finland

Following the invasion of Poland and a German-Soviet treaty governing Lithuania, the Soviet Union forced the Baltic countries to allow the stationing of Soviet troops in their territories under pacts of "mutual assistance." Finland rejected the Soviet Union's territorial demands and was invaded by communist forces in November 1939. The resulting conflict ended in March 1940 with Finnish concessions. France and the United Kingdom, treating the Soviet attack on Finland as tantamount to entering the war on the side of the Germans, responded to the Soviet invasion by supporting the USSR's expulsion from the League of Nations. In June 1940, the Soviet Armed Forces invaded and occupied the neutral Baltic States.

Stalin Toasts British Pact

Britain and Russia yesterday simultaneously announced the signing of a Pact declaring their full determination to defeat Hitler. The terms said:

1. The two Governments mutually undertake to render each other assistance and support of all kinds in the war against Hitlerite Germany;

2. They further undertake that, during this war, they will neither negotiate nor conclude an armistice or treaty except by mutual agreement.

The agreement came into force immediately on its signing in Moscow on Saturday by Sir Stafford Cripps, British Ambassador, and M. Molotov, Soviet Foreign Commissar. After the signing, Stalin joined in the toast to the Pact, drunk in champagne. Poland will be joined to the pact in the course of the next few days.

Negotiations between the Poles and the Russians have so far progressed speedily and satisfactorily. This is due as much to the willingness of the Poles to face the realities of the present situation as to the receptiveness of the Russians and their diplomatic contacts with the British and United States Governments. It would, of course, be paradoxical that the differences between these two neighbouring States, now allied to Britain for the overthrow of Hitler, should be allowed to remain unsettled.

Stalin's act in September 1939 when he occupied half Poland (by agreement with Hitler), will be repudiated. After this has been done, normal diplomatic relations will be restored and arrangements made for the release of the 200,000 Polish war prisoners held by the Russians, for service in the common cause.

Opposite above right: **Russian Leader, Josef Stalin.**

Opposite below: **In January 1940 the frozen bodies of Russian soldiers lie along the roadside after the Battle of Suomussalmi in Finland.**

Opposite above left: **After the Finns recaptured territory from the Russians in the Petsamo region of northern Finland, the bodies of the Russian casualties were collected together ready for burial. The corpses were permanently frozen into the positions in which they died.**

This page: **Russian tanks on patrol and in action on the battlefield in July 1941. Soviet armoured forces used a mix of self-propelled light anti-tank guns which could move at great speed whilst firing rapidly, along with much larger tanks equipped with a 6 inch gun set on a revolving turret.**

Germany invades Russia

One of the most significant moments of the entire war came on Sunday June 22, 1941: Germany launched Operation Barbarossa, its invasion of Russia. Hitler reneged on the Nazi–Soviet Pact of 1939; he had originally intended the attack for about a month earlier, but it had been delayed by a combination of weather and heavy fighting elsewhere – something which would prove to be important as it gave the Germans less time to advance east and northwards before the winter began. Churchill immediately pledged support for Russia, and during the summer the Americans agreed to extend their policy of Lend-Lease to Russia as well.

At first the Russians retreated from the advancing Germans. They took anything that could be useful to the invaders with them and simply destroyed everything else – not just supplies but fields of ripening crops, bridges and railways: a complete scorched-earth policy. German troops were besieging Russia's second city of Leningrad by September, the Ukranian city of Kiev fell in October and Hitler's troops had reached the outskirts of Moscow by the end of November. This was not as good for the Germans as it might have appeared. Not only was the bitter Russian winter now setting in, but the Russians were also well equipped to defend both Leningrad and Moscow. Towards the end of the year, on December 6, they launched a counter-attack against the Germans, who were now faced with the problem of surviving the savage weather as well as beating off the determined Russians.

Below left: The retreating Soviets destroy anything that might be of use to the advancing German armies. The same tactic had been used by Russian troops to defeat Napoleon more than a century earlier.

Below right: A combination of heavy bombardment and the Soviet scorched earth policy leaves very little for the invading Germans to claim as their own.

Bottom left: German troops advance through a burning farm. The crops, farmhouse and farm vehicles have all been destroyed.

Bottom right: Women help to construct defences around Leningrad as German forces advance.

Germans Thrusting At Leningrad

German armies were last night reported to be making three main attacks in their great offensive against Russia along a front of 1,500 miles; from Finland towards Leningrad; from East Prussia towards Moscow; and from Rumania towards the Ukraine.

These distances are great. A hundred miles of difficult country lie between the Finnish frontier and Leningrad. Moscow is 600 miles from East Prussia. The Ukraine is almost immediately menaced, but the territory stretches 600 miles into Russia.

A fourth thrust is being made in Poland. Berlin radio claimed last night that German troops had crossed the Bug River, which flows in an arc around Warsaw. Long columns were said to have penetrated deep into Russian territory.

Berlin correspondents of Swiss newspapers said the Germans were using several thousand tanks to drive an opening in the Russian front and were expecting "tremendous results."

The attack towards Leningrad is being made by German and Finnish divisions across the Karelian Isthmus - the battleground between the Soviet and Finland only 18 months ago.

Finnish sources admitted that Soviet aircraft had started fires at several points in Finnish territory. No details of the land fighting were available, but this is one zone where the Russians cannot afford to give ground easily. Leningrad, at the head of the Gulf of Finland and centre of a great military district, is the second city of Russia. Nearby is Kronstadt, home of Russia's Baltic Fleet.

Top: A Russian woman and her two sons are among the last to leave their town. Following Stalin's orders, the inhabitants laid waste to it themselves.

Middle left: Civilians are hanged by the Nazis near Smolensk. The Soviets intercepted this image of Nazi brutality and sent it to newspapers around the world.

Middle right: German troops wait by the roadside while a burning village is searched.

Right: A residential district burns in Kiev, the capital of the Ukraine region of the USSR.

Siege of Leningrad

The two-and-a-half year siege of Leningrad caused the greatest destruction and the largest loss of life ever known in a modern city. On Hitler's express orders, most of the palaces of the Tsars, such as the Catherine Palace, Peterhof Palace, Ropsha, Strelna, Gatchina, and other historic landmarks located outside the city's defensive perimeter, were looted and then destroyed, their art collections transported to Nazi Germany. Factories, schools, hospitals and other civil infrastructure were destroyed by air raids and long range artillery bombardment.

The 872 days of the siege caused unparalleled famine in the Leningrad region with disruption of utilities, water, energy and food supplies resulting in the deaths of up to 1,500,000 soldiers and civilians and the evacuation of 1,400,000 more, mainly women and children. Many evacuees died from starvation and the devastating bombardment. Piskaryovskoye Memorial Cemetery in Leningrad holds half a million civilian victims. Economic destruction and human losses in Leningrad on both sides exceeded those of the Battle of Stalingrad, the Battle of Moscow, or either of the atomic bombings of Hiroshima and Nagasaki. Leningrad is the most lethal siege in world history, and historians speak of the Nazi operation in terms of genocide, as a "racially motivated starvation policy" that was soon revealed to be an integral part of the Nazi plans for the extermination of 'untermenschen' which included all the slavic peoples of eastern Europe, among them the USSR.

Top: A German infantryman settles into a shell-hole to read the newspaper just received from home in August.

Above left: German troops slog through the heavy Russian snowfalls. The unrelenting bad weather conditions caused many setbacks for the Nazi army during the severe winter of 1941.

Above: A group of German soldiers pause for food and drink in the midst of the burning village of Witebsk during their summer advance.

Left: German tanks and infantry race across a Ukraine wheat field in August. The retreating Russians had been forced to withdraw but as they did so, set off a series of fires which destroyed the harvest that was ready to be gathered in.

Red Army holds out

Russia's Red Army had managed to hold out over the winter and had even some success in pushing the Germans back from Moscow in January. By late spring, however, the German Army had regrouped and a new campaign was planned. This time the intention was to strike towards the Crimea in the south, which would ultimately enable the Germans to take control of the Caucasus where there were significant oil reserves.

In June and July, the Germans captured Rostov and Sevastopol, but this initial success was not to last. The German army turned north in August, heading for the important city of Stalingrad; their advance was slowed by Russian resistance, which finally brought it to a halt in the suburbs of Stalingrad itself, forcing the Germans to settle in for a long siege instead of a swift advance. Stalingrad was desperately defended, with every patch of ground contested bitterly. Then, as the winter of 1942 began, the Russians launched a powerful counter-offensive, inflicting heavy casualties on the enemy and eventually surrounding the German positions both north and south of the city. Trapped between the counter-attacking troops and the city's desperate defenders, the German Sixth Army and the Fourth Panzer Division anxiously awaited a relief force accompanied by urgently needed food, ammunition and medical supplies.

JUNE 23, 1941

Ultimate Objective

The second German drive - from East Prussia - is being made across the former Baltic States of Lithuania, Latvia, and Estonia. This attack appears to have Moscow as its ultimate objective. Moscow would also be threatened from the north if Leningrad should fall.

Reports reaching Stockholm said a revolt which had broken out in Estonia was being successfully dealt with by Red troops. Some of the rebels seized ships in Tallinn harbour and opened fire on Russian troops in the capital.

Large formations of the Soviet Air Force have already attacked East Prussia, according to the Swiss radio. They were met by German fighters, and there were fierce and prolonged battles.

In the south, German and Rumanian masses are crossing the River Pruth into Bessarabia, the rich province taken by the Russians from Rumania after the collapse of France. Soviet troops are reported to be evacuating Bessarabia under cover of a defensive screen along the Pruth.

The German radio boasted of the superiority of the Luftwaffe over the Soviet air force. "The German pilots," said one of their war correspondents, "found the Russian airmen completely inexperienced and they behaved like children."

Three hundred divisions, or over 4,000,000 men will be locked in battle along this vast new front. Germany is estimated to have massed 125 divisions, including those she used against Greece - now policed by Mussolini. She has as allies 25 Rumanian and probably five or six Finnish divisions.

Russia's western army is believed to consist of 150 divisions. Many others are available, but the state of their equipment is doubtful.

Top left: German advance guards approach a property on the Eastern Front in early October 1941; the building is torched by departing Russian soldiers as the attackers look on.

Top right: At the end of July two Russian soldiers crouch behind their heavily-camouflaged machine-gun nest, poised for enemy approach.

Middle left: The Russians leave nothing behind to help the Nazis – a farmhouse burns in the mid-July advance.

Middle right: German troops pass the burned-out shell of the Electrical Industry building in Kharkov.

Left: The last of its inhabitants flee Kerch as German and Romanian divisions enter the city.

Pearl Harbor

On Sunday December 7, 1941, the war became a truly global conflict. Just before eight in the morning, Pearl Harbor, the US naval base in Hawaii, was attacked by almost 200 Japanese aircraft. The strike came without a declaration of war and caught the base and its anchored vessels completely unaware. An hour after the Japanese bombers had returned to their six aircraft carrier bases, a second wave of a similar size struck. In total, 19 warships were damaged or destroyed and more than 2,400 people were killed. The scale of the destruction might have been even worse had the US Navy's aircraft carriers not been at sea on manoeuvres.

Tension between the United States and Japan had been mounting for some years. Japan desired to be the dominant power in East Asia and the declining colonial presence of Britain, France and the Netherlands in the region had made this a real possibility. However, the United States, with its presence in the Philippines and interests in the resources of the East Indies, continued to pose a major hurdle. Japan felt squeezed by the United States since Washington had imposed an oil embargo and aided China in the Sino-Japanese War in response to Japan's aggressive expansionism. Attempts to reach a diplomatic solution to the dispute failed since Roosevelt was anxious not to be seen as appeasing Japan in the manner that Hitler had been by Britain and France prior to the invasion of Poland.

By November 1941 Japan's fuel supplies were running dangerously low so its navy resolved to capture the oilfields of the Dutch East Indies. Fearing that the United States would declare war as a result and convinced that a war was inevitable, Japanese pilots launched a pre-emptive strike on the US fleet.

Above: The destroyer USS *Shaw* takes evasive action as a Japanese bomb falls.

Middle: Smoke billows from the USS *Shaw* turning the blue Hawaiian sky black.

Right: The Japanese attack on Pearl Harbor severely disabled the US Pacific Fleet, allowing Japan to push into Southeast Asia with little opposition.

DECEMBER 8, 1941

Japan declares war on Britain and America

Japan to-night declared war on Britain and the United States after launching full-scale naval and air attacks on two of America's main bases in the Pacific - Pearl Harbour, in Hawaii, and Guam, between Hawaii and the Philippine Islands.

Already the Dutch East Indies have announced themselves at war with Japan, and the formal British and American declarations are expected in a matter of hours.

Quickly recovering from the first attacks, American warships steamed out of Pearl Harbour, and it was later reported that a Japanese aircraft-carrier had been sunk. Four Japanese submarines and six aircraft are also said to have been destroyed.

The Columbia Broadcasting System claims to have picked up a message saying that two British cruisers were sunk by Japanese planes attacking Singapore. This report is completely without confirmation. Another message, equally without support but well within the bounds of possibility, is that Japanese warships have been engaged by British and American naval units in the Western Pacific. This report emanates from the Tokio correspondent of a Japanese newspaper in Shanghai quoting an announcement by Imperial Headquarters.

Early reports that Manila, the American base in the Philippine Islands, had been raided were followed by messages that all is quiet there, apart from aircraft taking off either on reconnaissance or to engage Japanese shipping.

Below left: The huge propeller and part of the hull of the sunk Arizona.

Below right: A line of Japanese battleships with the Mitsu nearest the camera.

Bottom left: A massive cloud of smoke rises after the first wave of attacks, making accurate bombing more difficult. A Japanese plane can just be made out through the smoke.

Bottom right: The USS Arizona sinks, engulfed in smoke and flames.

Right: The President signs the declaration of war against Japan, just hours after delivering his speech to Congress.

Below: President Roosevelt addresses a joint session of the US Congress requesting a declaration of war against Japan.

Bottom right: Hundreds of residents of Tillamook, Oregon, meet to discuss civil defence in the event of a Japanese invasion of the West Coast.

Congress Declares War on Japan

Marines with fixed bayonets guarded the Capitol to-day as the United States Congress formally declared war on Japan. They voted 25 minutes after President Roosevelt, in a message denouncing Japan's aggression, had called for this action.

Mr. Roosevelt was frequently and loudly cheered during his address. He described yesterday as "a date that will live in infamy." The United States, he said, was at peace with Japan, and at her solicitation was still in consultation with her Government's representatives. "Indeed, one hour after Japanese air squadrons had commenced bombing the American island of Hawaii, the Japanese Ambassador and his colleague delivered to our Secretary of State a formal reply to a recent American message. It contained no threat or hint of war," he said.

"It will be recorded that the distance of Hawaii from Japan makes it obvious that the attack was deliberately planned many days or even weeks ago. "During the intervening time the Japanese Government has deliberately set out to deceive the United States by false statements and expressions of hope for continued peace.

"The attack yesterday on the Hawaiian Islands has caused severe damage to American naval and military forces. I regret to tell you that very many American lives have been lost. "In addition, American ships have been reported torpedoed on the high seas between San Francisco and Honolulu. Yesterday the Japanese Government also launched an attack against Malaya.

"Last night, Japanese forces attacked Hongkong. Last night Japanese forces attacked Guam. Last night Japanese forces attacked the Philippine Islands. "Last night the Japanese attacked Wake Island. And this morning the Japanese attacked Midway Island.

"As Commander-in-Chief of the Army and Navy, I have directed that all measures be taken for our defence, but always will our whole nation remember the character of the onslaught against us. "No matter how long it may take us to overcome this premeditated invasion, the American people in their righteous might will win through to absolute victory."

'A date which will live in infamy'

The day after the attack, President Franklin D. Roosevelt addressed a joint session of the United States Congress. Roosevelt called December 7 "a date which will live in infamy". Congress declared war on the Empire of Japan amid outrage at the attack and the late delivery of the note from the Japanese government breaking off relations with the US government – actions considered treacherous. Roosevelt signed the declaration of war later the same day. Continuing to intensify its military mobilization, the U.S. government finished converting to a war economy, a process initiated by the provision of weapons and supplies to the Soviet Union and Great Britain.

The Pearl Harbor attack immediately galvanized a divided nation into action. Public opinion had been moving towards support for entering the war during 1941, but considerable dissent remained until the attack when, overnight, Americans became united in opposition against Japan.

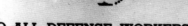

TO ALL DEFENSE WORKERS . . .

The President of the United States said:

"I APPEAL . . .

"to the owners of plants
"to the managers
"to the workers
"to our own Government employees
"to put every ounce of effort into producing these munitions swiftly and without stint. And with this appeal I give you the pledge that all of us who are officers of your Government will devote ourselves to the same whole-hearted extent to the great task which lies ahead.

"We must be the great arsenal of democracy. For us this is an emergency as serious as war itself. We must apply ourselves to our task with the same resolution, the same sense of urgency, the same spirit of patriotism and sacrifice as we would show were we at war."

★ ★ ★

Let's get squarely behind our President's appeal.

★ ★

Let's work together building that "GREAT ARSENAL OF DEMOCRACY" in record time.

★

Increase PRODUCTION! - That's our No. 1 job!

Let's go!

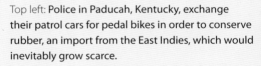

Top left: Police in Paducah, Kentucky, exchange their patrol cars for pedal bikes in order to conserve rubber, an import from the East Indies, which would inevitably grow scarce.

Top right: Japanese men leave a California hotel after being picked up by the FBI.

Middle left: Americans register for sugar ration books in May 1942. Sugar was America's first rationed commodity of the war.

Middle right: Factories engaged in war work were asked to put up this poster to inspire their employees.

Right: President Roosevelt is flanked by Vice President Henry Wallace, Speaker Samuel Rayburn, and his son, Captain James Roosevelt as he delivers his 'Infamy speech' in the House of Representatives.

The American war effort

The United States' unemployment problem ended with World War II as the demand for munitions, military vehicles and ships stepped up wartime production, creating millions of new jobs while the draft pulled young men into national service.

Women joined the workforce to replace men who had enlisted. Roosevelt stated that the efforts of civilians at home to support the war through personal sacrifice was as critical to winning the war as the efforts of the military. The war effort brought about significant changes in the role of women in society. At the end of the war, many of the munitions factories closed and those remaining sometimes replaced female workers with returning veterans; however women who wanted to continue working were able to do so.

Federal tax policy was highly contentious during the war, with Roosevelt battling a conservative Congress. By 1944 nearly every employed person was paying federal income taxes.

Many controls were put on the economy; the most important were price controls, imposed on most products and monitored by the Office of Price Administration. Wages were also controlled. In addition, the military imposed priorities that largely shaped industrial production.

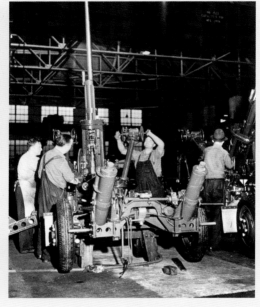

Top: Scenes during a battle just off Guadalcanal in December 1942. 33 Japanese planes attacked an American convoy but 32 of them were shot down. Here a bomb has just landed next to the American cruiser, *San Francisco* but the attacking aircraft has been successfully gunned down and plummets into the sea leaving a thick trail of smoke.

Middle left: Scenes from a tank factory demonstrate the method by which the treads were attached; fitted in two separate sections they were finally bolted together by hand.

Middle right: Final adjustments are made to an anti-aircraft gun carriage.

Right: Scout cars parked in lines as far as the eye can see at the Willys-Overland works in the USA, August 1942. Over 500,000 of the iconic Jeeps were made during the war, shipping for battle around the world.

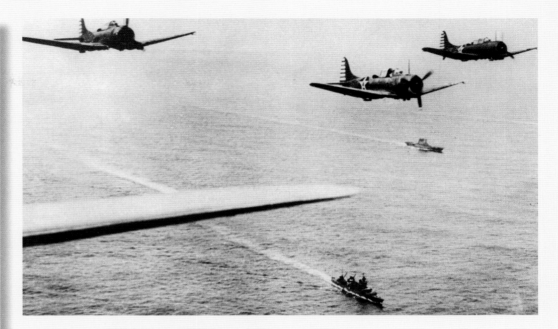

Cheers Greet All-In War On Axis

Germany declared war on the United States at 2 p.m. yesterday, half an hour after a similar declaration by Italy. Congress replied with America's declaration of war against the Axis less than five hours later.

Washington, Thursday

Five Japanese warships, including the 29,000-tons battleship95 Haruna, have been sunk by America's forces in the Pacific. Exactly an hour after the United States had declared war on Germany and Italy, amid the cheers of a unanimous Senate and Congress, the good news began to come in.

Wake Island, which all America had feared would be lost, was reported to be still fighting back. It has withstood three attacks by air and one by light naval forces.

It was learned that an American Army bomber had definitely sunk the battleship Haruna - protected, incidentally, by armour plate from Krupps, of Essen - leaving it ablaze and foundering after three direct hits. Then, only a few hours later, came the further news that a Japanese light cruiser, a destroyer, and two other naval units had been sunk.

Selective Service

The United States swingover from peace to war was swift but unflurried. By 86 votes to nil the Senate passed a Bill under which American expeditionary forces may be sent to any part of the world, and extended the length of service of the armed forces to the duration of the war.

Planning for the full utilisation of man - and woman - power went swiftly ahead. Selective service is to be broadened. Ten million men, the Director of Selective Service told questioners, could be made available to the Army and Navy.

Top: American scout-bombers and units from the Pacific Fleet working together in patrol operations in March 1942.

Middle: Factory workers fit the tracks onto an M-3 tank. These rolling arsenals weighed 28 tons, could travel at over 25 miles an hour and were armed with a 75mm field artillery gun, a 37mm anti-aircraft gun and four mounted machine guns. They were powered by a 400-horsepower Wright Whirlwind aviation engine.

Below: Just after they emerged from the production line in September 1942, four of America's new General Lee tanks with their 360-degree top turrets, are put through their paces on rugged terrain.

American women at war

Women took on many paid jobs in temporary new munitions factories and in old factories that had been converted from civilian products like car manufacturing. This was the 'Rosie the Riveter' phenomenon. 'Rosie the Riveter' became a cultural icon representing the American women who worked in factories that produced munitions and war supplies.

Women also filled many traditionally female jobs that were created by the war boom—as waitresses, for example. And they worked at jobs that previously had been held by men—such as bank teller or shoe salesperson. Nearly one million women worked as so called 'government girls,' taking jobs in the federal government, mainly in Washington, DC, that had previously been held by men or were newly created to deal with the war effort.

Women began to gain more respect and men realized that women actually could work outside the home. They fought for equal pay and made a huge impact on the United States workforce.

Top: Mrs Morton Stern is taking the fingerprint of Mrs Mabel Glenby at the headquarters of the American Women's voluntary services in New York City. In the background are other women who are registering for war work. The American Women's Voluntary Service (A.W.V.S) announced that 10,000 women had enrolled for defence training courses in the first week of the war.

Left: With New York skyscrapers looming through the clouds of gas, U.S army nurses at Fort Jay, Governors Island, New York, wear gas masks as they drill as part of defense precautions in December, 1941.

Above: Women workers, trained for aviation work, are busy on the assembly line of the Glenn L. Martin aircraft plant in Baltimore in February, 1942 where hundreds of bombers are being turned out. They have taken the place of the men called up for the armed forces.

Below left: Members of the American Women's Voluntary Service being received by the US squadron commanders, Lowell Beatty of New York and Harold Baker of Westchester Unit in Decmber, 1941. The women reported for instruction in coast guard patrol duty at 97th Street and Hudson River.

US Tanks for the Front Line

Design of the M-3 Tank commenced in July 1940, and the first were fielded in late 1941. The US Army needed a good tank immediately and not a perfect tank later, and coupled with Great Britain's demand for medium tanks immediately, the M-3 was brought into production by late 1940. It was well-armed and -armored for the period, but was withdrawn from front line duty as soon as the M-4 Sherman became available in large numbers.

Above: The last step in the manufacture of the M-3 medium tank was to lift them by crane into flat cars, clamp them down and cover them with tarpaulin. Cars loaded with U.S. tanks, having been thoroughly tested by army officers, would leave Detroit's Chrysler Tank arsenal on a daily basis.

Middle: At the start of the war, the Watervliet Arsenal was the only gun manufacturing plant in the US to turn out the famous 16 inch and 14 inch cannons for the army and navy. This is a general view of the shop where the big guns were made showing them in position in the huge machines where the workmen will turn them into finished products after 12 months of hard work. Under its defence program the government increased its personnel at the arsenal and kept the machines running 24 hours a day.

Below left: This photograph, taken at the Chrysler tank arsenal in April, 1942, shows a medium tank being carried overhead for convenience and quick handling. Fewer rivets were used in the new medium tanks than in the M-3s but for those that remained in the blueprints 125-ton 'cold' riveting machines such as this would save much time and leave no doubt that the rivets were in to stay.

Below Right: Soon after war was declared the grim reality of the conflict comes to San Francisco as big ramparts of sand bags are hastily constructed in front of one of the telephone company's buildings.

Southeast Asia falls to Japan

The conflict in the Pacific escalated rapidly. On December 10, 1941 the British navy suffered an appalling blow when two of its largest battleships, the *Repulse* and the *Prince of Wales*, were sunk by Japanese bombers. Japan made several lightning-fast strikes throughout the area, and by the end of the year the US bases at Guam and Wake Island had been captured. Hong Kong fell on Christmas Day. Japanese forces moved swiftly in an attempt to seize control of Southeast Asia following the attack on Pearl Harbor and their run of victories in Malaya, Hong Kong, Thailand and the Philippines. They now launched attacks throughout the Pacific; in January 1942, Manila, the Dutch East Indies, Kuala Lumpur and Burma were all invaded.

Burma

This put the Allies under immense pressure. British troops in Malaya were forced to retreat to Singapore by February. The city fell on February 15, and about 80,000 British and Australians were captured. Later in February, Japan attacked Australia itself, bombing the northern city of Darwin. Then the Japanese landed on the island of Java on February 26, defeating British and Dutch naval forces in the Battle of the Java Sea. By early spring, it seemed that the Japanese were almost invincible. British troops had been forced to withdraw across the mainland of Burma towards the Indian border, and the Japanese were continuing to capture islands throughout the western Pacific.

Above: A Japanese soldier during a skirmish in Burma.

Middle: One of the US Navy's amphibious trucks brings supplies ashore at New Caledonia in the South Pacific. American troops landed on the Free French island-colony in April 1942.

Left: A scout group of British, American, Chinese and native Kachin troops wades through a river in the Burmese jungle.

Japan and China

The Second Sino-Japanese War, July 1937–September 1945, was the largest Asian war in the 20th century. It also made up more than 50% of the casualties in the Pacific War if the 1937-1941 period is taken into account.

From December 1937 events such as the Japanese attack on the USS Panay and the Nanking Massacre swung public opinion in the West sharply against Japan, increasing fear of Japanese expansion. This in turn prompted the United States, the United Kingdom and France to provide loan assistance for war supply contracts to the Republic of China. Furthermore, Australia prevented a Japanese government-owned company from taking over an iron mine in Australia, and banned iron ore exports in 1938. Japan retaliated by invading and occupying French Indochina (present-day Vietnam, Laos and Cambodia) in 1940, and successfully blockaded China from the import of arms, fuel and 10,000 tons per month of materials supplied by the Allies through the Haiphong-Yunnan Fou railway line.

To pressure the Japanese to end all hostilities in China, the United States, Britain and the Dutch East Indies began oil and steel embargos against Japan. The loss of oil imports made it impossible for Japan to continue operations in China. This chain of events set the stage for Japan to launch a series of military attacks against the Allies following the raid on Pearl Harbor by the Imperial Japanese Navy on December 7, 1941.

DECEMBER 27, 1941

Hong Kong's last stand

The full story of the Battle of Hongkong was issued by the War Office last night.

It starts with December 8, when the Japanese attacked our troops on the mainland and we withdrew into 'Gindrinkers Line,' and ends with Christmas Day when the last of the island garrison was forced to capitulate.

The Hongkong garrison consisted of two British, two Canadian, and two Indian battalions and the Hongkong Volunteer Defence Force. The geographical features of the colony, states the War Office, its isolation, and the fact that its only aerodrome was on the mainland precluded the possibility of air support.

On the morning of December 8, a Japanese division, with a second division in immediate reserve, crossed the frontier on the mainland. Demolitions were made, and our troops withdrew. There was patrol activity, and a men-carrier patrol ambushed and annihilated a Japanese platoon on Castle Peak road.

On the morning of December 11, strong enemy pressure developed on our left flank, held by the Royal Scots. Two companies were driven off by heavy mortar fire, but the situation was stabilised by using all available reserves. The Royal Scots suffered severe casualties. By midday it was decided to evacuate all the mainland except the Devil's Peak position.

Stonecutters Island was heavily bombarded all day. The island was evacuated during the night of the 11th after demolitions had been made.

The island was sporadically bombarded by artillery and from the air. The civil population was reported to be calm, but their morale considerably shaken. Monetary problems and rice distribution gave cause for serious anxiety.

December 13 was a difficult day. The enemy sent a delegation to negotiate surrender. The proposal was summarily rejected by the Governor (Sir Mark Young).

On December 16 serial bombing and artillery shelling were increased. One enemy aircraft was brought down into the sea.

On the 17th aerial bombardment was directed against the Peak wireless station and other places. No military damage resulted.

On December 22 the enemy landed further troops on the north-east coast. A counter-attack on the 21st from Stanley towards Ty Tan Tak had failed, although a certain number of the enemy were killed at the cost of about 100 Canadian casualties.

On December 23 some ground on Mount Cameron lost during the night was recaptured by the Royal Marines, but counter-attacks by the force at Stanley towards Stanley Mound failed. However, the Middlesex Regiment successfully repulsed a determined attack at Leighton Hill.

It was impossible to conceal the fact that the situation had become exceedingly grave. The troops, who had been fighting unceasingly for many days, were tired out. The water and food supply was desperate. The reservoirs and depots were in enemy hands.

On December 24 the enemy continued to subject the garrison to heavy fire from dive-bombers and mortars, and by means of incendiary bombs set the countryside all round Mount Cameron on fire.

On December 25 the military and naval commanders informed the Governor that no further effective resistance could be made.

Far left: A senior officer from the Chinese army salutes wounded troops after the North Hunan battle in July 1942.

Centre: A Chinese machine-gunner in position ready for attack, July 1942

Left: Chinese soldiers stride out in March 1942.

Battle for Singapore

The Japanese Twenty-Fifth Army invaded Malaya from Indochina, moving into northern Malaya and Thailand by amphibious assault on December 8, 1941. The attack was timed to coincide with the Japanese attack on Pearl Harbor, which was meant to remove the United States' capability of intervention in Southeast Asia.

The Battle of Singapore was fought in the Southeast Asian theatre of World War II when the Japanese Imperial Army invaded the Allied stronghold of Singapore. Singapore was the major British military base in South East Asia and nicknamed the "Gibraltar of the East". The fighting in Singapore was short and sharp – from 8 February to February 15, 1942.

The fall of Singapore to the Japanese brought about the largest surrender of British-led military personnel in history. Around 80,000 British, Australian and Indian troops were captured to join 50,000 prisoners of war, taken by the Japanese in the Malayan campaign. Britain's Prime Minister, Winston Churchill, described the fall of Singapore to the Japanese as the "worst disaster" and "largest capitulation" in British history.

The invasion of Malaya was driven by the country's valuable natural resources needed by Japan in the Pacific War against the Allies; Japan's needs had been intensified by the trade restrictions enforced by the Allies before the outbreak of war. Singapore, on a peninsular island to the south, was connected to Malaya by the Johor–Singapore Causeway. The Japanese viewed it as a strategic port which could be used as a launch pad against other Allied interests in the area, and to consolidate the invaded territory.

FEBRUARY 16, 1942

Fortress Falls

Singapore has fallen. The first official news of its capture by the Japanese was given by Mr. Churchill in his broadcast last night. He described it as a "heavy and far-reaching military defeat" for the Empire. So far no further details are available from British sources. According to Axis radio reports, the greater part of the British and Australian garrison were evacuated to Sumatra.

Thirty or more ships were anchored in Singapore harbour on Friday night, said Berlin. The next morning they had all gone. A Batavia dispatch last night said a party of Australians evacuated from Singapore had reached Java.

Japanese Imperial Headquarters issued a brief communiqué announcing that the Singapore garrison surrendered unconditionally at 12.30 p.m., British time, yesterday. It was arranged that 1,000 British troops should remain in Singapore City to maintain order until the Japanese forces completed occupation.

Left & above: **Scenes of destruction in Singapore at the end of January 1942 after Japanese bombers left a trail of havoc. Malaysian rescue workers were already on hand and intent on clearing the wreckage.**

Left: American tank crews on manoeuvres in England.

Below: British and American troops arrive in port in advance of the Allied invasion of North Africa, November 1942.

Bottom left: American marines land in Iceland on their way to Britain.

Bottom right: Britain was awash with Allied troops. Here Winston Churchill visits Czechoslovak troops with exiled Czechoslovak President Eduard Benes.

Top left: American GIs manning a Howitzer launch an attack on Japanese troops in Burma.

Top right: Men of Britain's 14th Army patrol through swamps in Burma.

Above: Speeding at treetop level, a US Douglas A20 attack-bomber strafes Japanese planes on the ground at Lae, in New Guinea.

Middle right: Marines board an LCM landing craft in the Aleutian Islands before setting off to push the Japanese off Kiska Island.

Right: US troops fire on Japanese positions on the Aleutian island of Attu. The Japanese navy attacked the Aleutians to try to divert the Americans from Midway.

America's first victories in the Pacific

The Battle of the Coral Sea took place on May 4-7, 1942. American aircraft carriers off New Guinea intercepted a Japanese invasion force heading towards Papua and the southern Solomon Islands. This was the first naval battle in which all the fighting was done by the pilots of planes launched from aircraft carriers; it was also the first defeat for the Japanese. There were losses on both sides, but the Japanese fleet was turned back with the sinking of one of its aircraft carriers, making the Coral Sea America's first victory in the war with Japan.

Midway and Guadalcanal

One month later, four more Japanese aircraft carriers were destroyed in the Battle of Midway, severely reducing their capabilities. This heralded a clear change in the Allies' fortunes in the Pacific theatre: the balance of both air and sea power was now tipping in favour of the Allied forces. Allied attacks were launched in the Solomon Islands, and the first landings took place at Guadalcanal on August 7. At first Allied forces met little resistance, but the Japanese troops were very swiftly reinforced and fierce fighting was to rage for the rest of 1942. Naval battles also continued with the Americans inflicting further heavy damage to the Japanese navy and to a supply convoy off Guadalcanal in November. The island was finally won in February 1943 at a cost of thousands of lives. Within days the Americans moved to assist the Australians in pushing the Japanese out of New Guinea. The Australians had already dealt the Japanese their first defeat of the war at Milne Bay in September 1942 and with the additional US forces they were able to win back control of the island by the end of 1943.

Top and middle: **Pilots in America were on constant standby in case of an attack on their shores.**

Right: **Americans gather to enrol for the US Air Force in New York.**

Dwight "Ike" Eisenhower

After the Japanese attack on Pearl Harbor, Eisenhower was assigned to the General Staff in Washington, where he served until June 1942 with responsibility for creating the major war plans to defeat Japan and Germany. He was appointed Deputy Chief in charge of Pacific Defenses before becoming Chief of the War Plans Division. He was then appointed Assistant Chief of Staff in charge of Operations Division under Chief of Staff General George C. Marshall, who spotted talent and promoted accordingly.

In 1942, Eisenhower was appointed Commanding General, European Theater of Operations and was based in London. In November, he was also appointed Supreme Commander Allied Force of the North African Theater of Operations. In February 1943, his authority was extended as commander of AFHQ across the Mediterranean basin to include the British 8th Army which was under the command of General Bernard Montgomery.

Top: The assignment of Brigadier General Dwight D. Eisenhower (left) to be Chief of The General Staff's War Plans Division was disclosed on February 19 by the War Department. Eisenhower succeeded Major General Leonard T. Gerow (right), who was shifted to command of the 29th Division.

Middle: General Eisenhower watches Charlton Athletic take on Chelsea in the Southern Cup Final at Wembley Stadium. Arsenal manager George Allison sits next to him ready to explain the rules.

Left: This is one of the first pictures to be received in Britain of the US Flying Fortress, which had been in action against the Japanese in the Philippines. Here the pilots are seen consulting a map beside their giant machine.

DECEMBER 15, 1941

Who Fights Whom

Thirty countries are now at war. This is the line-up:

Allies

United States; British Empire; Soviet Russia; China; Belgium; Czechoslovakia; Greece; Netherlands; Norway; Poland; Yugoslavia; Free France; Costa Rica; Cuba; Dominican Republic; Guatemala; Haiti; Honduras; Nicaragua; Panama; Salvador.

Axis

Germany; Italy; Japan; Finland; Hungary; Rumania; Bulgaria; Croatia; Slovakia.

Top: US Liberator bombers at an American air base in England.

Right: U.S Navy scout bombers circle in formation above their aircraft carrier home in the Pacific in November 1942.

Bottom right: The camp at Manzanar, California, that housed more than 60,000 Japanese citizens and Japanese Americans during the war.

Below: US Ordnance crew loading up a Boeing Flying Fortress of the Hawaiian Air Force Bomber Command in March 1942; they are seen carefully handling a 300-pounder.

The Americans arrive in Britain

Meeting in Washington in December 1941, Churchill and Roosevelt agreed that the Allies should concentrate on winning the war in Europe before turning their attentions fully towards the Pacific theatre. This 'Germany First' policy had its critics, but it was agreed that the US and Britain would be stronger fighting together, and that logistically Britain had to confront the Nazi threat first. Nevertheless, the US kept piling the pressure on Japan, winning key battles at Coral Sea and Midway during 1942.

American troops had begun landing in Britain within weeks of the attack on Pearl Harbor and Hitler's subsequent declaration of war on the US; throughout 1942 they were to arrive in vast numbers. These were the GIs (their equipment was stamped 'General Issue' – hence the name) and they were widely welcomed in Britain.

The GIs proved especially popular with children – they were seen as purveyors of treats that had become impossible to find, such as chocolate and sweets. They were also very popular with numerous British women, some 20,000 of whom would become 'GI brides' by the end of the war. As a result of this, many British men would complain that the Americans were 'oversexed, overpaid and over here'.

Top: A US army Jeep makes for an unusual sight on a London street.

Middle: American soldiers enjoy a Bank Holiday fair in Hampstead, 1942.

Far left: American military relax as the landlord of the village pub serves beer.

Left: Many women were thrilled that the arrival of the GIs meant that luxury items such as stockings became easier to obtain. Until then many women had painted their legs to give the impression of a seam.

Right: Eleanor Roosevelt tours through buildings destroyed in the Blitz in London in October 1942.

Right: A British ATS with an American sailor at Speakers' Corner in London.

Far right: Armed with a carbine, a US soldier stops a bus in a London street in May 1944 to check identity papers of all military personnel on board.

Below: The first contingent of American soldiers land in Northern Ireland after being shipped across the Atlantic.

The Baedeker Raids: Britain Blitzed again

Right: The ruins of St Andrew's Church in Bath, gutted by fire after a Baedeker raid in April 1942.

Below: York's 15th- century Guildhall in flames, after a raid in retribution for RAF attacks on Baltic ports.

Bottom: Searching for victims in the ruins of St John's Roman Catholic Church which received a direct hit. One of the priests was killed.'

The Baedeker Raids took place from April 1942 to the end of June. The name came from Baedeker travel guides of Britain as the press reported that this was how the targets were selected. Instead of attacking the industrial towns and cities, suddenly all the picturesque tourist cities such as Bath, Norwich, Exeter, Canterbury and York became targets. They did not have the air defences of the larger cities and consequently 1,637 were killed with 1,760 injured. Over 50,000 homes were lost. It was believed that these raids were in response to the Allied bombing of Lübeck in northern Germany. It had been targeted as a base used to supply German troops on the Russian front.

Far left: A comic moment as Pioneer Corps come across a relic from the past in the rubble of bombed Bath.

Left: During a raid on the city of Cambridge in August 1942, the University Union Society's building suffered the effects of blast damage.

Below left: Bomb damage to one of Bath's beautiful Georgian Crescents.

Below right: Thick grey dust covered the houses and roadway after the havoc caused in a Bath thoroughfare by Nazi raiders.

German bomber losses

Baron Gustav Braun von Stumm, a German propagandist is reported to have said on April 24, 1942 following the first attack, "We shall go out and bomb every building in Britain marked with three stars in the Baedeker Guide."

Some noted buildings were destroyed or damaged, including York's Guildhall and the Bath Assembly Rooms, but on the whole most escaped — the cathedrals of Norwich, Exeter and Canterbury included. The German bombers suffered heavy losses for minimal damage inflicted, and the Axis' need for reinforcements in North Africa and the Russian Front meant further operations were restricted to hit-and-run raids on coastal towns by a few Focke-Wulf Fw 190 fighter-bombers. Deal, Kent was one of these towns and was hit hard, with over 30 civilian dead including many women and children, most of whom are buried in the Hamilton Road Cemetery in Deal.

Top: Firemen hosing down the smouldering embers of a building in the centre of Canterbury.

Middle left: This is the Kent Hospital in which women patients were killed during the night raid. Among the debris Sister Gantry crawled, giving morphia injections to the injured women while rescue work went on.

Middle right: The Archbishop of Canterbury inspects damage to the Cathedral caused by the raid in June 1940.

Left: Norwich suffered extensive bomb damage during World War II, affecting large parts of the old city centre and Victorian terrace housing around the centre. The heaviest raids occurred on the nights of 27/28 and 29/30 April, 1942.

Top left and right: **Plymouth was heavily bombed by the Luftwaffe, in a series of 59 raids known as the Plymouth Blitz. Although the dockyards were the principal targets, much of the city centre and over 3,700 houses were completely destroyed and more than 1,000 civilians lost their lives.**

Above: Following an air raid on Dover on March 23, 1942 that left 13 people dead, a demolition squad works to clear the damage and debris in a bus garage.

Left: Two women pick their way through debris in a badly battered street in Exeter. A total of 18 raids between 1940 and 1942 flattened much of Exeter's city centre. In1942, as part of the Baedeker Blitz 160,000 square metres of the city, much of it adjacent to the central thoroughfares, High Street and Sidwell Street, were levelled by incendiary bombing. Many historic buildings were destroyed, and others, including the grand Cathedral of St Peter in the heart of the city, were damaged.

Advancing through Russia

Germany renewed its plans to attack Moscow but on June 28, 1942 the offensive re-opened in a different direction. Army Group South took the initiative, anchoring the front with the Battle of Voronezh and then following the Don river southeastwards. The grand plan was to secure the Don and Volga rivers first and then drive into the Caucasus towards the oilfields, but operational considerations and Hitler's vanity required both objectives to be attempted simultaneously. Rostov was recaptured on July 24, when the 1st Panzer Army joined the fray, and then the Group drove south towards Maikop.

Meanwhile the 6th Army was driving towards Stalingrad, for a long period without support from the 4th Panzer Army, which had been diverted to help the 1st Panzer Army cross the Don. By the time the 4th Panzer Army had rejoined the Stalingrad offensive, Soviet resistance had stiffened. A rush across the Don brought German troops to the Volga on August 23, but for the next three months the Wehrmacht would be fighting the Battle of Stalingrad street-by-street.

Towards the south the 1st Panzer Army had reached the Caucasian foothills and the Malka River. At the end of August, Romanian mountain troops joined the Caucasian spearhead, while the Romanian 3rd and 4th armies were transferred following their successful clearing of the Azov littoral. Taking up position on either side of Stalingrad they released German troops for the proper fighting.

The advance into the Caucasus became bogged down, with the Germans unable to fight their way past Malgobek to the main prize of Grozny. Instead they switched the direction of their advance to approach Grozny from the south, crossing the Malka at the end of October and entering North Ossetia. In the first week of November, on the outskirts of Ordzhonikidze, the 13th Panzer Division's spearhead lost momentum and the German troops had to fall back. The offensive into Russia was over.

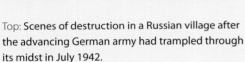

Top: Scenes of destruction in a Russian village after the advancing German army had trampled through its midst in July 1942.

Next to top: Crew-members of a Russian armoured train line up for inspection just before they leave for the front line in August 1942. The train had been built by the railwaymen of the Moscow junction and was presented to the Red Army to aid their fight against the Germans.

Above left: Russian Marines engage the enemy on the Black Sea coast, July 1942.

Above right: German soldiers close in on a gutted factory during street fighting in the city of Stalingrad during the first two weeks of October 1942.

Right: Russians man the anti-aircraft battery of the battleship Parizhskaya Kommuna. The ship was part of the Soviet Black Sea Fleet which was helping soldiers with the defence of Sevastopol in June 1942.

FEBRUARY 19, 1942

German Terror of Fire, Rope and Bullet

Negley Farson, the Daily Mail's world-famous correspondent in Russia, cables to-day the first independent eye-witness account of the atrocities carried out by the Germans. He has talked with the victims and seen the mute evidence of the German gallows in the village streets, and he says: "I have seen and heard enough of atrocity stories in various parts of the world to be sceptical, but nobody could doubt these people."

Moscow, Wednesday.

The reasons for the ferocity and determination with which the officers and soldiers of the Red Army are battering the Germans across White Russia can be found in the recently-liberated Soviet towns and villages.

I spent yesterday on the snowclad plain of what was once the prosperous farming district of Lotoshino, 100 miles north-west of Moscow. There I saw a gallows, with the ropes still dangling from it, on which the Nazis had hanged eight civilians - one being Tatiana Peskovatszkaya, 26-years-old woman health administrator for the Lotoshino district.

I talked with a brave but weeping 15-years-old boy who had been made a prisoner by the Germans, was beaten, and saw his mother and sister led off to be shot. I listened to a half-demented father who saw many of his family killed and whose 18-months-old baby was frozen to death as he carried it in his arms.

I talked with bitter-faced "partisans" who for two months had waged guerilla warfare against the Germans from a hideout in the depths of forest and swamp.

If ever I have seen horror, this was it. I and two other correspondents who talked with these stricken and still fighting people are completely satisfied that the Russians are not exaggerating: as they themselves state: "These things are true. We know that because we have both suffered and seen it. But thousands of our people are still unaccounted for - and we are afraid of what we shall find."

"Awful Area"

The great plains around Lotoshino are now beginning to be spoken of by the Russians as the "awful area." It was the last part of the territory known as the "Moscow region" from which the Nazis were driven out late in January. Before fleeing the frustrated, outraged Germans killed 994 civilians. Five hundred and seven of these were shot.

At the village of Mikulino-Gorodische Germans first tried to gas the inmates of an asylum. Then they had them out in batches of eight or ten to be shot. A hundred and fifty-three civilians died either from hanging or torture or were driven out of their homes, in 40 deg. below zero, to freeze to death.

Out of 32,000 people living in this former contented farming district, 25,000 are supposed to be alive. The thousand that the Germans are know to have killed themselves leaves 6,000 still unaccounted for. Of these 1,500 are from Lotoshino itself.

Top left: Red Army soldiers man an anti-aircraft machine gun, keeping up a deadly defence against attacking German bombers in September 1942.

Top right: A farmhouse in the background burns as German troops continue to push along the Kharkov front in August 1942.

Middle: New Red Navy torpedo boats set out on a mission in the Black Sea.

Above: Rows of dead Ukranian citizens are lined up along the ground in July 1942. German soldiers killed them due to food shortages: they wanted to ensure that any food available went to the invading troops.

Battle for Stalingrad

The German army under General Paulus finally reached Stalingrad after a gruelling advance to launch its attack on August 15. The 14th Panzer Division attacked from the north while Luftwaffe bombers blitzed from the air. A week later, although progress had been made in the northern suburbs, the southern part of the city was still resisting the German advance. The siege continued into winter with the city now a symbol of the hubris of the opposing leaders, Hitler and Stalin, each determined to possess the city whatever the cost. Germany failed to realise the impact of the 20 mile sprawl of the city along the banks of the Volga. The Russians kept close to their enemy, making it difficult for the Germans to deploy heavy artillery and the city's ruined streets were impassable to heavy German armour forcing the conflict into hand-to-hand fighting.

Victorious Russians push west

Temperatures plummeted to 24 degrees Celsius below freezing – and the Germans were running out of supplies of food, medicine and ammunition, but Hitler refused to permit surrender – nor could he manage to supply them, effectively condemning the army to a form of mass suicide. By December, there was little doubt about the ultimate result, and January 31 brought a massive defeat for the Germans, forcing Paulus to capitulate, disobeying Hitler. On February 2, 1943 the last of the German forces finally surrendered. The Russians took over 90,000 prisoners, amongst whom were twenty-four generals; many more, on both sides, had died. This was the German army's greatest-ever defeat and a major turning point on the Eastern Front. The Russians now began to push the Germans back to the west.

Top: **The ruins of Stalingrad's Factory District, where much of the fighting took place.**

Middle: **A Russian mortar unit drags heavy equipment using sleighs as they move towards a ridge on the Southern Front in January 1943. Their warm clothing and headgear gave them a distinct advantage over the inadequately-clad Germans.**

Left: **Members of a family crouch over the body of their father, murdered during a massacre in the town of Kerch. The bandaged man on the left of the picture was wounded in the head during the massacre and lay still, covered with earth and corpses, until the Nazis departed.**

Right: :**The scene of Nazi terror against the civilian population of Russia in Rostov-on-Don.**

Top: Armed Russian workers take up defensive positions on the roof of their factory.

Above: Russian troops capture a German tank as it attempts to penetrate defences in the city of Stalingrad.

Left: A Russian anti-tank crew on the outskirts of the city.

Stalingrad Army Wiped Out

Field-Marshal Paulus, Commander-in-Chief of the German Sixth Army and Fourth Tank Army at Stalingrad, was captured by the Russians yesterday a few hours after he had been promoted to the highest rank by special proclamation from Hitler's headquarters. He was seized with his staff when Soviet troops stormed the Ogpu headquarters in the heart of the city and completed the greatest disaster that has befallen Germany in this war.

It is now revealed as a disaster of unsuspected proportions. Instead of 220,000 men, the trapped army consisted of 330,000 troops, it was announced by Moscow in a special communique last night.

In addition to the Sixth Army, the Fourth Panzer Army has been trapped and destroyed. Thirteen German and two Rumanian generals and 46,000 troops have been captured. Five thousand were taken prisoner with Marshal Paulus yesterday.

Booty taken between January 10 and 30 includes 744 aircraft, 1,517 tanks, and 6,523 guns.

Annihilation Of The German Troops

Here is the full story as told in the special despatch: "Our forces on the Don front between January 27 and January 31 completed the annihilation of the German troops surrounded west of the central part of Stalingrad.

"In the course of the fighting, and from the depositions of enemy generals now prisoners in our hands, it was ascertained that by November 23 the German forces there numbered at least 330,000, if the auxiliary engineering and police units are taken into account, not the 220,000 previously thought.

"As is known, the German forces encircled before Stalingrad between November 23 and January 10 had lost up to 140,000 from the action of our artillery, bombing from the air, the action of our land troops, sickness, frost and exhaustion.

"In view of this data the victory of the Soviet forces before Stalingrad assumes even greater importance. The number of prisoners between January 27 and 31 increased by 18,000 officers and men.

"In the course of the general offensive against the encircled enemy forces our troops captured 46,000 officers and men in all.

"To-day, our forces captured General Field-Marshal Paulus, commanding the group of German forces before Stalingrad, consisting of the Sixth Army and the Fourth Tank Army, his Chief of Staff, and the whole of his staff."

FEBRUARY 9, 1943

Life Begins Again Among Ruins of Stalin's City

BY HAROLD KING

I am in Stalingrad - the city of desolation, of masses of wrecked machinery, twisted rails, frozen bodies, and street after street of gaunt, ruined houses. Peace of sorts, however, has come since the destruction of Paulus's German Sixth Army of 330,000 men.

General Chuykov, the man who defeated the Germans, is here. I met him in a dug-out on the bank of the Volga. There I also saw Paulus, embittered and sallow-faced, with the other German and Axis generals he led into captivity.

When I entered the city, around me everywhere, as far as I could see, was a desolation never imagined even in a hideous dream. The worst scenes in London, Coventry, and Plymouth are overshadowed.

I walked the battlefields with Russian officers as my guides between the minefields. For two days I walked and walked, covering 30 miles from the north of the city to the south and then to the west.

Stalingrad once housed 400,000 people. To-day there is hardly a single house standing in the six miles between the square of the Heroes of the Revolution, in the centre of the city, to the famous October Revolution factory in the north.

The October Revolution factory - where Rodimtsev's Guards put up their savage defence - is an indescribable mass of wrecked machinery, bricks, and twisted rails. Now, in Stalin's city of steel, Stalingrad, men are at work again. They are clearing, shovelling, moving anything in their way to reopen communications. Women are there too.

Young General

The battlefield has been largely cleared of dead, but here and there a frozen body lies face up. A leg sticking through the snow betrays the grave of a soldier.

In a dimly lit dug-out bored out of a 100ft. cliff on the bank of the Volga, Lieut.-General Chuykov, commander of the 62nd Soviet Army, told me the story of Paulus's defeat. Vasily Ivanovich Chuykov is 42 - one of Stalin's young generals. He is handsome, weather-lined, and his deep-set brown eyes are easily moved to smile.

"My army - the 62nd - was in action against the German Sixth Army from July 22, when the first clash occurred south-west of Kietskaya," he said. "The battle for Stalingrad itself began on September 14, and the bloodiest day of all was a month later, on October 14, when the Germans brought in five new or re-manned divisions with two tank divisions and hurled them into a front only three miles wide.

"They had an incredible number of guns, and their planes were making 2,500 flights a day. "The noise was so tremendous that one could not hear shells and bombs exploding, nor see more than five yards because of the smoke. "The vibration was so immense that if a glass were put down on the table here in this dug-out it was smashed to atoms.

"On the bloody October 14 I had 61 officers of my staff killed or wounded. "Then the front became stabilised. "The story of my 62nd is the story of two armies locked in a deadly grip from September 20 to February 2. Neither side could disentangle itself.

"The Germans made no tactical errors - but they made one big strategical error. That was when they made Hitler supreme commander."

Top: **Soldiers raise the Red Flag above a building in a recaptured part of Stalingrad.**

Middle: Stalingrad residents welcome reinforcements from the Red Army.

Above inset: **Once the Germans had been defeated, these women were free to emerge from the basement which had been their home for the duration of the battle.**

Above: The Russian Operation Uranus to relieve Stalingrad involved the deployment of over 10,000 heavy guns, almost 1,000 tanks, and over 1,000 aircraft. Having surrounded the Axis forces the Red Army attacked to the north on November 19, and to the south two days later, rapidly gaining the advantage. Hitler commanded Field Marshal von Manstein's Don Army group to relieve the trapped Axis armies. However, this offensive was repelled on December 12 and 13 and withdrawn on Christmas Eve.

Siege of Leningrad continues

In northern Russia, the siege of Leningrad continued. At the beginning of 1943 up to 5,000 people were dying each day, mainly due to starvation and disease. By the spring thaw, supplies were getting through by sea, boosted by the American extension of lend-lease to Russia. Refugees were also being evacuated but the death rate remained high.

Operation Spark

The encirclement was broken in the wake of Operation Spark – a full-scale offensive conducted on two fronts. This offensive started in the morning of January 12, 1943. After fierce battles the Red Army units overcame the powerful German fortifications to the south of Lake Ladoga, and on January 18, 1943 the Leningrad and Volkhov Fronts met, opening a 10–12 km wide land corridor, which could provide some relief to the besieged population of Leningrad.

The siege continued until January 27, 1944, when the Soviet Leningrad-Novgorod Strategic Offensive expelled German forces from the southern outskirts of the city. This was a combined effort by the Leningrad and Volkhov Fronts, along with the Baltic Fronts. In the summer of 1944, the Finnish Defence Forces were pushed back to the other side of the Bay of Vyborg and the Vuoksi River.

Top: Many Soviet civilians trapped in Stalingrad had to make their homes amongst the rubble, in basements, or even in shell holes.

Middle left: Refugees in the battered streets of Stalingrad.

Middle right: A Russian soldier takes cover amongst rubble in Leningrad.

Right: A Red Army patrol launches a counterattack on the outskirts of Leningrad.

Right inset: Red Army anti-aircraft gunners poised for a low level attack by German planes on the Russian positions in the Northern Front in March 1943.

Atlantic convoys

The Battle of the Atlantic passed its climax by May 1943. In the winter months up until February, losses to the North Atlantic convoys had been somewhat reduced, but the German U-boat fleet continued to grow and coupled with a breakdown in Allied intelligence in March, German submarines began once more to inflict heavy losses on the convoys, particularly in the mid-Atlantic gap where shipping could not be protected by air cover. That month, approximately 475,000 tons of shipping was lost, and Britain's lifeline was almost severed. However, by April, a dramatic increase in air support and in the number of escort vessels meant that Allied sinkings fell to around half the number of the previous month. At the same time, with improved radar systems, effective intelligence, and more VLR (Very Long Range) aircraft, U-boat losses began to rise. By the end of May, almost 100 submarines had been destroyed, and the remainder of the U-boat fleet was withdrawn. From the summer onwards the rate of shipbuilding surpassed the rate at which the Germans were able to effect losses, and although the U-boats would return to the North Atlantic in the autumn with improved weaponry and radar, some 40 of them were destroyed in the last four months of the year.

Above: **Churchill addresses the nation in June 1942. From June 18–25 he had been in the USA for talks with Roosevelt. Their topics for discussion included the protection of shipping, the diversion of German forces from the Russian front and atomic research.**

Below: **A German submarine pictured just moments before being sunk by US Liberator bombers.**

Raid on Dieppe

In 1942, the Allied forces were not yet ready to mount a full-scale invasion of Western Europe, but it was decided to launch a large, though somewhat speculative, raid on the French port of Dieppe. Originally planned for July, the mission was postponed until August due to poor weather and given the codename Jubilee. The attack took place at dawn on August 19 and involved just over 6,000 troops, the majority of whom were Canadian, aided by British and Free French Commandos, and a small group of American Rangers. The troops were supported by eight destroyers and around 70 airborne squadrons. The plan involved landing at five separate positions along the coastline and eliminating resistance on the flanks, before units converged on the town of Dieppe itself with a frontal assault timed to occur 30 minutes after the initial landings. However, the main attack force was pinned down on the beaches, coming under heavy fire from German positions in sea-front buildings. Although some infantry managed to infiltrate the town, they became engaged in fierce fire-fights and lacked the back up of tank regiments, which came ashore late and had difficulty negotiating the sea-wall. The supporting air squadrons also suffered heavy losses. By the time the operation was called off in the afternoon it had proven a terrible failure, with the loss or capture of over 3,000 men. Although lessons were learnt that would no doubt ultimately reduce the loss of life on D-Day, the cost of these lessons had been severe.

Top: **The scene in the White House State Dining Room, Washington, U.S.A., on July 2, 1942. Representatives of the 26 United Nations, each stand beside their own flag as President Roosevelt dedicates them anew to the winning of the war. The representatives of Mexico and the Philippines added two more signatures to the Pact. Seated at the table, from left: Dr. Francisco Castillo Najera (Mexican Ambassador to the United States), President Roosevelt, Philippine President Manuel Quezon, and U.S. Secretary of State Cordell Hull.**

Above: **Aircrew of the first Hurricane Squadron that flew to Dieppe.**

Far left: **Independence Day was celebrated in London on July 4, 1943 by thousands of American service men. The traditional haycart ride was made by one party which went into Hyde Park, and lunched in the cockpit.**

Left: **Major General J.H. Roberts (right), commander of the Canadian forces at Dieppe.**

Chapter Six

Invasion of North Africa

The start of 1942 saw something of a stand-off in North Africa: both sides were regrouping on either side of the Gazala Line. Rommel launched his next attack on the British in May, as his Wehrmacht colleagues were attacking in Russia. The Panzer Army Afrika outflanked the British and forced them to make a rapid withdrawal to Tobruk – which was lost by June. Following that, the British Eighth Army retreated eastwards to El Alamein. Here it was possible for them to be reinforced, both swiftly and to a considerable extent, via the Suez Canal. There were sustained German attacks during July and August, but the British were able to hold the defensive Alamein Line. They were ready to strike back by October, under the inspirational command of General Montgomery, who was sent to lead the Eighth Army in August. During the night of October 23 an enormous artillery bombardment began, followed by a frontal assault against Rommel's forces. Progress was steady though initially quite slow, but the advance picked up speed and Rommel began to retreat on November 3. The Germans were then rapidly pushed back into Libya.

Left: **Operation Torch beachhead in November 1942.**

El Alamein and Operation Torch

On November 8, 1942 a large-scale invasion of French North Africa was launched under the command of US General Dwight Eisenhower. It was known as Operation Torch, and had the honour of being the largest seaborne expedition in history until it was dwarfed by the Normandy landings.

Stalin had been demanding that the Allies open a second front in Europe to relieve some of the pressure on the Red Army, which was defending an enormous front. Roosevelt agreed with the strategy in principle, but was advised against it by his generals. Churchill was also sceptical; he had authorized 'a reconnaissance in force to test the enemy defences' at the French port at Dieppe in August 1942. It was a disaster. The force was withdrawn after only nine hours, by which time thousands of troops – mostly Canadians – had been either killed or captured. Instead, Churchill advocated opening a new front in North Africa. By capturing Tunisia, the Allies would severely disrupt the enemy's supply lines and could engage them on two fronts.

Top: American troops wade ashore at Arzeu, having been delivered from their ships by landing craft.

Upper left: Troops bring stores ashore on the North African coast during the Torch landings.

Upper right: Wading through the Mediterranean Sea, American troops come ashore in Algeria.

Above left: Part of the vast armada of ships which sailed to Africa in order to open a new front on the west of the continent. Although protected by accompanying warships, many of the vessels carrying troops were actually ocean liners.

Left: Britain's Royal Navy had a major role in the world's greatest combined operation when the 500 ship convoy safely transported Allied troops to French North Africa where simultaneous landings were made at strategic points. A landing craft leaving a transport off Algiers in November 1942.

Top: The Torch landings, commanded by General Eisenhower, began on November 8 with troops deployed at Safi and Casablanca in Morocco, and on beaches at Algiers and Oran in Algeria. After brief conflicts with French forces Admiral Darlan, commander of Vichy France, ordered a ceasefire on November 11, and French cooperation was assured. The Allies now began to close in on the Axis armies from both sides, forcing them into Tunisia.

Above left: An American-built Maryland bomber of the South African Air Force strikes a German supply convoy in the Libyan desert.

Above: Medium bombers of the U.S. Army Air Force in the Middle East are seen flying in formation over the desert in late October 1942. The planes are camouflaged so that they blend into the background colour. These are the planes that are harassing the supply lines and bases of the Axis in North Africa.

Left: Since the occupation by the Allied troops, Algiers was for the first time raided by German aircraft in November 1942.

Pushing Germany out of Africa

There was little resistance to the Allied landings, and Admiral Darlan, the commander of Vichy France, whose forces were occupying the area, ordered a ceasefire just two days later. He also appealed to the French navy to leave Toulon, where they were based, and join the Allies. Hitler immediately scrapped Marshal Pétain's collaborationist Vichy government and ordered the full occupation of France, which took place on November 11. The French immediately scuttled their fleet to deny the Germans additional naval power.

By the end of January 1943 Montgomery's army had pushed the Germans back westward from Egypt through Libya and General Eisenhower was pushing east. Trapped between the two, the position of the Axis forces was hopeless. Rommel himself left for Europe, handing over to General von Arnim. The Axis army – about 250,000 men – surrendered to the Allies in May.

Right: **Old Glory, the American Flag, flies above the ruins of a North African town.**

Below: **The liberated French population of Algiers give the V-for-Victory sign as American troops march through the town.**

Top left: The first operational task of the United States Army in the European theatre of operations, the occupation of French North Africa was begun on November 8 by U.S. Rangers simultaneously landed at strategic points. Here, an American officer is in conversation with villagers at a point near Oran where a landing was made without opposition.

Top right: America's General Eisenhower (left) with Britain's General Montgomery (right). After pushing the Germans out of Africa, the two men would lead the Allies to victory in Western Europe.

Above left: Italian soldiers are driven through the streets of Algiers on their way to internment camps. American troops were charged with maintaining order as locals poured onto the streets to jeer at the POWs.

Above right: Captured Italians are driven through Algiers to internment camps shortly after the Torch landings.

Left: Led by a standard bearer, US troops march towards an airfield near Algiers on the first day of Operation Torch.

NOVEMBER 5, 1942

Rommel Retreats in Disorder

Rommel's Afrika Corps - pride of the German Army - and his Italian allies are in full and disorderly retreat. His second-in-command has been killed, the commander of the Afrika Corps (General von Thoma) is in our hands with other high officers and 9,000 prisoners; and 260 of his tanks and 270 of his guns have been captured or destroyed.

Every available Allied aircraft has been flung against the fleeing Axis columns in day and night attacks. The Eighth Army is racing forward in relentless pursuit.

This tremendous news was given to an eagerly awaiting world late last night in a special communiqué from British Middle East Headquarters. Two hours later it was revealed that the Axis pocket near the coast had been completely overrun and that the Italians in one sector had asked for an armistice to bury their dead.

Over 9,000 Prisoners Captured

Here is the text of the British communiqué. It was broadcast to Germany and Italy again and again with all the resources available to the United Nations:

"The Axis forces in the Western Desert, after 12 days and nights of ceaseless attacks by our land and air forces, are now in full retreat. Their disordered columns are being relentlessly pursued by our land forces and by the Allied air forces by day and night.

"General von Stumme, a senior general who is said to have been in command during Rommel's absence in Germany, is known to have been killed. So far we have captured over 9,000 prisoners, including General Ritter von Thoma, Commander of the German Afrika Corps, and a number of other senior German and Italian officers.

"It is known that the enemy's losses in killed and wounded have been exceptionally high. Up to date we have destroyed more than 260 German and Italian tanks and captured or destroyed at least 270 guns.

"The full toll of the booty cannot be assessed at this stage of the operations. In the course of the operations our air forces, whose losses have been light, have destroyed or damaged in air combat over 300 aircraft, and destroyed or put out of action a like number on the ground.

"At sea our naval and light forces have sunk 50,000 tons and damaged as much again Axis shipping carrying supplies to North Africa. The Eighth Army continues to advance."

Top: A Victory Parade held in Tunis on May 20, 1943 when units from the Allied Forces marched through the town. All the Allied Commanders were present and the salute at the march past was taken by General Eisenhower, General Alexander, General Anderson and General Giraud. Spitfires swoop low over the parade as American troops march past.

Above right: Allied flags are hoisted over the Allied HQ in Algeria on November 25, 1942. Sir Andrew Cunningham, General Anderson of the First Army and General Clark were present.

Above: Her left wing and engine nacelle riddled by flak, a B26 (Martin Marauder) of the U.S. Army Air Forces flies home to a safe belly landing after a bombing raid in Tunisia in April 1943.

Left: In the ancient ruins of the Carthage amphitheatre, the First Army and its leader General Anderson gathered in June 1943 for thanksgiving after their North African victory. The band and choir were from the Anti-Tank Regiment. General Anderson, who read the lesson, sat among his senior officers before the improvised altar. Behind him, tier upon tier, were the men of the First Army.

Above left: **General Nogues, French Commanding Officer in Morocco and Resident General, salutes the flag of the US Western Task Force in November 1942.**

Above right: **General Eisenhower and General Giraud inspect a Guard of Honour of French troops during a victory parade in Tunis, Tunisia in May 1943.**

Left: **General Keyee and General Nogues review French and American forces taking part in a joint parade in Casablanca. The soldiers pass the stand while receiving the officers' salutes in December 1942.**

Uprisings in Warsaw

From November 1939 Warsaw's Jewish population was forced to move into a ghetto, which was sealed off from the rest of the city the following year. Jews from all over Poland and Europe were sent to live in the Warsaw Ghetto where thousands died from starvation and disease. From July 1942 the Nazis began a major purge of the Ghetto and hundreds of thousands of people were sent to their deaths at Treblinka concentration camp. In early 1943, after news of the exterminations had reached the Ghetto, the remaining population rose up in rebellion. Using weapons that had been smuggled in or improvised, the rebels held out against the German army for almost a month. Thousands were killed during the uprising and the survivors were deported to death camps or executed on the spot.

The following year, the Polish Home Army, the main Polish resistance movement, rose up in rebellion hoping to liberate Warsaw before the fast-approaching Soviet troops arrived. The uprising began on August 1, 1944 and the 50,000 strong Polish Home Army met with some early successes. However, the Germans soon sent in reinforcements and the Luftwaffe began a relentless bombardment of the city. The rebels were slowly worn down and no relief came from Soviet forces, which had stopped just short of the city – ostensibly on the orders of Stalin who did not want the Polish Home Army to take over. With more than 200,000 dead and much of the city destroyed, the rebels surrendered on October 2, 1944. The Russians seized the city three months later.

Above: Men, women and children taken from a building at gunpoint following the failed uprising.

Left: Members of the Polish resistance await the arrival of the Nazis following their surrender.

Below: The ruins of Warsaw following the failed uprising in August 1944.

DECEMBER 11, 1942

Massacres by Gas in Poland

Grim details of the German "mass extermination" drive in Poland are given in a Note handed to all Allied Governments yesterday by the Polish Foreign Minister. The Note outlines a report which I was yesterday shown at the headquarters of the Polish Ministry of Information. This states that well over 1,000,000 Jews have perished in the past three years.

Seven thousand men, women, and children are carried off daily to the "extermination camps." Half the Jewish population of Poland must be annihilated before the end of this month - the order comes from Himmler, adds the report.

In the spring of this year the mass murder campaign became viciously thorough. The news came through that a new extermination camp had been opened at Sobibor in Wlodawa county and the daily deportations began. I quote from the report:

"The Germans cordoned off a whole block of houses and ordered everybody to leave their homes and assemble in the yard. Anyone who failed to get out quickly enough or who tried to hide was killed on the spot. "All infirm, old, and crippled people were also killed in their homes. No consideration was shown for families, wives were torn away from husbands, small children from their parents."

Packed Into Goods Trucks

Then they were packed into goods trucks - 120 in a truck with space for 40. They choked for lack of air, but the trucks were sealed and the trains set out. Deportees were carried off to three execution camps, Treblinka, Belzec, and Sobibor. Here the trains were unloaded, the condemned stripped and then killed either by poison gas or electrocution. From two to ten thousand people have been killed in this manner in a few hours. By the end of September this year 250,000 Jews had been eliminated. Whole families in Poland commit suicide by gas or cyanide. To prevent people taking poison the chemists' shops in the ghetto have all been closed.

The Note handed to the Allied Governments - it is already being considered - expresses the confident belief that they "will share the Polish Government's opinion as to the necessity not only of condemning the crimes committed by the Germans and punishing the criminals but also of finding means of offering the hope that Germany might be effectively restrained from continuing to apply her methods of mass extermination."

Top: Polish Jews are rounded up in Warsaw and marched to a concentration camp in March 1940.

Above: The Warsaw Ghetto burns as the Nazis try to suppress the uprising in April 1943.

Left: German soldiers massacre Jews in newly-occupied Poland in retaliation for the death of a German soldier.

Resistance and collaboration

During the Second World War the Nazis controlled a vast swath of Europe from France to the Soviet Union. Throughout their occupied territories and vassal states the Germans found people prepared to work with them and people intent upon working against them. Those who collaborated usually did so because they were sympathetic to Nazi ideology or were pragmatists, willing to work with whoever was in charge. They assisted the Germans by forming puppet governments, deporting Jews and arresting members of the resistance; some even joined volunteer units of the dreaded Waffen SS. Those opposed to German occupation or to Nazi ideology joined organized resistance movements or engaged in individual acts of defiance. Their activities ranged from hiding Jews and sabotaging communications to killing collaborators and providing intelligence to the Allies. Many others did not actively participate in resistance or collaboration and simply tried to survive the occupation – these people have sometimes been criticized as passive collaborators.

The reaction to the German occupation was not uniform across Europe; there was inevitably more resistance activity wherever the German presence was stronger and German rule more direct. Different national groups also responded to the German presence in different ways and some nations even welcomed the Germans as liberators from other oppressors – such was the case in Croatia and Estonia where the Germans were regarded as liberators from Serb and Russian domination respectively.

Français ! souvenez-vous

ici habite un

COLLABORATEUR

Ce papillon ne peut être apposé sur la porte d'un COLLABORATEUR qu'après enquête et autorisation des Services du Contre Espionnage.

Above: In celebration of the birthday anniversary of the Voluntaires Françaises – the French ATS – General de Gaulle took the salute at a parade and inspection in London in November 1942. Colours were presented to the Voluntaires and decorations – some of them posthumous – were presented by the General. In this picture, General de Gaulle posthumously awards the Croix de Liberation to Lieutenant Ria Hackin who was drowned at sea while on duty. Madame Mathieu (the former tennis player) is receives the medal.

Left above: Marshal Pétain inspects French troops at Châteauroux, in unoccupied France. Pétain ruled Vichy France in collaboration with the Nazis in order to spare southern France from direct German rule. The Vichy government actively supported Nazi racial policies against the Jews, and thousands were rounded up, placed in concentration camps, and later transported to death camps in the east.

Left below: French Resistance fighters are drilled on the edge of a field close to the treeline so they can duck for cover.

Left inset : 'Here lives a collaborator'. Anyone suspected by the Resistance of collaborating with the Germans might have woken to find this sign posted on their front door during the night.

Top left: Vidkun Quisling, wartime Premier of Norway, gives the Nazi salute as he inspects German troops in Norway.

Top right: Resistance fighters carry out target practice in the foothills of the French Alps.

Above left: Italian Resistance fighters launch an attack against Fascists in a Milan street.

Above centre: Vidkun Quisling awaits his trial in Oslo at the end of the war. Appointed upon the orders of Hitler, his name has become synonymous with treasonous collaboration.

Above right: A still from a film smuggled out of France reveals daily life in the French Resistance. When possible, the day began with the raising of the Tricolour.

Left: The Allies drop supplies to the Resistance in Nazi occupied Belgium.

Allied offensives in the Pacific, 1943–44

Midway proved to be the last great naval battle for two years. The United States used the ensuing period to turn its vast industrial potential into actual ships, planes, and trained aircrew. At the same time, Japan, lacking an adequate industrial base or technological strategy, a good aircrew training program, or adequate naval resources and commerce defense, fell further and further behind. In strategic terms the Allies began a long movement across the Pacific, seizing one island base after another. Not every Japanese stronghold had to be captured; some, like Truk, Rabaul, and Formosa, were neutralized by air attack and bypassed. The goal was to get close to Japan itself, then launch massive strategic air attacks, improve the submarine blockade, and finally (only if necessary) execute an invasion.

In November 1943 US Marines sustained high casualties when they overwhelmed the 4,500-strong garrison at Tarawa. This helped the Allies to improve the techniques of amphibious landings, learning from their mistakes and implementing changes such as thorough pre-emptive bombings and bombardment, more careful planning regarding tides and landing craft schedules, and better overall coordination.

The US Navy did not seek out the Japanese fleet for a decisive battle, as Mahanian doctrine would suggest (and as Japan hoped); the Allied advance could only be stopped by a Japanese naval attack, which oil shortages (induced by submarine attack) made impossible.

Below: **US Air Mastery on Guadalcanal.** 'Wildcat' fighter planes lined up and ready for US Navy and Marine pilots at an airfield on Guadalcanal Island. Although US Marines had withdrawn from the Island, the Marine Air Force was still there fighting hard with Army and Navy pilots. Up until February the Japanese had lost 876 planes – five times that of the American losses.

Burma 1943

The Japanese invasion of Burma in 1942 had successfully cut off supply routes to China along the Burma Road and placed Japanese troops dangerously close to the Indian border. Japanese commanders had hoped that Indian forces in the area would revolt against the British. However, although some captured soldiers were formed into an army to fight against the Allies, colonial Indian divisions, which had fought alongside British troops in North Africa, were redeployed to Burma in 1943 where they fought with great distinction. Now under the overall command of Lord Mountbatten, British troops were reinforced and received greater air support, enabling them to maintain defensive positions deep in the Burmese jungles; the employment of guerrilla tactics would result in some successful campaigns against the Japanese. Major General Orde Wingate formed and led the 77th Indian Infantry Brigade, otherwise known as the Chindits, which adopted the tactic of 'Long Range Penetration', operating in columns deep inside enemy territory, sabotaging infrastructure and ambushing Japanese troops. Although they were eventually ordered to withdraw as air-drops became more difficult, the Chindits had proven that damage could be inflicted on the Japanese in difficult jungle territory.

Above: General Frank Merrill and some of his staff discuss new methods to hamper the Japanese headquarters somewhere in the Burmese jungle.

Middle: American soldiers waving a greeting from one of the convoy ships arriving at an Australian port, with thousands of U.S. troops and war materials in June1942.

Left: Native stretcher bearers in New Guinea rest themselves and their casualties in the shade of a coconut grove en route from the front lines near Buna to hospitals in the rear. In skirmishes and large engagements, United States troops killed over a thousand Japanese in five days.

Bombing Germany

For the first two years of the war, Britain did not launch a comprehensive air offensive against Germany's cities. There was strategic bombing of military and industrial targets within Germany, but it was not until 1942 that Britain began indiscriminately raiding Germany with the intention of breaking civilian morale. Arthur 'Bomber' Harris took charge of Bomber Command in February 1942 and began planning for the aerial bombing of German cities. The test case for the new tactic was the historic city of Lübeck in northern Germany, which was struck on the night of March 28, 1942. The town's old buildings were easily set alight by the incendiary bombs dropped by the RAF, causing widespread destruction and loss of life.

1,000-Bomber Raids

Two months after Lübeck, Harris assembled his bombers for a strike against Cologne, an industrial city on the Rhine. Operation Millennium, as it was codenamed, employed 1,047 aircraft, making it the largest fleet yet seen in aerial warfare. The raid was originally intended for Hamburg, Germany's second-largest city and a major site of U-boat production, but it was switched to Cologne because of poor weather. On the night of May 30, the aircraft flew in a tight stream, maintaining height and speed, both to avoid collisions and to limit German radar detection. The mission was achieved more quickly than had ever been attempted, even for a much smaller force. Although some of the crews missed their intended target, almost 900 planes bombed Cologne, releasing 1,455 tons of bombs, two thirds of which were incendiary devices.

Top: **Bombs plunge towards targets in Berlin.**

Middle: **Improved targeting systems enabled these US bombers to strike even through dense cloud.**

Middle inset:**The bomb doors are open and a one-ton bomb commences its journey of destruction during a mission over Germany in October1942.**

Right: **The ground crew of the 'Hells Angels' attend to their plane, a veteran bomber of the Eighth Air Force, and one of the most prolific Flying Fortresses of the war.**

Seven Days of Fire at Hamburg

Fires have now been raging for a week without intermission in Hamburg, most devastatingly bombed city in the world. The war industries and dockyards of Germany's greatest port are being methodically razed by air bombardment, the like of which has never been seen before.

Hundreds of R.A.F. heavy bombers on Thursday night stoked up the flames by again dropping over 50 tons of bombs a minute during an attack which lasted for three-quarters of an hour – the third 2,300-tons assault in six days.

From 45 miles away the pilots could see the fires started last Saturday when Bomber Command made its first obliteration onslaught. They left new fires in the industrial areas of the port, which welded with the others into an overall conflagration. In six days and nights about 7,500 tons of bombs have crashed on to Hamburg – a rate of nearly 70 tons a minute.

Every night since last Saturday our crews have seen the flames, for Mosquito bombers have been over on the three nights when a heavy attack was not made. Crews of the heavy bombers of the United States Eighth Army Air Force saw them, too, when they made their precision attacks in daylight on Sunday and Monday.

Day By Day

Never before in the history of air warfare has an attack of such weight and persistence been made against a single industrial concentration. No other target in Germany has hitherto had more than one 2,000-tons attack.

This is a diary of the blows:

Saturday (night): R.A.F. 2,300-tons raid.
Sunday (day): U.S.A.A.F. Fortresses.
Sunday (night): R.A.F. Mosquitoes.
Monday (day): U.S.A.A.F. Fortresses.
Monday (night): R.A.F. Mosquitoes.
Tuesday (night): R.A.F. 2,300-tons attack.
Wednesday (night): R.A.F. Mosquitoes.
Thursday (night): R.A.F. Giants, 2,300 tons.

The total of bombs dropped on Hamburg in these six days is equal to the weight dropped by the Luftwaffe on London in the whole of the blitz period 1940-41. The greatest weight that fell on London in one night was 450 tons.

The R.A.F. on Thursday found Hamburg a fortress city. Great and more powerful defences had been rushed into the area. The Germans must have brought guns and searchlights from other places just as likely to be Allied bomber targets. Luftwaffe chiefs have switched extra squadrons of night fighters to the port even at the risk of making their air screen round other zones perilously thin.

This strengthening of defence is reflected in the growth in R.A.F. losses - 28 in the latest attack, 18 on Tuesday night, 12 on Saturday.

US Air Force

The US Army Air Force initially favoured performing daylight raids over Europe to ensure greater precision, even on long-range missions when distances precluded fighter support. During 1942 and the early months of 1943, part of their success could be attributed to the fact that much of the German fighter force was in Russia and North Africa. However, during the summer of 1943 American losses soared. German defences had been much improved, and their fighter pilots learned to attack bombers head-on, taking advantage of poor frontal defences. In turn, the Americans were prompted to devise the means of surmounting these problems. Amongst the most important developments was detachable 'drop tanks', (below) which allowed extra fuel to be carried by supporting fighter planes on long-range bombing missions. By early 1944, US fighters were accompanying bombers as far as Berlin, and in the event of an engagement with enemy fighter planes, the fuel tanks could simply be discarded.

Above: A B17 Flying Fortress crew study the new remote-controlled chin-turret which provided better protection against frontal fighter assaults.

Left: A Halifax bomb-rack shows every foot of space packed with high explosives and incendiaries. The cargo has just been loaded and N.C.Os check over the fuses.

Flying Fortress

The US B17 Flying Fortress was amongst the most effective bombers of the conflict, flying more combat missions than any other bomber and serving in every theatre of war throughout the conflict. It was also produced in the largest numbers, with some 12,726 being manufactured between 1935 and 1939.

The B17 was held in high regard due to its toughness and ability to withstand enemy fire but many were downed, mainly during daylight raids.

Above: Crew members of the 'Little Twink' were reunited after their plane was shot down over Germany. Only two of the seven that bailed out survived, whilst the pilot and two others rode out a crash landing.

Left: Part of a massive formation of US bombers returns from a raid in Germany.

Below: Factories and an airfield in Berlin burn after heavy bombing. Initially, Berlin was spared the worst of the aerial onslaught because it was too far away for the RAF to mount a sustained campaign. However, improved technology and the arrival of the Americans changed that and Berlin was bombed severely from November 1943 until the last months of the war.

JULY 26, 1943

Hamburg Bombed Again

U.S. Follow RAF in Daylight

Heavy bombers of the U.S. Eighth Army Air Force pounded Hamburg yesterday, a few hours after the R.A.F. had launched the mightiest air attack yet on Germany's greatest port. The U.S. planes flew in daylight. The British bombers flew by night, to drop over 2,300 tons of bombs in 50 minutes, and to raise a smoke pall four miles high, which was still hanging over Hamburg when the Americans arrived. Simultaneously with this daylight attack, another force of United States "heavies" raided the naval base at Kiel. Meanwhile medium United States bombers, under R.A.F. fighter protection, struck at targets in Holland and Belgium without losing a single machine.

The Luftwaffe tried in vain to stem the onslaught. Big air battles were fought along the North Sea coast from Holland to Heligoland Bight. R.A.F. Spitfires carved a path through enemy fighters for Mitchell bombers to attack the Fokker aircraft factory at Amsterdam. Though the Mitchells met heavy flak they were unhampered by German planes, and bombs fell right across the target.

Similar strong opposition was put up by the Luftwaffe when airfields at Woensdrecht, in Holland, and Courtrai, in Belgium, were bombed by Typhoon bombers, and industrial targets near Ghent were attacked by American medium bombers.

Dog Fights Across The Channel

Dog fights ranged across the Channel on the way home. Three German fighters were shot down in the operations and many more were severely damaged. Another enemy plane was destroyed last evening, when R.A.F. fighters kept up the round-the-clock offensive. Two motor vessels near Le Havre were set on fire.

A new phase of round-the-clock bombing of the enemy in the West has begun on an unprecedented scale. Judged even by the standards set in the spring, the weight of the attack is breathtaking. The virtual annihilation of enemy industrial plants, naval docks, and air depots by day, and whole towns by night can be expected as weather conditions permit. The record 2,300-tons raid on Hamburg may be regarded as a sample.

Non-stop from early Saturday until a late hour last night, thousands of British and American aircraft, from four-engine bombers to stratosphere fighters, have been engaged this week-end. In ground organisation and generalship alone it is the greatest test to which air power has ever been put. So far it is stated to be "going extremely well." This terrific new offensive, timed by the waning of the moon and a return of more helpful weather generally, was begun by the United States heavy bombardment forces on Saturday, when for the first time they attacked targets in Norway.

Top: US airmen report back to an officer following a successful raid on industrial sites near Berlin. The markings on the back of the navigator's jacket indicate the number of missions he has completed.

Above: Aircrews ready to embark on another daylight bombing mission over Germany.

Left: Medium bombers of the US Army Air Force in the Middle East fly in formation over the desert in October 1942. Camouflaged to blend with the landscape, they harass Axis forces and their supply lines in North Africa.

Hamburg and Dresden

The RAF proceeded to bomb Germany relentlessly by night, and from 1943, they were joined by the American Air Force (USAAF) which bombed by day. This ceaseless round the clock bombardment never directly achieved its aim of forcing Germany into submission by breaking civilian morale, but it did play a vital role in wearing Germany down in preparation for the overland invasion.

In late July 1943, the RAF and the USAAF launched Operation Gomorrah, a series of devastating raids on Hamburg. Almost 3,000 sorties were flown over the city leading to the deaths of an estimated 40,000 people, most of whom perished in a great firestorm that engulfed the city on the night of July 27. A firestorm caused by a heavy raid on Dresden killed a similar number of people in February 1945. Dresden was singled out for the raid because it was an important transport hub and was being used to send troops and supplies to the Eastern Front. The death toll was higher than might have been expected because Dresden's population had swelled in number as a result of the thousands of refugees who had poured into the city in the empty trains returning from the front.

Above: Despite massive damage to the tail of this B17, the pilot managed to return from his bombing mission over Germany and land safely back in Britain.

Below: Bombs exploding across a wide area of Berlin, striking the Templehof marshalling yards, Anhalter Station and other parts of the railway system.

MAY 19, 1943

Dam Water Spouted 1,000ft. Up

Air Chief Marshal Sir Arthur Harris last night described the attack on the German dams as "a major victory in the Battle of the Ruhr."

Conveying his "warmest congratulations to all concerned on brilliantly executed operations," he said: "To the aircrews I would say that their keenness and thoroughness in training and their skill and determination in pressing home their attacks will for ever be an inspiration to the R.A.F. "In this memorable operation they have won a major victory in the Battle of the Ruhr, the effects of which will last until the Boche is swept away in the flood of final disaster."

Wing Commander Gibson, who was in charge of the whole operation, personally led the attack on the Mohne dam. After he had dropped his mines he flew up and down alongside the dam to draw the fire of the light A.A. guns emplaced on it.

Guns were poking out of slots in the walls of the dam. His gunners fired back as he repeatedly flew through the barrage and this had the effect of making some of the enemy gun-fire waver. A flight lieutenant who dropped his mines later was in a better position to see what happened to the dam.

"I was able to watch the whole process," he said. "The wing commander's load was placed just right and a spout of water went up 300ft. A second Lancaster attacked with equal accuracy and there was still no sign of a breach.

Sheet of Water

"Then I went in and we caused a huge explosion up against the dam. It was not until another load had been dropped that the dam at last broke. I saw the first jet very clearly in the moonlight. I should say that the breach was about 50 yards wide."

One pilot said that the jets were so powerful that they were hurtling out horizontally for at least 200ft.

A D.F.M. sergeant was the last to see the Mohne dam. He was returning from the attack on the Sorpe dam. "I found some difficulty in finding the right end of the reservoir," he said, "because the shape had already changed. "There was already a new sheet of water seven miles long, and it was spreading fast."

"When we attacked," one pilot said, "you could see that the crown of the wall was already crumbling. There was a tremendous amount of debris at the top. Our load sent up water and mud to a height of a thousand feet."

Top: A United States 8th Air Force Bomber Command Station 'somewhere in England'. The station was equipped with Liberator planes, and with all-American crews, these giants of the air dropped their bombs on Germany and Italy, or on enemy-occupied countries, to hamper or to destroy the enemy's war effort. Liberator bombers taxiing up to take off for the start of an operational patrol at the base early in April 1943.

Middle: Low-flying RAF bombers strike a power station in Cologne.

Left: The computerised gunsight of a Flying Fortress which was able to account for factors such as range and windspeed, ensuring greater accuracy even in difficult conditions.

Below left: The Mohne Dam is successfully breached by a bouncing bomb during the 'Dambuster' raids of May 1943.

Massive strikes on Berlin

In the autumn of 1943, mass raids were launched against Berlin. Air Marshal 'Bomber' Harris had long believed that the destruction of several major German cities would be enough to end the war. Although the RAF and USAAF had inflicted serious damage on Germany, and no doubt forced the military to direct resources away from offensive campaigns, the losses of Allied planes and crewmen were also severe. Over a four-month period in 1943, more than 1,000 bombers and their crews were lost.

However, in 1944, with the advent of the US long-range P-51D Mustang fighter, the Allied raiders, particularly the Americans who continued to fly daylight missions, were guaranteed a little more protection.

Top left: A Berlin street following an RAF raid in retaliation for heavy bombing in London the previous week.

Above: Berliners gather to survey bomb damage in a central street.

Middle: Members of the German Safety Service tackle a blaze caused by incendiary bombs.

Left: Berliners clear away debris following an air raid.

Top left: Bombs fall on industrial targets in Berlin.

Top right: A huge bombed-out area shows the scale of the damage in this part of Berlin.

Left: Three pictures show bomb damage being cleared away from homes and shops in Berlin, destroyed by Allied air raids.

The liberation of Italy

The Allied victory in North Africa in May 1943 altered the state of play in the Mediterranean, making an attack on Italy possible. Italy was in bad shape: the country had lost an estimated 200,000 soldiers in North Africa, more than 200,000 were fighting on the Eastern Front, and about 500,000 were deployed in the Balkans. So when American, British and Canadian troops invaded Sicily in July 1943, the island fell within just six weeks. This rapid defeat in Sicily, combined with the devastating bombing of the mainland, led to the overthrow of Mussolini by the Fascist Grand Council; he was arrested and sent to prison.

By September, the Allies had crossed to the mainland and the new Italian government surrendered. However, this did not bring peace as the German occupation forces continued to resist the Allied advance. Italy was now treated as another of Germany's vassals: Jews were rounded up and deported to Auschwitz, partisans were executed and the country was plundered of its historic artworks. German glider pilots even rescued Mussolini from his remote mountain prison and made him leader of their new puppet state, the 'Italian Social Republic'.

Top: British troops kick down the door of SS Headquarters in Florence.

Far left: A church in Turin damaged during Allied air raids on the major industrial centres in northern Italy on August 8, 1943.

Above: Italian soldiers in Sicily surrender.

Left: As food grows scarce, the grounds of Milan Cathedral are turned into a cornfield.

JULY 26, 1943

Duce Sacked By His King

King Victor Emmanuel of Italy has dismissed Mussolini and appointed Marshal Badoglio as "Prime Minister and Chief of Government." This sensational news, which may soon put Italy out of the war, was broadcast by Rome radio at 10.45 last night.

Here is the text of the announcement:

"H.M. the King has accepted the resignation from the post of Chief of Government, Prime Minister, and Secretary of State, of his Excellency Cavaliere Benito Mussolini. The King has appointed as Chief of the Government, Prime Minister, and Secretary of State, his Excellency Marshal of Italy Pietro Badoglio."

This was followed by the reading of proclamations by the King and the new Premier.

The King's message said: "Italians: From to-day I assume the command of all the armed forces. In the solemn hour which has occurred in the destinies of our country, each one must again take up his post of duty. No deviation can be tolerated. "Every Italian must stand firm in face of the grave danger which has beset the sacred soil of the Fatherland." Italy, by the valour of her armed forces, by the determined will of all Italians, will find again the road to her future destiny." Italians, I feel myself to-day indissolubly united more than ever with you in unshakable belief in the immortality of the Fatherland."

Taking Over

Marshal Badoglio said: "Italians: On the orders of the King Emperor, I am taking over the military government of the country with full powers. The war continues." Italy, grievously stricken in her invaded provinces, in her ruined towns, maintains her faith in her given word, jealous of her ancient traditions. Ranks must be closed round the King Emperor, the living image of the Fatherland and an example for us all." The commission which I have received is clear and concise: It will be scrupulously executed. And whoever imagines that he can interrupt a normal development or who seeks to trouble public order will be struck without mercy.

"Long live Italy. Long live the King."

The broadcast was concluded with the national anthem. The Fascist anthem was omitted. The King's proclamation was dated "July 25, 1943," and not, as was the previous custom, "21st year of the Fascist era."

Appeal

Only ten days ago, with the invasion of Sicily well under way, Mr. Churchill and President Roosevelt appealed to the Italian people to rid themselves of Mussolini and surrender.

Early this morning the German radio was still silent on the tremendous change which has now come about in the war situation. Not so Rome. As if anxious that London and Washington should realise its full implications as soon as possible, Rome radio repeated the news solemnly and slowly in English at midnight. Both proclamations were read at almost dictation speed.

Top: Anzio lies in ruins in the aftermath of Allied raids in preparation for the landings in January 1944.

Middle: Monghidoro, just south of Bologna, is liberated by the Allies in October 1944.

Right: Italian partisans search for German stragglers in the town of Cesena following its liberation.

The fall of Rome

After encountering some initial difficulties at Salerno, the Allies raced through southern Italy in September 1943. They reached Naples at the end of the month to discover the population of the city had already risen up and pushed the Germans out. The lightning advance ground to a halt in November after the Germans retreated to the 'Gustav Line', a highly defendable position running across the country from the Tyrrhenian to the Adriatic Seas.

Attempts to break the Line during the winter proved costly to the Allies, so a surprise landing was made north of the Gustav Line, at Anzio, on January 22, 1944. In February the Germans counter-attacked in this area and the Allied advance came to a halt. To relieve the pressure on their men at Anzio, the Allies launched an invasion across the Gustav Line at Monte Cassino, the site of an ancient Benedictine abbey. The town did not fall until three months later, and only after the town and abbey had been completely reduced to rubble with great loss of life. With the Gustav Line breached, the Allies linked up with their comrades at Anzio and marched on Rome, liberating the city on June 4, 1944.

Mussolini executed

The Germans continued to resist in Italy for almost a year, and it was not until April 29, 1945 that they finally surrendered. The day before, Mussolini and his mistress had been captured and executed by Italian partisans. Their bodies, along with fifteen others, were hung upside-down from the girders of a petrol station in Milan.

Top and middle: **First news of Italy's surrender reaches London.**

Right: **Allied troops receive a rapturous welcome in the streets of Rome.**

Opposite bottom: **After days of determined fighting under appalling weather conditions and in the face of stiff enemy resistance, the vital mountain barrier of Mt. Cassino, which barred the Allied advance on Rome, was in Fifth Army hands. Here, German prisoners captured on the Mt. Camino sector walk through mud and water back to POW compounds in mid-December 1943.**

Great Allied Landings Near Rome This Morning

British, American, and Canadian troops, in force, were landing at various points in the "heart of Italy" early to-day. The report was given at 3 a.m. by the Allied radio at Tunis, broadcasting to Italy. It was picked up and issued by the American Office of War Information in New York.

Reports to Stockholm from Swedish correspondents on the Italian frontier said the landings were being made at Gaeta, south of Rome; Civita Vecchia, north of Rome; and Pisa Marina, north of Leghorn. Other landings were said to be going on at Naples, Genoa, and in Sardinia.

The reports to Stockholm added that the Italian garrison in Corsica yesterday overpowered the Germans and took control of the island. The Milan garrison was said to be preparing to give battle if the Germans should attempt to occupy the city.

Algiers reported at 1.30 this morning that Marshal Badoglio has ordered the complete hold-up of all ships, trains, and trucks carrying German troops in Italy.

Allies Give Orders

At 5.30 last evening all hostilities between Italy and the Allies ceased. The unconditional surrender of Hitler's foremost partner had been accepted and an armistice granted. All the Italian Armed Forces immediately came under Allied orders.

Geneva reports late last night said that all Italy has received the news of the capitulation with "explosions of joy." Demonstrators in Milan, Turin, Como and all northern industrial areas last night cheered the Allies and the Eighth Army.

Eisenhower In Italy

Up to an early hour to-day there was no indication of any military reaction or move by the powerful German forces stationed in Northern Italy. It was expected last night that the Germans would at least make some move to prevent the Italian Fleet from falling into our hands by bombing the warships in their ports or at sea on their way to Allied bases. Yet there was no news of anything.

The first news of Italy's unconditional surrender was given to the world in a dramatic broadcast announcement from General Eisenhower, C.-in-C. Allied Forces in the Mediterranean.

Top: Seventeen merchant ships in the liberated Italian port of Bari are bombed in a surprise German raid in December 1943.

Above inset: A great welcome was accorded to the first British troops entering Maida, in the province of Calabria, on the heels of the retreating enemy. The welcome, in September 1943, was organised by several English-speaking inhabitants who had lived in America, and who made rough American and British flags. Nearly 140 years ago, during the Napoleonic Wars, Maida was the scene of a battle when British troops invaded Italy under the command of Sir John Stuart. London's Maida Vale is named after the area.

Above: The people of Naples greet the Allies after evicting the Germans themselves.

Cassino Abbey bombed to a ruin

Front-Line troops of the Fifth Army watched in awed silence to-day the destruction by bomb and shell of Cassino Abbey. They looked on at the terrible bombardment with memories of comrades who had fallen under the guns of the Germans entrenched behind the abbey walls.

It had to be done - this razing of one of the great monuments of the Western World. And it has been done thoroughly after repeated warnings and with all due consideration for civilian life.

Seven waves of Fortresses, Mitchells, and Marauders have reduced the monastery to ruins. When I turned away from the scene an hour ago, the great, grey oblong monastery was nothing but a jagged silhouette against the pale blue sky. The German guns mounted in the abbey have been silenced. No longer is it the strong fortress dominating Cassino and denying us access along 'Highway Six' to Rome.

Doubtless there will be argument for many years to come about the deed that was done between 9 a.m. and 2 p.m., but I don't believe there was one man on our side of the Rapido Valley to-day who felt any regret or remorse, or, indeed, any other emotion save acute interest.

The attack was directed not only against the monastery but against the system of pillboxes and strong-points on the slopes below it.

Top left: American artillery pounds Monte Cassino in February 1944. The abbey was initially spared, but the Allies began shelling it to deny the Germans a key observation post on the Gustav Line.

Top right: Monte Cassino Abbey lies in ruins after the battle.

Middle: Cassino fell to British troops of the 8th Army and Polish troops captured the famous Abbey. British infantrymen pass Sherman tanks during mopping-up operations in Cassino, May 26, 1944.

Left: Not a single building is left undamaged during the Allied offensive on Monte Cassino.

Rome Ours: Germans Flee North

The city of Rome was firmly in Allied hands by midnight. The liberation of the first capital of Hitler's Europe came four years to the day after the last British troops were evacuated from Dunkirk. And General Alexander, the last man to leave Dunkirk, was in command of the victorious armies.

The city fell after a day of confused, sometimes bitter fighting, much of it in the city itself. Most of the fighting was in the south-east of the capital - well away from Vatican City - and the final entry was made at 7 p.m. by Highway Six through the Maggiore Gate.

Troops from the Anzio beachhead were the first to enter. Supported by tanks, they drove the Germans back to the edge of the ancient Forum. After that resistance, except for snipers, appears to have collapsed. At 1.30 this morning it was reported that the Germans had been driven into the northern suburbs; an hour later that the hotly pursuing Allied troops were beyond Rome, leaving behind only sufficient troops to mop up the German rearguards and snipers. Sporadic fighting was then reported to be in progress in the north-western suburbs of the capital.

The march into Rome had early yesterday promised to be a triumphal entry. The first troops advancing on the city were greeted by the Italians with flowers and cheers. "It was like a country drive," said one correspondent. Then resistance grew rapidly. Minefields guarded by mortars and machine-guns blocked the path of the Fifth Army. Snipers began to appear. Groups of infantry formed "pockets" to try to hold up the Allied advance.

Top: Minturno, two miles beyond the Gargliano river, fell to the British on January 2, 1944. The advance guard there met with an even stiffer resistance from the Germans, anxious of their Gustav line positions. Infantrymen are trying to clear a road through the rubble of the ruined and empty village of Tufo, perched on top of a hill, in the front line. The job was made more difficult by constant enemy shellfire.

Above far right: Guards of the 5th Army camped on rocky ground before moving forward into the front line.

Above: RAF Spitfires stand-by, ready to take off from an advanced landing field in Italy. The Spitfires covered for Allied bombers and also went out on offensive sweeps.

Right: British infantrymen, covered by machine gunners, dash through the town of Aquino. The town, which was strongly defended by the Germans, fell to troops of the 8th Army in the early hours of May 25. It had been mined and booby-trapped by the enemy before withdrawing.

1944:
Japan in retreat

The hard-won success of Guadalcanal led to a determined advance, codename Operation Cartwheel, by Allied forces through the Solomon Islands and New Guinea during 1943. Japanese forces had a major HQ in the town of Rabaul on the island of New Britain, garrisoned by around 100,000 troops, and this now became a strategic goal for the Allies in the Pacific Campaign. In the Battle of Tarawa, a heavily fortified atoll that held the key to the recapture of the Marianas, the Allied beach landings in November were met by the first heavy Japanese resistance at the beachhead to date; this would provide useful experience for future Allied landings such as Iwo Jima – but with a high cost in casualties. In the game of chess played out in the Pacific Islands, the steady pushing of the Allied forces could only have one conclusion but the delaying tactics of the totally committed Japanese Imperial Army made progress slow and the loss of life very high – on both sides. But the first months of 1944 proved the tide had turned on Japan.

Above: US Marines attack a Japanese strongpoint during the landing at Tarawa, where some of the 'bloodiest fighting of the campaign took place' to establish an Allied bridgehead on this central Pacific base. Two Marines – barely visible in their camouflaged cloaks – can be seen crouching behind the shattered stumps of palm trees, having tossed dynamite sticks seen exploding on the Japanese strongpoint.

Middle: Marines on the littered beach at Tarawa covered their ammunition and other gear with camouflaged shelter-halfs in case the Japanese tried an air attack.

Far left: A sub-machine gun in one hand and a grenade in the other, a soldier marches at the head of his men in pursuit of Japanese defenders of New Britain Island in the Southwest Pacific. US troops, in a two-pronged drive, advanced to new positions on the north and south coasts of New Britain and by March 27, 1944 were less than 170 miles away from the major Japanese base at Rabaul.

Left: Marines advance across desolate Darry Island in the wake of fleeing Japanese, as the Marines took Eniwetok Atoll in the Marshall Islands. The palm trees were either uprooted or defoliated by the bombardment before the leathernecks came ashore to clean out the holed-up Japanese in February 1944.

Above left: US Marines plunge through the surf at Cape Gloucester, New Britain, after disembarking from a landing craft to push a jeep to shore. An amphibious vehicle nears the beach during landing preparations on the Southwest Pacific island on December 26. Some Marines carry stretchers so that the wounded can be removed to medical stations promptly. US landing forces captured the twin air strips on Cape Gloucester in the initial attacks and then pressed on inland in their campaign against the Japanese.

Above right: American Marines wading ashore at Cape Gloucester, New Britain, had rough surf as well as the enemy to contend with. But they beat both. Other troops can be seen on the beach.

Middle left: A Japanese soldier, cornered by US Marines on Namur Island, holds out his arms in surrender while another Japanese digs his way out of a blasted blockhouse where twenty Japanese were trapped. An enemy soldier lies dead at the foot of the wrecked stairway (centre). Namur was the northern part of Kwajalein Atoll and one of the Japanese island fortresses in the Central Pacific taken by US forces leading up to the seizure of Kwajalein in the Marshall Islands, February 1944.

Middle: American assault troops splash across a shallow stream, near Aitape, where they formed small patrol groups to seek out Japanese defenders of the coastal base on Northern Guinea. US amphibious forces stormed ashore at Aitape and at two points flanking Hollandia, to the west, on April 22, 1944, gaining control of an additional 150 mile stretch of the Northern New Guinea coast for the Allies. Supplementary landings six days later aided in blocking escape routes for an estimated 60,000 Japanese troops entrapped in that area of the Southwest Pacific island.

Bottom: US amphibious tanks line a beach, bringing in supplies to American Marines who landed on Japanese-held Emirau Island in the St. Matthias group of the Southwest Pacific. An amphibious car pulls a truck ashore (left, centre), while in the background, troops form a chain in the surf to convey materials to the beach. US Marines captured the island on March 20, 1944, to complete encirclement of Japanese remnant garrisons on New Britain, New Ireland and the Northern Solomon Islands.

No-One To Leave Britain: Official

Britain becomes a sealed fortress from midnight on Thursday. From that hour no one will be allowed to leave this country until further notice except for business of urgent national importance which cannot possibly be postponed.

New restrictions announced on behalf of the Government by the Home Office last night turn Britain into a state of self-imposed military siege. People who have received exit permits to leave the country either by sea or air will not be allowed to use them unless they leave within the 60 hours from 12 noon to-day.

The new restrictions, says the announcement, have been imposed "for military reasons." "These restrictions will remain in force until further notice, but they are temporary, and will be relaxed as soon as military considerations permit."

The new ban is the last clamp on the Second Front security measures, which began with the ban on travel between Britain and Ireland at midnight on March 12. That was followed by another midnight order which came into effect on April 17, forbidding foreign diplomats from leaving the country, and requiring that all diplomatic bags being sent abroad should be censored. Only the diplomatic staffs representing the United States and the Soviet Union were exempted from this unprecedented measure.

Right: Restrictions announced on behalf of the Government by the Home Office on April 24, 1944 turned Britain into a state of self-imposed military siege. People who had exit permits to leave the country either by sea or air would not be allowed to use them unless they left within two days.

Above: Britain's fortified coastline. By May, 1944 only people with business interests in the area were allowed near the south coast of England. People exempt from the ban of visiting the coast didn't require individual permits, but they did have to satisfy police or Service authorities that they were exempt. The challenge could come at any time. The War Office advised all 'exempts' to carry documents showing reasons for their presence in the banned belt.

Holiday Coast to be Closed

The British coastline facing Hitler's Europe is to be closed to the public on April 1. A 10-miles deep belt stretching from the Wash round to Land's End will be banned to all, with few exceptions.

"Operational reasons" was the explanation given by the War Office last night, when eight new "protected" areas were listed - making up the biggest banned area of the war.

This major augury of decisive events ahead forbids all who were not living in the banned belt on April 1 from entering or being in it after that day. Chief exemptions are members of the Forces on duty, M.P.s, and certain Government officials. Other classes are exempt, but the Government hope they will keep out except in cases of urgent need.

So the Order - which comes as a surprise to the resorts - means that most seaside summer holidays must be sacrificed this year for "operational reasons."

The belt is made up of large areas of Norfolk, Suffolk, Essex, Sussex, Kent, Hampshire, Dorset, Devon, and Cornwall. Parts of Fife, Midlothian, and East Lothian come under a separate Scottish Order.

Top: Paddling in the sea around Britiain's coastal areas became an impossibility.

Above: This woman was determined to make the most of her day at the seaside. By May 21, 1944 beaches along the south coast were closed for 'operational reasons'.

Above left: As the beaches around Britain's shores were fortified against invasion with mines and barbed wire, children, like these boys, could only gaze longingly at the sea.

Left: Although almost 2,000 yards of the beach had been cleared for access by the military at Angmering this is the closest these mothers and children could get to the sea.

Chapter Seven

The Battle of Normandy

Preparations for the invasion of Occupied France had proceeded apace in Britain throughout the winter of 1943 and the spring of 1944. The Dieppe raid in 1942 had cost many lives, but it had also shown that it was going to be virtually impossible to capture and hold a major French port. 'Operation Overlord' was therefore planned to land on the less well-defended Normandy beaches to the east of the Cherbourg peninsula. This meant that a vast invading army would have to be both deployed and supplied without the advantages of a proper harbour, so artificial 'Mulberry' harbours were built to be towed across the English Channel to the landing beaches. In preparation for the invasion, special landing craft and amphibious vehicles were built, and large numbers of troops started assembling in southern Britain. In addition, a pipeline named 'PLUTO' was constructed to be laid across the seabed from the Isle of Wight to Normandy to ensure this enormous army had enough oil supplies once the invasion was underway.

The overall commander, General Eisenhower, gave the order for the long-awaited attack on the Normandy beaches to begin on June 6, 1944: D-Day. Soon after midnight a vast invasion fleet of nearly 7,000 vessels closed in on the designated beaches, and parachutists and glider-borne troops landed behind German lines in Normandy. At first light, after an initial assault from thousands of aircraft, the invasion proper began.

Five beaches were designated for the landings; the Americans landed at the westernmost beaches, codenamed 'Utah' and 'Omaha', while the British, supported by the Free French, came ashore further east at 'Gold' and 'Sword' beaches. The landing at 'Juno', in the middle of the two British beaches, was undertaken by the Canadian military, under the command of the British.

By the end of the first day some 130,000 men had landed in Occupied France and were able to establish a bridgehead in Normandy. This had come at a cost of many lives, especially at Omaha beach, where the preliminary aerial bombardment had missed the German defences along the sea wall. As the Americans came ashore, the Germans fired relentlessly from their pillboxes, gunning down hundreds of men before the beach was finally taken.

Left: **Allied troops form up on their Normandy beachhead while under heavy fire early on D-Day, June 6, 1944.**

D-Day rehearsal

Operation Overlord was planned with the utmost secrecy to ensure that the German Command would continue to believe that the logical Allied invasion point would be the Pas de Calais area. Amazingly, the secret was kept even though the whole of Britain effectively became a transit and training camp for the forthcoming landings. The massed troops underwent training to prepare them for the landings. The most notorious, Operation Tiger, set out to create realistic conditions for the 30,000 participating troops in the last week of April 1944. In nine troop ships, the US forces were to land on Slapton Sands in Devon where similar geography and terrain to their Normandy objectives were found. The convoy was intercepted by German E-boats and in the ensuing attack three transports were damaged or sunk, taking over 500 lives. Further misfortune hit over 300 more troops who made it to the beach but ignored important markers, and walked into a friendly fire zone. SHAEF Commander Eisenhower had decided his men should be exposed to the most lifelike enactment and a British heavy cruiser provided a barrage on the coastline with live ammunition as the men beached. In total, 749 soldiers and 197 US Navy personnel were killed. The tragic loss of these men was kept secret for several months and the names released with the casualties of D-Day.

Above: **American army preparations for D-Day on Slapton Sands, Devon. 749 GIs were killed when one of these training exercises went horribly wrong.**

Left: A DUKW amphibious troop carrier, known to all as 'Duck', boards a Tank Landing Ship or LST. American designed and built, based on a GM truck and engine, the DUKW could transport over water and land. Heavy duty pumps would keep the craft afloat when holed by gunfire and the driver could alter the air pressure in the tyres whilst driving, allowing the vehicle to negotiate soft sand and mud or normal road surface. Over 2,000 DUKWs were supplied to Britain under the US Lend-Lease programme; the name looks like an acronym but it is just GM's coding for the vehicle's specifications.

Left: General Dwight D Eisenhower talks with paratroopers of the 101st Airborne Division on 5 June prior to embarking on their spearhead mission that would successfully secure strategic positions just beyond the Omaha beachhead in the early hours of D-Day.

Below left: Taken during a training exercise just before D-Day, this photograph shows some of the equipment needed for the landings. The barrage balloon offers some protection from enemy aircraft and here army engineers are practising with slat and wire temporary road surfaces to enable vehicles to move over the soft, fine sands of the Normandy coast.

Below: Loading the last pieces of equipment before setting off to join the invading armada out in the Channel. This photograph emphasises the planning and logistics of Operation Overlord in which not only the troops had to be transported across the Channel, but all the weapons, vehicles and equipment needed, together with systems to help feed and support the soldiers.

The greatest armada of all time

To meet the logistical challenge of beach landings, specially adapted craft were constructed, some of which had already seen service in the Pacific. As the Allies would not have control of the ports in Northern France and the beaches on which the landings were to take place would not have deep anchorage, the Mulberry Harbour was created – a collection of floating quays to be towed to just off Omaha beach and ballasted to the seabed, enabling materials to be unloaded from ship to shore.

The combined air and sea landings began in the early hours of 6 June 1944 with British and US airborne forces parachuting and gliding to secure key inland objectives. The largest seaborne invasion force in history set out from assembly points all around the southern coast of Britain: some troop-carrying landing craft, like the DUKW, had to be loaded with troops just offshore from the beaches – bigger landing craft sailed across the English Channel already loaded – a miserable experience for the troops on board as these shallow-draft vessels were not designed for open sea. Nevertheless, the preparations for D-Day gave successful results in most cases, with American forces landing on Omaha and Utah beaches in the west, adjacent to the Cotentin peninsula; British and Canadian forces landed on Gold, Juno and Sword beaches to the east.

Top and middle: 5,000 ships, manned by nearly 200,000 naval personnel, made this the largest invasion armada of all time and on the fiirst day more than 175,000 troops were transported along with their armament, vehicles and supplies.

Left: US Infantry attacked Omaha and Utah beaches next to the Cherbourg peninsula; seen aboard their landing craft, they are about to beach. Shells are bursting on the shore from a naval barrage but the men look calm, protected by the armoured ramp down which they will soon run to meet the enemy. These craft carried a platoon – around 30 men – possibly a jeep and, apart from the armour at the front, were mainly constructed in plywood to a design by a US timber merchant called Andrew Higgins and were widely known as 'Higgins Boats'.

'Good Hunting' - Montgomery

The voice of General Montgomery, giving a stirring message to his troops before they set out, was heard in the B.B.C. war report last night. General Montgomery said:

"The time has come to deal the enemy a terrific blow in Western Europe. The blow will be struck by the combined sea, land, and air forces of the Allies, the whole constituting one great Allied team under the supreme command of General Eisenhower.

"On the eve of this great adventure, I send my best wishes to every soldier in the Allied team. To us is given the honour to strike a blow for freedom which will live in history: and in the better days that lie ahead men will speak with pride of our doings.

"We have a great and righteous cause. Let us pray that the Lord, mighty in battle, will go forward with our armies and that His special Providence will aid us in the struggle. "I want every soldier to know that I have complete confidence in the successful outcome of the operations we are now about to begin.

"With stout hearts and enthusiasm for the contest, let us go forward to victory, and as we enter the battle let us recall the words of a famous soldier, spoken many years ago. These are the words he said:

"He either fears his fate too much
Or his deserts are small,
Who dares not put it to the touch
To gain or lose it all."
"Good luck to each one of you. Good hunting on the mainland of Europe!"

Above: The landings were no party for the infantry. They had to descend into landing craft down rope nets from their troop ships and in many instances wade ashore under fire - all with their full equipment. Here British troops are about to join their welcoming party of heavy armour already occupying the beachhead.

Left: Heavily laden GIs wade ashore where half-tracks wait to help with their loads and give a shield in the first vulnerable moments ashore. In the distance a file of troops heads inland.

JUNE 8, 1944

Stern Test At Any Moment

In the second beachhead area on the Cherbourg peninsula American airborne forces were reported by the Germans to have linked up with troops landed from the sea.

General Eisenhower yesterday crossed the Channel to the beachhead area in a British warship, accompanied by Admiral Ramsay. For 4½ hours he cruised off the invasion beaches and held a series of conferences with General Montgomery, Rear-Admiral Kirk, and field commanders, whose names are still secret.

After his return it was learned at Supreme Headquarters that the programme is working out as planned, and on time. The stern test of attack which may develop at any moment will be met with a full measure of confidence and material resources.

Early this morning the German radio reported that strong Allied air fleets were attacking Lorient and Nantes, both U-boat bases, and the port of St. Brieuc, all in Brittany. Dummy paratroops were said to have been dropped at St. Brieuc.

Last night the weather showed considerable improvement. The sea was reported to be "fairly calm."

Above & left: These pictures shows well the broad shelving beaches selected for the Normandy landings. While they offered easier landings to the Allied forces they also offered deadly sweep of fire for defenders. The landings were prepared with extraordinary care, including geological surveys months before the invasion - made by British mini submarines. If the Germans had in any way expected the Allied landings the slaughter would have been horrific. The low tide on June 6 allowed the beaches to be cleared of mines and other obstacles, nonetheless the operation was laden with risk.

Top: General Eisenhower, Supreme Commander of the Allied invasion, plans 'Operation Overlord' from his headquarters in Britain.

Above: A barrage balloon floats over this bustling beachhead. On the distant ridge can be seen the hospital tents marked with red crosses. Thanks to intensive RAF Bomber Command activity during the run up to D-Day, the Luftwaffe was more or less neutralised, with airfields destroyed and radar knocked out. Targets were chosen with care - focus was given to the Pas de Calais while systematically destroying the rail infrastructure across northern France.

Right: American troops, carrying full equipment, wade ashore. The American landing beaches, Omaha and Utah, were farther west than the British and Canadian landing points. Troops moved out into the Cherbourg Peninsula as well as pressing south.

Top: After the initial onslaught, the flood of men and material continued for weeks; around 600,000 military personnel would come ashore on Omaha beach.

Above: Barrage balloons gave local cover to the invasion beaches: more encouraging to the soldiers was the constant stream of Allied bombers overhead.

Left: The scene on the beach in the first few days after the landings - unloading supplies, in this case the wooden slat and wire runners that were essential to get the vehicles moving onto firm ground.

The last act

June 6, 1944, will stand as one of the memorable days of all time. Upon this day was launched the greatest act of war in history - the invasion of Europe. This day saw well begun the campaign which will end the war in an Allied victory.

The Germans are beaten, and they begin to know it. Rome was one portentous symbol in their darkening sky. The Allies have the advantage in men, material, morale - everything. On the Eastern Front Russia awaits her moment. No secret weapon or tactical trick can save the Third Reich now.

This is the thought that must be uppermost in our minds as we watch unfolding the gigantic combined operation of the Allied land, sea, and air forces.

'The battle,' says Mr. Churchill, 'will grow constantly in scope and intensity for many weeks to come.' It will go well at one moment and not so well at the next. The fortunes of war will not always favour us.

After nearly five years of mingled triumph and disaster the British people are not likely to be led astray by excessive hope or unreasoning despair. Rather will they respond to the words of the King, who last night asked for a revival of the crusading spirit which sustained us in the dark days.

A great team

There have been warnings from high places. 'A long period of greater effort and fierce fighting lies ahead,' says President Roosevelt. General Eisenhower gives an inspiring Order of the Day to his troops, but, he says: 'Your task will not be an easy one.'

These warnings spring not from apprehension but from a just appraisal of the situation. They are based on the confidence so well expressed by General Montgomery: 'We are a great allied team.'

The mighty forces sweeping across the Channel are equipped with all the best that modern science and ingenuity can provide, and are trained to the last ounce. Supporting them is the terrifying punch of 11,000 war-planes, and transporting them are 4,000 large vessels, besides many thousands of smaller ones, backed by the power of six battleships and numerous other naval craft.

We can but marvel at the extent and intricacy of the operation. Beside these hosts of craft and myriad of aeroplanes, the record armadas of North Africa and Sicily become small.

According to plan

Of the actual fighting we know little, but things are going well. 'The operation is proceeding in a thoroughly satisfactory manner,' says Mr. Churchill, and nothing could be more emphatic. It may be that these landings are among the feints which the Prime Minister mentioned some weeks ago. The Germans appear to expect landings elsewhere. Let them speculate. We are content to wait on events.

Events are inspiring enough. The largest massed airborne landing yet attempted anywhere has been successfully made. Other troops have pushed several miles inland from the beaches.

There will be many conflicting reports in the next few days. Those which do not come from official sources or accredited correspondents should be treated with reserve.

The first three days will be the most critical. If our fine men, who carry with them all our thoughts and hopes, can establish themselves firmly during that time, the first big obstacle will have been victoriously overcome.

Top: Fellow German soldiers carry their wounded comrade to an evacuation barge just eight days after D-Day. At this stage, troops were still being landed from Britain and the ships which delivered them were busy taking POWs back to detention camps.

Above: An aerial view of Omaha beach on the morning of D-Day. Military vehicles attempt to exit the beach while small dots of men and beach obstacles can be seen in the water.

Front Now 100 Miles Across and Troops Still Pour In

The first historic day of Europe's liberation has gone completely in favour of the Allies.

"We have got the first wave of men through the defended beach zone and set for the land battle," said Admiral Ramsay, Naval C.-in-C., last night. "Naval ships landed their cargoes 100 per cent." Our troops and tanks are firmly ashore at many points along 100 miles of the Normandy coast from Cherbourg to Le Havre. They are ten miles inland at Caen; five miles inland at the base of the Cherbourg peninsula. The sea is rough on the beaches but reinforcements are pouring in. German coastal batteries have been mostly silenced. Casualties among both airborne and assault landing troops have been much lower than expected. Losses at sea were "very, very small." Against the 7,500 sorties flown by the Allied Air Forces the Luftwaffe put in only 50.

1,000 Troop Carriers In First Air Blow

Twenty-four hours have sufficed to smash the first fortifications of Hitler's vaunted West Wall. The Allied Navies and Air Forces, operating in unheard-of strength, have put the first wave of General Montgomery's armies safely ashore on the magnificent beaches of Normandy according to plan.

"Impregnable" strongpoints built up over three years by the famous Todt Organisation crumbled in a few hours under 10,000 tons of bombs and shells from 600 warships.

Minesweepers have swept away the mines. Engineers have cleared the underwater "fences," "pyramids," and "hedgehogs." Troops and guns and tanks are flowing on to the shore of France.

At Supreme Headquarters this morning there was a feeling of optimism that all was going well. Airborne operations, in which well over 1,000 planes and gliders took part, were particularly successful.

Weather was the biggest worry of the invasion commanders. A strong north-west wind sent white horses racing over a grey sea.

Above: Early on, in the first days of the invasion, the Allies began to take prisoners. Here a German soldier surrenders to the Americans.

Left: Captured on D-Day+1, these German prisoners are marched by British soldiers through a French village under the gaze of the local inhabitants.

Operation Cobra

Despite the complete surprise achieved by the Allied landings, German resistance was strong, particularly from a Waffen SS Panzer Division that was recuperating in the area before going back to active service. This succeeded in holding back the planned speed of the Allied advance. It would not be until July 18 that the Allied forces were able to break out from the Normandy coast beachhead in 'Operation Cobra', with General Patton striking into Brittany and Montgomery's 21st Army group heading into Belgium towards the Rhine.

Top: Two injured POWs, guarded by an American Military Policeman, wait in a jeep as a 'duck' amphibious vehicle passes through a liberated village. It is D-Day+4 and already the tricolour flies from the public building on the left.

Above: The main street of the town of Isigny, famed in peacetime for the quality of its dairy produce. Lying between the two American beachheads, the town was attacked by both sides from the air, from the sea and by fighting on land but was liberated within the first few days of the invasion.

Right: When the town of Ste Mère-Eglise, inland from Utah beach, was captured after fierce fighting, this German sniper was taken prisoner. Here he rides to captivity on the bumper of an American jeep.

Tank Groups

Pilots returning late last night said our troops were moving inland. There was no longer any opposition on the beaches. "We saw our tanks moving up on Caen. We could see no enemy infantry at this point near the coast."

The Germans report that Caen is the main invasion point. A big beachhead, they said, has been established between Bayeux and the mouth of the Orne River, north of Caen. Other landings have been made farther east, and "the once fashionable beaches of Deauville and Trouville have been the scenes of bloody combat."

Allied paratroops, according to the Germans, were landed around Caen and on both sides of Lisieux, 15 miles inland from Trouville. Allied tank groups were also reported by Berlin to be operating in the Carentan-Isigny area, five miles inland at the base of the Cherbourg peninsula.

Heavy fighting is in progress along the whole 19-miles stretch of road between Carentan and Valognes, at the northern end of the peninsula. Parachute troops established themselves on both sides of the road, said the German News Agency, and later in the day were reinforced by glider-borne troops. The road from Carentan to Valognes (Route Nationale 13) is the main highway from Paris to Cherbourg.

Above: The threat of Nazi invasion and the devastation of the Blitz might have subsided but the people of Britain suffered a new assault as the first V1 bomb landed on London on June 13. Evacuation of civilians continued. Here some of the 400 evacuees moved into Prestwich in Greater Manchester, are helped out by a friendly 'clippie' and an ARP officer.

Left: A grim scene from June 1944 in the once quiet Normandy town of Pont l'Abbé. Carrying all they have managed to salvage from their wrecked homes, these women and children hurry past a German military vehicle and its driver, killed in the Allied advance.

Destruction of Caen

One of Normandy's principal cities and strategically placed for road and river transport, Caen suffered a terrible fate in the aftermath of D-Day; Montgomery had set its early liberation as a priority target but an unexpected German Panzer counterattack halted the British spearhead and it was not until July 7 that Canadian forces entered Caen after it was heavily bombarded. Over 1,000 civilians died before the final liberation on July 18.

Top: **The Curé of Caen walks amidst the ruins of the town while German shelling continues.**

Above: **Eight days after D-Day, the leader of the Free French, General Charles de Gaulle, lands on the Normandy beaches.**

Right: **These young German soldiers claimed to be 18 years old but look little more than 14 or 15. They wait with other POWs to be shipped back to England for internment less than a week after D-Day.**

Progress beyond Normandy

As Operation Overlord pushed forwards in Western France, breaking out from the Normandy Bocage from July 18, Allied Forces marched steadily northwards in Italy, liberating Rome on June 4; the capture of the strategic Adriatic port of Ancona on the same day as the Normandy breakout, marked the inevitable collapse of Northern Italy.

The scale of Allied bombing over Europe became immense. On June 20 alone, the US 8th Air Force sent out over 1,500 bombers with fighter escorts to attack strategic targets. 191 B 24 Liberators were directed to the Misburg oil refinery near Hanover when 169 planes dropped high explosive bombs in a daylight raid.

Nearly 400 US 8th Air Force B-17 bombers hit Hamburg on June 18; it would not be the last raid but already the port city was devastated. The strategic bombing of German cities at this stage of the war would be hotly debated in years to come, but this was not yet the height of the terrible destruction wrought from the air by Allied forces.

Above and middle: While the Allies were beginning the assault on the Germans in northern France, fighting continued in Italy. An attack at Anzio in January 1944 was the beginning of an attempt to force German troops out of the parts of Italy they still occupied after the defeat of Mussolini. By June, the Allies were making good progress. A German soldier holed up in a dug-out in Piedmont waves a flag of surrender before emerging from his hiding place.

Left: French troops man an anti-tank unit as it rolls through Bolsena in Italy around the time of Operation Overlord. The M3 half-track tows an M3 37mm gun that was no match for the legendary German 88 anti-tank gun, which had four times the range and much heavier ammunition.

Above: Billowing smoke following the raid on Misburg oil refinery when 169 planes dropped high explosive bombs in a daylight raid.

Right: Moeneckeburg Strasse, a prominent business street in Hamburg, following the bombing on June 18.

Left: British infantry in Caen, searching for snipers in wrecked streets, look at a direction board. Before the invasion, Caen had a population of 60,000. On June 6, leaflets were dropped by Allied aircraft, urging the population to disperse into the countryside. Only a few hundred left. Later in the day British heavy bombers attacked the city, aiming to slow the flow of German reinforcements. There was huge destruction. Eight hundred civilians lost their lives in the 48 hours following the invasion. Streets were blocked by rubble, and ambulances could not get through. Notable buildings such as the Palais des Ducs, the church of Saint-Étienne and the railway station were all destroyed or severely damaged.

Liberation of France

The Germans were not prepared for the invasion force to come ashore at Normandy. They had been fooled into believing that the attack would come along the coast near Calais, by considerable decoy activity. Nevertheless the fighting was bitter and the men encountered stiff resistance across Normandy. Within a few days the Allies began linking up their five beachheads as ever more troops poured ashore. All the plans for increasing and supplying the invasion force worked with good effect and, on June 27, American forces captured the port of Cherbourg. On July 18 Caen was taken after prolonged fierce fighting and the Allies began to push out of Normandy towards Paris.

A second invasion force landed in the south of France near Toulon on August 15 and drove the Germans northwards along the Rhone valley. In all their advances the Allies were given invaluable assistance by the French Resistance, who harried the retreating Germans. The village of Oradour-sur-Glane in central France was to pay the price for increased resistance activity: members of the 2nd SS Reich Panzer division massacred the entire village on June 10 as they made their way to the front in Normandy.

Above left: The war is over for this German officer who displays his Iron Cross and Infantry Assault Badge. He was captured after the successful completion of the three-week campaign to secure the Cotentin Peninsula and its most important prize, the port of Cherbourg which was extensively sabotaged by the defending Nazis.

Above right: The insignia on this 18-year-old wounded German soldier shows him to be Waffen SS. The recently formed 12 SS Panzer Division was composed of Hitler Youth born in 1926 and led by veteran officers. The division was newly activated in Normandy and engaged the Allied invaders from June 7 with enduring ferocity. A regimental commander, Kurt Meyer, was tried for War Crimes and convicted of massacring 140 captured Canadian troops early in the fighting.

Right: A boy of fourteen captured in Coutances after sniping at American soldiers.

Above: In the ruins of Carentan at the base of the Cotentin Peninsula, firemen clear rubble after the liberation of the town by US forces. Field Marshal Erwin Rommel instructed the German defenders of Carentan to fight to the last man and the battle was bitterly fought in close combat.

Middle: A long column of Germans being marched away from the front line after being captured by the Americans in the fighting for the outer defences of Cherbourg.

Left: The German garrison at Cherbourg numbered over 20,000 and had nowhere to go, cut off by the advancing American troops. Defeat was inevitable but their demolition squads rendered the port unusable until mid-August. The last defenders were silenced on July 1 and the captured troops were marched to the Omaha beachhead.

Bayeux celebrates

The town of Bayeux celebrates Bastille Day, liberated after four years of German occupation. It was the largest crowd ever seen in the town, many people having travelled from the nearby town of Caen which had suffered terrible damage in the fighting. Crowds were also swelled by Allied troops and, as the accompanying caption iterated, 'members of the Maquis who, but a few hours before, had been fighting behind the German lines'.

Top: Bayeux's Bastille Day procession. In it were not only French, British and American troops and prominent citizens but also men of the Maquis who, but a few hours before had been fighting behind the German lines.

Above: British troops play a celebratory football match against a local French team.

Left: Another scene in Bayeux on Bastille Day but this time with a reminder that the liberation struggle is not over. As the people celebrate, tanks roll past on their way to the front.

Bayeux Is Captured - Official

Capture of Bayeux and the crossing at several points of the Bayeux-Caen road by Allied troops was announced by Supreme Headquarters at 1.30 this morning. The first step has been taken towards the isolation of the Cherbourg peninsula.

Bayeux, an old Norman town with a normal population of about 6,000, lies five miles inland. It stands athwart National Highway 13, from Cherbourg to Paris, and the main line railway.

Earlier the Germans reported that British were driving towards Bayeux from their beachhead in the Caen area after landing 100 tanks at one point.

A further indication of the favourable development of operations in this area was a German report that new airborne landings have been made in the Falaise-Argentan area, 32 and 40 miles inland from the Caen beachhead.

Communiqué No. 4, issued from SHAEF - Supreme Headquarters Allied Expeditionary Forces - shortly before midnight, announced that airborne operations were resumed on a "very large scale" yesterday morning. They were made in the rear of the German forces confronting our men on the beaches.

Above: The main street of the small town of Creully in Normandy with American and British troops alongside local inhabitants on their way to Mass. By this time only part of France had been liberated and large numbers of people from behind the German lines fled to liberated towns like the one pictured here.

Middle: Three German prisoners being marched out of the industrial town of Colombelles which fell after heavy bombardment from the air.

Far left: These German artillery engineers, captured near Caen, were originally stationed at Dieppe before being sent to fight as infantry.

Left: The batman of a captured German general continues to observe rank, carrying his superior's kit, in particular a smart leather briefcase.

Battle of Falaise Gap

Following the breakout from the beachhead, Allied forces began an encircling movement to trap the German armies in the area of Normandy centred on the town of Falaise. The Battle of Falaise Gap was a pivotal conflict, whereby German forces, instructed to hold their position and resist the overwhelming Allied offensive, knew they were about to be surrounded but fought desperately to keep an avenue of escape. On August 21, the Allies finally closed the gap, trapping an estimated 50,000 Germans and creating a clear route to Paris which was liberated on August 25.

Left: A German tank pushed off the road by advancing armour during the drive to Falaise starts to burn. On the right a medical orderly is ready to give assistance to the Canadian soldier who has fallen, but was uninjured.

Below: In the late stages of the Allied breakout from Normandy, code-named Operation Cobra, US forces under George Patton captured the coastal town of Avranches, the gateway to Brittany. After a massive aerial bombardment and an irresistible armoured advance, Germans fled their strategic defensive positions, some of them even crossing the dangerous sands of the bay to reach Mont St. Michel. Despite a fierce counterattack, the liberation of Avranches on July 31 held, allowing a rapid advance to Le Mans. Many Germans were trapped and surrendered – here a column of 2,000 prisoners is escorted by US troops.

Left: As the Allies pushed west from Normandy parts of Brittany were liberated. The citizens of Rennes come out to cheer the Americans as they enter the town.

Below: In brilliant August sunshine American tanks, watched by the local people, rumble through the streets of Avranches.

Bottom: Red cross aid for the advancing Allied forces.

MENU *5
FIRST HALF OF
5 RATIONS

Saint-Lô devastated

Saint-Lô was almost totally destroyed (95% according to common estimates) during the Battle of Normandy, earning the title of "The Capital of the Ruins" from Samuel Beckett. The Operation Cobra breakout had St-Lô as its first important capture - of necessity as it was positioned on a strategic crossroads. Prior to engaging the determined defenders, the main lines of defence were carpet bombed then pounded by Allied artillery. American money paid for a new hospital after the war in some recompense for the devastation. At one point it was mooted that the town should remain a ruined monument to the invasion but it was rebuilt and its historic buildings restored.

Main picture: **The town of St-Lô in Normandy in August 1944. The battle for the town was particularly fierce, the Germans mounting a strong defence, and by the time it was liberated there was hardly a building left standing in the centre.**

Above: **A much-decorated German soldier is captured. His medals include: first and second class iron crosses, a wound badge, the Russian medal and a sharpshooter's medal.**

Inset: **Mlle. Marie Jose Ruella, aged 74, refused to leave her home in the village of Amayé-sur-Orne despite the shelling and was the only person left to welcome the British troops as they passed through the village.**

Left: In this daylight raid on Berlin by Allied bombers, German government buildings including Hitler's chancellery are thought to have been hit.

Below: Burnt-out Luftwaffe fighters lie in pieces in their maintenance hangar at Paris's Le Bourget Airport – at first a target for the attacking Allies who had set about destroying every airfield available to the Germans in France, and now for the Germans who wanted to deprive the Allies of a strategic base next to Paris.

Bottom: A road is cleared through the ruined town of Villers-Bocage. Craters have been filled in and obstructions removed so that convoys of troops and equipment can be moved to new forward areas.

Above: The town of Falaise, the centre of two weeks of fierce fighting, is a collection of ghostly ruins, pictured here after it was finally taken by Canadian forces on August 17.

Middle: A British Bren-gunner takes up position on the Caen-Vire road on the outskirts of the village of Jurques.

Left: Paratroopers land in southern France to herald an Allied beachhead landing on a 100-mile coastal strip from Nice to Marseille on the morning of August 15, 1944.

The Allies great offensive

In all their advances the Allies were given invaluable assistance by the French Resistance, who harried the retreating Germans. Liberating troops finally reached Paris on August 24, where serious street fighting had broken out some days before. General de Gaulle entered the French capital in triumph on the following day, though there were still outbreaks of sniping.

The Allies had reached Belgium by September, and Antwerp and Brussels were also liberated. The American troops then passed through Belgium and reached the German border, where they encountered a major obstacle: the River Rhine. General Montgomery devised Operation Market Garden in the hope of seizing vital bridgeheads, an audacious attempt to land airborne troops behind German lines and capture crossing points. The early stages were successful, but the British 1st Airborne Division met with strong German resistance at Arnhem in the Netherlands. In addition, the troops sent to relieve them were held up, then withdrawn, having sustained heavy casualties; the Rhine remained, for the moment, under German control. Then in December, the Germans launched a surprise counter-attack in the Ardennes. This pushed the Allies back some 40 miles, creating a bulge into the Allied lines – and it became known as the 'Battle of the Bulge'.

At the same time that the Allied forces were fighting their way through Western Europe, the Russians were advancing from the east. Minsk fell on July 3 – the Red Army captured 100,000 German soldiers – and by the end of the month they had advanced into the western part of Poland. The Warsaw uprising began on August 1 with the Polish resistance fighting the German garrison. However, Stalin halted the Russian advance and left the fighters, who were essentially anti-communist, to their fate. German revenge was terrible and some 200,000 Poles died.

It was obvious that Germany's defeat was inevitable by the middle of 1944, but Hitler refused to consider any form of surrender. He placed his faith in a new generation of secret weapons that would, he believed, inflict devastating damage on Britain. The first of these was the V1, a pilotless flying bomb, which began falling on London and south-east England from June. They caused casualties and heavy damage, as well as a dip in morale – most people had thought that the dangers of the Blitz had passed. The threat from the V1 decreased as the Allied troops overran the launch sites in northern France. Between June and early September, it is thought that almost 7,000 were launched; over half were destroyed before reaching their intended targets. London came under attack from another German 'wonder' weapon, the V2, from September onwards. These, in contrast to the V1s, were long-range rockets and were fired from sites in places still controlled by the Nazis. The renewed threat from the skies revived the need to evacuate children from the threatened areas, and some 200,000 mothers and their children had left London by the end of July.

American-led forces continued their 'island-hopping' offensive in the Pacific, inexorably moving towards Japan and, on June 19–20, the Battle of the Philippine Sea took place between fleets of aircraft carriers. As with the Battle of the Coral Sea, neither fleet actually came within sight of the other and most of the damage was done by planes launched at a distance from the aircraft carriers. The American fleet sustained few losses, but inflicted grievous damage to Japanese air and sea power in the Pacific, thereby opening the way to the recapture of the Philippines.

Left: The delicate spire of Rouen Cathedral rises above the rubble left behind after the fierce fighting that led to the Allies' successful capture of the city.

Island-hopping

After securing Guadalcanal and New Guinea in 1943 the Americans continued with their offensives in the Pacific, jumping from island to island, moving ever closer to Japan in a strategy known as 'island-hopping'. In the summer of 1944 the US liberated Saipan, Guam and Tinian in the Marianas Island chain, and the invasion of Peleliu and Angaur in the Palau island group followed shortly after. The capture of these islands helped put America's B-29 bombers within range of Japan's main island, and from June 1944 the US Army Air Force began a bombing campaign against Japanese cities with the intention of forcing the country into submission. In 1945, the bombing became relentless, especially in Tokyo, where thousands of people were killed in firebombing raids, but the Japanese government still refused to surrender.

Top: A long line of amphibious tanks arrives ashore at Tinian Island in the Marianas chain, August 1944.

Middle: American paratroop reinforcements float down from transport planes to a beachhead in support of an amphibious Allied landing on Noemfoor Island, about 100 miles west of Biak Island and 800 miles from the Philippines on July 2, 1944. On the beachhead, vehicles and men of the amphibious force awaited them. The Allies gained control of three Japanese-built airstrips in their five-day capture of the strategic island off the north coast of Netherlands New Guinea. Noemfoor gave the Allies another forward base from which to mount their growing attacks on the enemy.

Left: An American tank patrols Garapan, Saipan's main city. Captured from the Japanese on July 9, 1944 after 24 days of bloody fighting, Saipan was one of the larger Mariana islands, with a substantial civilian population, of which an estimated 22,000 Japanese died. The Japanese garrison numbered 30,000 and was wiped out in the battle which cost nearly 3,000 American lives with 10,000 wounded.

Above left: On September 15, US and Australian troops landed on the island of Morotai virtually unopposed; the beaches they chose were unsuited to unloading vehicles and equipment and the troops, including General Douglas MacArthur, had to wade chest-high through the sea. Morotai and its airfield were important to the later invasion of the Philippines and the Japanese knew this well: reinforcements poured into the island and although Allied forces controlled it, Japanese resistance continued until the end of the war, when around 600 remaining troops surrendered.

Above: Installations at the Japanese air base on Woleai Island go up in smoke as planes of a US Navy Carrier task force blast the base during an attack on enemy strongholds in the Western Carolines of the Central Pacific. Planes were wrecked and the airstrip temporarily put out of operation. Surface units and carrier-based aircraft of the American force sank or damaged 46 Japanese ships, destroyed 160 planes, probably wrecked 54 others and bombed enemy bases during the three-day assault.

Middle: On September 17, US marines haul an anti-tank gun ashore from their landing craft during the invasion of Angaur, another of the Palau islands which had to be taken en route to the Philippines. The small garrison of Japanese fought hard but the battle was over by September 30.

Left: The Battle of Peleliu, one of the small coral islands of Palau, was controversial; the airfield there was of little strategic importance and although the US attackers expected a quick victory, the Japanese had prepared for invasion with great care. From the first landing on September 15, US forces faced determined opposition until November 27 when almost the entire Japanese garrison of 11,000 had been wiped out. This battle was a preview that prepared the US military for similar defensive tactics in Iwo Jima and Okinawa.

Paris liberated

The liberation of Paris was completed on August 25, 1944 after 10 days of civil and military disobedience on all sides. The Allies had no plan to liberate Paris at this stage in the war, but wanted to make all haste to Berlin to end the conflict. The large population of Paris, and intelligence reports that the German occupiers were poised to destroy the city around them, increased Allied determination to skirt round a potential Stalingrad. But a general strike in Paris from August 15 and overt action in the streets by the Free French Resistance, led the French commander, General Leclerc, to disobey his battle orders from General Bradley and send an advance guard into the city with the promise of reinforcements to follow. Seeing that the die was cast, Bradley permitted Leclerc to fulfil his promise and in the event the German commander, General Dietrich Von Choltitz, disobeyed Hitler's orders to devastate the city; instead Choltitz surrendered.

Left: **A French tank stands before the Arc de Triomphe as the capital is reclaimed.**

Below: **Thousands of American troops with their equipment march down the Champs Élysées.**

Left: Senior Nazi officers are escorted by Free French Resistance under the watchful eyes of US troops. They provide a public spectacle outside the Hotel de Ville - the Town Hall of Paris.

Below inset: Marking the liberation of Paris, the first edition of the Continental Daily Mail to have been printed since June 1940 is published on August 28.

Bottom: US tanks and transport line the square outside the Hotel de Ville, providing grandstand views for the elated people of Paris who are in a party mood.

Daily Mail

CONTINENTAL EDITION

MONDAY. AUGUST 28, 1944.

Liberation Edition

The Continental "DAILY MAIL" reappears this morning - the first British newspaper to resume publication in Paris. It is in abbreviated form, but it is an earnest of the happier days that have come to Paris and many liberated areas of France.

This edition ends the gap in publication which began on Monday, June 10, 1940, the last publication date of the Continental "Daily Mail" in Paris before the German occupation.

For this edition special stories have been written by two brilliant "DAILY MAIL" writers :

Alexander CLIFFORD, who reported the BRITISH 8TH ARMY'S magnificent victory in North Africa and is now with the BRITISH ARMY in France.

Noel MONKS, who was well known to Continental "Daily Mail" readers before the war.

German 7th Army's Huge Losses

BY ALEXANDER CLIFFORD

Normandy, Sunday.

The freeing of Paris was one of the most exhilarating moments of history. And it is natural that it should have overshadowed the fact that the German Seventh Army is still being defeated in Western France.

SALUTE THESE MEN

The liberators of Paris were the troops of General Hodges' First American Army which included the 2nd French Armoured Division. This news was officially released last night, and with it the story of a gesture of courtesy made by General Hodges.

A letter was prepared as the official document which will shortly hand back the control of Paris from the American

Stirring Scenes at Liberation of Paris

BY NOEL MONKS

Paris, Sunday.

I came into Paris with an American advance column at noon on Friday, and I confess unashamedly that as we rounded a corner south of the Porte d'Italie and I saw the Eiffel Tower standing clear and strong above the city of Paris.

Germans in Paris surrender

THE battle for Paris is over. General Leclerc's tank columns broke into the capital early yesterday and in less than 12 hours' fighting smashed German resistance. The end came suddenly last evening when Leclerc, according to the Patriot radio, delivered an ultimatum to the general commanding the German garrison. The two, with the Maquis chief of Paris, then went to Montparnasse Station, where the terms of the capitulation were signed.

Under these, the German general at once ordered the cease fire. His men, unarmed, were to assemble at selected points to await orders. Their arms were to be piled and handed over intact.

At about the time Leclerc dictated his terms to the German, and while fighting was still in progress, General de Gaulle entered the city. Huge crowds greeted him with the 'Marseillaise' and cries of 'Vive de Gaulle!' to which he replied: 'I wish simply and from the bottom of my heart to say to you, Vive Paris!'

Top: While elsewhere in the city Parisians celebrate, French troops fire at the remnants of the German army who have holed-up in defendable positions.

Middle: A group of GIs and a member of the Resistance work to flush out German snipers, barricaded in buildings in the Paris streets two days after the liberation.

Left: Fighting in Paris was sporadic - the Germans had good military strength but used it sparingly; however they continued atrocities against the population to the very last and took refuge in pre-planned fortifications. The Free French hunted them down - the men here are advancing on a government building in which around 500 German soldiers had holed up and eventually surrendered.

Top: De Gaulle makes his way through the crowds on the Champs Élysées in Paris.

Above: General de Gaulle flew in from his Algiers HQ to join the advance of French troops into Paris. He made a famous speech from the Hotel de Ville, emphasising the French role in liberating Paris. The following day, de Gaulle led a victory parade under the threat of sniper fire and took the salute with other Allied leaders in the Place de la Concorde.

Above left: General Leclerc's armoured division passes through the Arc de Triomphe

Left: Food supplies were sent almost immediately to Paris by the Allies. Here British troops and local women chat alongside a lorry loaded with flour.

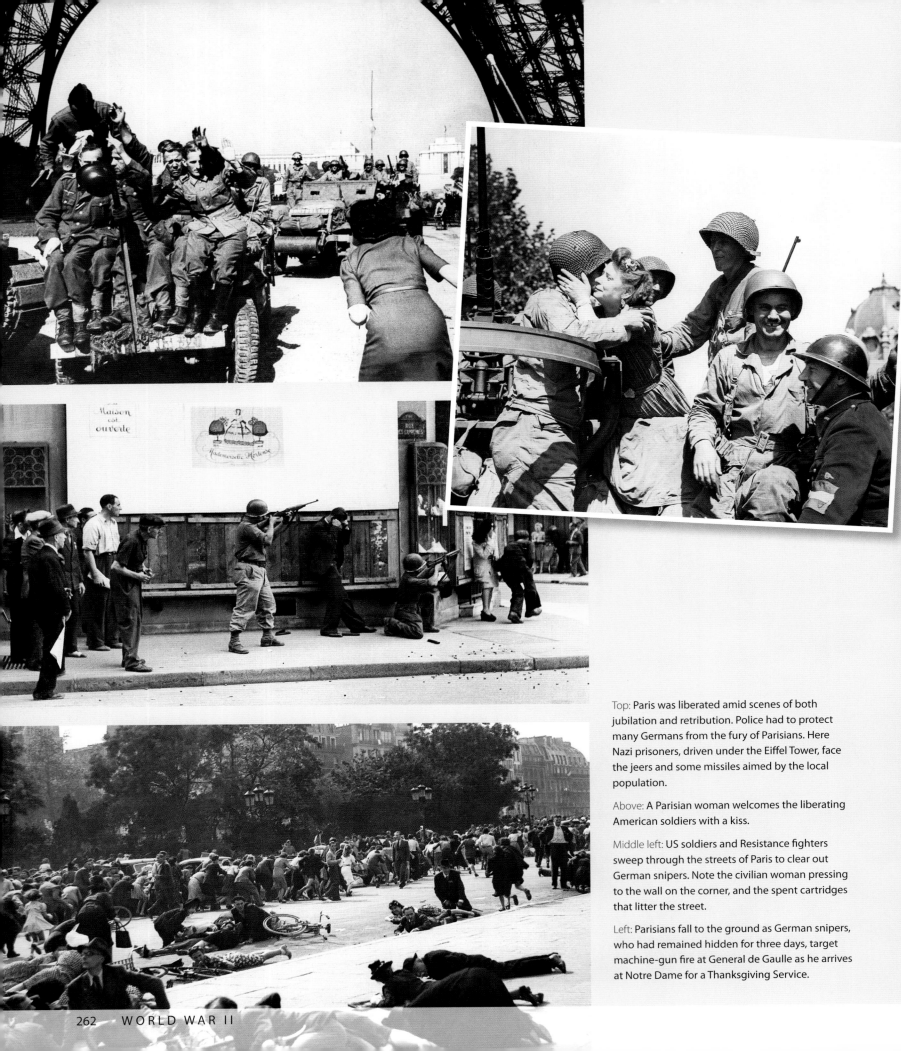

Top: Paris was liberated amid scenes of both jubilation and retribution. Police had to protect many Germans from the fury of Parisians. Here Nazi prisoners, driven under the Eiffel Tower, face the jeers and some missiles aimed by the local population.

Above: A Parisian woman welcomes the liberating American soldiers with a kiss.

Middle left: US soldiers and Resistance fighters sweep through the streets of Paris to clear out German snipers. Note the civilian woman pressing to the wall on the corner, and the spent cartridges that litter the street.

Left: Parisians fall to the ground as German snipers, who had remained hidden for three days, target machine-gun fire at General de Gaulle as he arrives at Notre Dame for a Thanksgiving Service.

Top: A woman leans forward to curse this captured German soldier as he is marched at gunpoint through the streets of St-Mihiel in Northern France.

Above: By the third week in August the Allies had been fighting on French soil for ten weeks and while in some areas German resistance was relatively light, in many others the fighting was fierce. Here exhausted soldiers catch a few moments sleep in the Normandy countryside.

Left: A jeep drives along the causeway to the world-famous landmark of Mont-St-Michel which the Germans had evacuated in early August as the American army pushed through into Brittany. The island and its buildings were undamaged.

Above: A German prisoner in Brest hands a 'safe conduct' pamphlet to Lt W. F. Kinney of Chicago. The pamphlets were shot over the German lines carrying a guarantee of good treatment to those who surrendered.

Above right: Canadian troops 'clean up' in May-sur-Orne, Basse Normandie, as they search house-to-house for enemy soldiers.

Right: A German soldier is captured on the road to Brussels by a Welsh corporal.

Far right: The church at Aunay-sur-Odon is badly damaged, but the spire remains intact despite the surrounding devastation, which engineers are bulldozing to clear the road.

Above: As British forces pushed north towards the Rhine they met many waterways that had to be bridged: engineers raised pontoon crossings to replace those demolished by retreating Germans. Here M10 tank destroyers of 77th Anti-Tank Regiment, 11th Armoured Division, cross a Bailey bridge over the Meuse-Escaut (Maas-Schelde) canal at Lille St Hubert (St Huibrechts) on September 20, 1944.

Middle: British tanks speed along the cobbled highway into Belgium while German prisoners are held at the roadside. Liberating Belgium was another piece of the jigsaw which would open a route to the River Rhine whilst giving the Allies the strategic port of Antwerp; however, although Belgium was liberated in the first week of September, Antwerp would not be effective as a port until the end of November, when the Scheldt Estuary area was finally cleared of doggedly resistant German troops.

Left: The scene in the submarine pens at Brest as the town surrendered. It was from Brest that many of the German U-boats left to harry shipping in the North Atlantic.

Right: Before they evacuated Florence on August 11, the Germans destroyed every bridge but one over the river Arno. British sappers, however, were soon on the job and astounded the people of Florence by the speed with which they replaced one of the bridges. The Bailey Bridge, which they built, was erected on the pylons of the former Ponte San Trinith.

Right middle: Parachutes fill the sky over the coast of Southern France after the 12th Air Force Troops Carrier Air Division C-47s carried men and supplies to the dropping zones over the new beachhead, somewhere between Nice and Marseilles.

Below: U.S. Eighth Air Force bombers attacked synthetic oil plants over a wide area of Germany on August 16. A B17 Flying Fortress can be seen as it passes over the burning plant at Rositz, located about 21 miles south of Leipzig.

Below right: Before this R.A.F. Bomber Command has carried out its offensive against the Germans by night, but now its heavy four-engined Lancasters and Halifaxes pounded German positions in the field and strongpoints in Normandy and Brittany, in support of the Army, by day. Nearly one hundred Lancasters of R.A.F. Bomber Command fly by daylight to attack enemy positions in the field.

Above left: Women branded as Nazi collaborators stand dejectedly after receiving the common punishment of having their hair shorn. One with her baby, whose father was a German, carries a bundle of belongings, forced to abandon the community that has rejected her, while the local population expresses vigorous disapproval.

Above right: As the Netherlands came under Allied control, Nazi collaborators were quickly arrested. Uncertainty over Dutch loyalty to the Allied cause contributed to Market Garden's failure: British intelligence believed the Dutch Resistance to be compromised by Nazi double agents and ignored vital intelligence. Germany had appointed an Austrian governor to rule the Netherlands, banning all political parties except the National Socialist Party whose members were then promoted to key positions.

Left: The French Resistance was renamed 'French Forces of the Interior' by de Gaulle giving them more regular national status.

Brussels liberated but slow progress in Holland

By September 2, the Allies had liberated Brussels, and were moving across Belgium towards Germany. With their freedom restored, Belgian civilians and reistance groups began to round up German troops and Nazi sympathisers.

The old town of Bruges was liberated by Canadian forces around September 15, and despite days of fighting, the town itself was unscathed.

Top: The Belgian resistance was known as the White Army and, with Allied assistance, they played an important role in securing the country. The Allies drop supplies including arms and ammunition to support them.

Above: A group of prisoners brought in by Belgian resistance fighters.

Middle: A British armoured squadron supports troops holding a bridgehead near Gheel in Belgium, where German resistance was fierce.

Left: An Allied transport convoy crosses a pontoon bridge in Belgium.

Above: Canadian troops liberate Bruges in mid September and are cheered by the local people. The ancient city was of less importance than its connected port of Zeebrugge, which the German occupiers had made into a heavily defended fort - part of the Atlantic Wall; it was the beginning of November before Zeebrugge fell. 15 days of fighting preceded the taking of Bruges but little damage was done to the historic town.

Right: British tanks moving into the Belgian capital are cheered on by locals.

Above left: German prisoners march under guard through Antwerp. The speed of the Allied advance took the German defenders of Antwerp by surprise and the port was liberated on September 4. Despite its importance to the Allied supply lines - by now seriously overstretched - it would take another three months to oust Germans from control of the waterway leading to the port, which was many miles upstream on the River Scheldt.

Above inset: As German troops retreated from Brussels, they left the Palais de Justice burning in their wake.

Above right: A Belgian who had worked for the Gestapo, is captured and handcuffed by police in Grammont.

Left: Belgian police and civilians round up a group of 'Quislings', or Nazi sympathisers. The name was derived from Vidkun Quisling, the Norwegian politician who had collaborated with the Nazis following the German invasion of Norway in 1940.

Top: British tanks and their crews are mobbed by ecstatic Belgians as they pass through Brussels.

Above: British troops in Brussels enjoy an ice cream.

Left: Allied troops and transport moving into the Belgian capital are cheered on by locals.

Operation Market Garden

By September, Allied forces were advancing into Belgium and Luxembourg and plans were being put in place to secure the Rhineland and Ruhr in readiness for an assault on Holland and then Germany itself. General Eisenhower, who was in overall control of the Allied forces in Europe, favoured maintaining a wide offensive line along the whole of the front, but as the advance slowed, he looked to Generals Patton and Montgomery, who were controlling forces in the region, for suggestions. There was some argument over what form such an assault should take. Patton wished to attack along the heavily defended Siegfried Line to capture Metz, whilst Montgomery wished to bypass these defences, cross the Rhine at Arnhem and capture the German 15th Army from behind their lines, whilst also cutting off the launch sites from which V1 and V2 rockets were being fired at London and other cities. The final plan was Operation Market Garden, which involved dropping paratroopers into the region in advance of infantry and armoured divisions in an attempt to secure vital crossing points across the Rhine. Bridges were successfully secured at Veghel, Grave and Nijmegen, but the British 1st Airborne and Polish 1st Independent Parachute Brigade suffered heavy casualties at Arnhem after troops sent to relieve them failed to break through German defences.

Top: Montgomery's daring plan to rush mechanised forces forward to the Rhine in the Netherlands centred on Operation Market Garden, the largest airborne attack in history, involving over 30,000 troops to secure the lower Rhine, giving a direct route into Germany. US airborne troops are pictured in their transport plane before takeoff.

Middle: Liberation snowstorm descends on Holland. The Dutch landscape is covered with Allied parachutes while others can be seen still falling. This was just one of the many landings of Market Garden.

Right: Descending paratroops fill the skies, jumping from C-47 transports with their equipment. Although brilliantly conceived, Market Garden differed from previous Allied campaigns with no rehearsals, no diversionary attacks and limited tactical planning that depended on achieving a sequence of separate objectives culminating in the bridge over the Rhine at Arnhem. Weaknesses quickly became apparent: commanders had ignored intelligence of German strength in the area, radio communications failed and deadlines lagged. Men fought with outstanding bravery and determination but at the end of the nine-day battle on September 25 there were nearly 8,000 Allied casualties, dead, wounded or taken prisoner.

SEPTEMBER 26, 1944

Arnhem front

Alexander Clifford, in a delayed cable, tells below the story of the first corridor battle.

The Germans have tried the obvious thing. They cut through our corridor behind us, and - if you like to put it that way - technically surrounded us.

The moment came at noon on Friday. It was a long time before anyone worked out exactly what happened. But the effective news was that German tanks and infantry were across our lines about 17 miles north of Eindhoven. All convoys must halt. The attack came from Germany itself. It may have been combined with an attempt to rescue some of the estimated 70,000 Germans who are partly cut off in Western Holland. Its main purpose was certainly to cut the axis.

From that moment the campaign abandoned all the rules again and became a series of personal adventures of each individual. For many truck drivers it meant sitting patiently by the roadside and listening to the firing ahead. For the men on the Arnhem front it meant the queer feeling that they were no longer fighting at the end of lines of supply but were temporarily in a military vacuum. For me it meant that I was cut off from my kit, which I had left in a little inn in the village where the Germans had attacked. It had been a gay, clean little inn, with an innkeeper who still managed to provide comfort and good Dutch food. And now the German mortars were falling on it.

Good humour

For the men on that section of the road it meant a sudden inferno of battle at a spot technically 30 miles behind our front lines. British and German trucks were blazing along the road and out into the fields. The possibility had been clearly enough foreseen. We always knew we could deal with anything of the sort if it occurred, and around Nijmegen there was a great deal of good-humoured banter as people who had been cut off began to go round trying to find billets for the night.

In the desert one would have joined some unit and slept in its laager. Here in civilised Europe one hardly knew what to do. In the end I and those with me decided to sleep on the billiards tables of a wayside pub. We ate sumptuously off German rations which we found in a train at Nijmegen railway station.

The night was a succession of wild alarms. Dutchmen, either honestly misinformed or deliberate Fifth Columnists, kept streaming in to tell us that the Germans were a mile away, that the British were evacuating Nijmegen, and so forth. None of it was remotely true. But the whole position was so unorthodox that it was understandable.

There was plenty of shooting during the night. But as often happens near the front, when morning came no one knew what it had been about. The only certain news was that the Germans were still across our path. Tanks had been sent to deal with them.

I followed down behind the leading patrol. It was necessary to reach that little inn quickly if any of my kit was to be saved. The Germans were reported to have been in the village itself for quite a few hours.

The ruptured stretch of axis was a trail of wrecked vehicles. It was almost like Normandy again, for the fields were strewn with dead cows. The tarmac was churned to dust where swerving tanks had ground it up. Half a dozen cottages along the way were still burning.

Methodical

While our patrol was still passing through all this we looked up and saw a new mighty phase of this three dimensional campaign. The sky filled fuller than I have ever seen it with planes and gliders. They came low, flying in steady and majestic patterns. They were simply reinforcements for the front. The Germans began to shoot at them. It was alarming to hear how near the Germans still were to the centre-line of our axis. They were firing from the nearest woods two fields away and their bullets were spangling the cloudy sky all round the great air fleet.

They got some hits. Extraordinarily few in the circumstances, but they could hardly help getting some. A towing plane began to burn and circled from the rest. Two or three gliders slipped loose and swung round towards what they knew were our lines.

But the Germans had given their positions away and firing broke out savagely once more from our land forces. A battle started chaotically among the fields and copses and farmhouses round about. It looked chaotic. But there was plenty of method in the way the Germans were being elbowed aside. You could piece it all together by watching the positions of the tanks along the roads and the places where the anti-tank guns were being dug in and the columns of smoke where our shells were falling.

And then we came to the gay, neat little village in whose inn we had left all our kit. Now it was empty and splintered and broken. It was grey with a pall of dust. Its streets were a tapestry of fallen branches and loose tiles and scattered bricks.

The inn itself was windowless and derelict. The innkeeper and his family were alive - they were down in the cellar steadfastly singing hymns. Almost everything they possessed was broken. Their yard was full of dead chickens. We dug what remained of our things out of the wreckage of our bedrooms. An American paratrooper came and told us to be quick about it, the village still wasn't very healthy.

Top: Later, in October, the Allies were able to make more progress in Holland. Here British troops advance along a ditch during an attack on the village of St Michielsgestel outside 's-Hertogenbosch.

Above: Polish soldiers take cover in a wrecked farmhouse, just 400 yards from the enemy line at Hooge Zwaluwe in Holland.

Above: A dramatic photograph, taken on August 24 but not released to public view until mid-September, shows the last moments of two of the few remaining ships of the German Kriegsmarine in Western Europe: the heavy destroyer Z24 in company with the torpedo boat T24 had escaped destruction in the recent Battle of Ushant and both had been discovered near the mouth of the River Gironde by Beaufighters of Coastal Command's RAF 236 and RCAF's 404 squadrons on a routine patrol out of Davidstow Moor. They attacked with rockets and cannon blazing in a hail of anti-aircraft fire from the enemy ships. All the Beaufighters were damaged but made it back to base. Later reconnaissance could only find oil-slicks remaining of the two German craft.

Above inset: 500-ton U-boat 243 is surrounded by a hail of bullets as a depth-charge erupts in a plume close to the stricken vessel in the Bay of Biscay.

This was the first kill of Flying Officer W B Tilley of the RAAF; along with his colleagues of 10 Squadron, he was trained to fly the Short Sunderland flying boat that, equipped with radar, could detect enemy submarines on the surface. The Sunderland carried out convoy escort duties throughout the war.

Left: Canadian troops row themselves ashore from this troopship in September. More than a million Canadians fought in the Allied forces across every theatre of war. Landing with the British on Juno, Gold and Sword beaches on D-Day, they deployed northwards after the Battle of Falaise Gap; moving along the Channel coast reaching Dieppe, the scene of a military debacle that cost Canadians dearly in 1942, liberating Calais and ending in the Scheldt area where Canadians took a prominent part in ousting Nazi forces from September to October.

Above: **Although in their hasty evacuation of the important town of Namur, Belgium, the Germans destroyed the bridges over the river, Belgian workers soon had this one capable of carrying pedestrian traffic. US Army engineers speedily threw pontoon bridges across, enabling Allied armour to continue the drive against the retreating enemy.**

Above right: **The people of Dieppe are able to see their beach again after four years of German occupation when the coastal area had been off-limits to civilians.**

Middle left: **The amazing scene in the Rome Supreme Court on September 23,1944 as officials and a US officer pleaded for order after demonstrators had burst in demanding the death of Pietro Caruso, former fascist Police Chief of Rome. Caruso's trial was put off, and the mob, incensed, lynched a hated trial witness, Donato Carretta, the sadistic former governor of Rome's infamous Regina Coeli Prison.**

Above: **A US 'Long Tom' 155mm field gun is towed across a Bailey bridge over the River Sieve outside Borgo San Lorenzo a short distance north of Florence in northern Italy. By September 11, elements of the British 8th Army were advancing on the central section of the German Gothic Line - a fearsome defence around 10 miles deep that took advantage of the Apennines which cross Italy almost unbroken from east to west at this point. Despite a fierce two-pronged attack by the 8th and 5th Armies, the Gothic Line held, aided by terrible winter weather.**

Left: **Salvaged parts of V1 bombs that fell on southern England in great numbers from June 1944. These fragments were studied by the Ministry of Aircraft Production's Experimental Station to discover possible deterrents. Despite the use of artillery barrages around the coast and patrols by specialist Tempest aircraft, nearly 1,000 'buzz-bombs' reached their targets causing 6,000 deaths and nearly 18,000 wounded. Capturing or destroying the launch sites in northern France and then in Holland relieved Britain, but the flying bombs continued to devastate cities like Antwerp that were still in range.**

Opposite: A long column of German troops files out of Aachen as the town finally surrenders to the Americans.

Top: The quality of German forces defending Aachen was mixed - from hardened Panzer companies to units comprising young recruits and convalescents. However, the fortifications of the city made up for the uneven quality of the troops and as well as slowing the US advance they cost around 5,000 Allied casualties. There was a strong will to defend the town - its defenders were now on home ground rather than an alien occupying force; moreover, Aachen was the seat of Charlemagne, founder of the First Reich, heavily symbolic to the Nazi regime.

Middle: As heavy fighting continues during October, German refugees leave Aachen. American troops, meanwhile, head deeper into the town.

Above: British troops advance cautiously across open countryside towards the town of Venray, an important road and rail junction.

Left: German POWs march out of Aachen under the gaze of local civilians, some of whom are clearly now refugees.

Below: Three Canadian soldiers march down the deserted Boulevard Pasteur in newly captured Calais, its famous clocktower in the background. The town was liberated on October 1 after the German garrison surrendered, having released 20,000 civilians during a 24-hour truce.

Top & lower right: Pictures taken from a film made by the RAF Film Production Unit during the great daylight attack on Duisburg by more than 1,000 RAF heavy bombers on October 14 when over 4,500 tons of high explosives and incendiaries were dropped on Germany's vital Ruhr communications centre in the space of 25 minutes. Within a few hours, this devastating blow – the heaviest single attack yet made on any German industrial city – was followed by a night assault of even greater weight. The top picture shows a 4,000 pound bomb and a shower of incendiaries leaving the bomb bay of an RAF Lancaster high above Duisburg.

Below: German mines being cleared.

Below inset: Smoke billowing from multiple targets in Bergen. The German U-boat fleet had been forced out of its bases on France's Atlantic coast and had moved to heavily built bunkers in the Norwegian port. Two RAF raids set out in 1944 to destroy the concrete pens but hit many civilian targets, including a school. Around 250 Norwegian civilians died in these two raids.

Bottom: An oil refinery near Gelsenkirchen in Germany, devastated by RAF and US Air Force bombing.

Top left: In Holland, Allied tanks advance through the streets of Schijndel, near Tilburg.

Top right: American 4.2 mortar shells land in the small village of Le Tholy as the Allies move through northern France.

Right: Allied bombers now met little opposition from the Luftwaffe in the air and could freely bomb targets in Germany. The riverside wharves are obscured by the plumes of smoke from exploding bombs.

Above: Squadron Leader JH Iremonger with members of 486 Squadron briefing his New Zealander pilots at their base, Grimbergen, in Belgium. This was one of five Tempest Squadrons now located in Europe which had made its name defending Britain against V1 flying bombs. The Hawker Tempest, designed by Sidney Camm and based on the Typhoon, was fast at low altitude - and thus able to keep pace with the rocket-propelled V1s; the Tempest pilots learned the weak points of the buzz-bombs and had excellent kill-rates.

Roosevelt told to carry on

Franklin Delano Roosevelt (also known by his initials, FDR) was the 32nd President of the United States, leading his country during a time of worldwide economic crisis and world war. The only American president elected to more than two terms, he forged a durable coalition that realigned American politics for decades. FDR defeated incumbent Republican Herbert Hoover in November 1932, at the depths of the Great Depression. FDR's combination of optimism and activism contributed to reviving the national spirit. At the Tehran Conference, Roosevelt and Churchill told Stalin about the plan to invade France in 1944, and Roosevelt also discussed his plans for a postwar international organization. For his part, Stalin insisted on the redrawing of the frontiers of Poland. Stalin supported Roosevelt's plan for the United Nations and promised to enter the war against Japan 90 days after Germany was defeated.

Above right: In 1944, 62-year-old Franklin Delano Roosevelt stood for an unprecedented fourth term and was re-elected President, despite his declining health. Excited service personnel track the progress of the election in the US forces social club - hosted at Rainbow Corner on Shaftesbury Avenue in London's Soho. There they had access to food, dancing and attractive companions 24 hours a day.

Right: An iconic photogaph from the war showing a Japanese Torpedo plane crashing in flames as a result of a direct hit from carrier anti-aircraft guns during operations near Saipan in the Marianas.

Left: One minute after midnight on October 22, the British Second Army under General Dempsey started a drive for 's-Hertogenbosch, a Dutch railway and communications centre vital to the Germans. Infantry troops are pictured in a trench captured during the advance.

Below: Troops of the American 9th army enter the captured town of Linnich, which is on the banks of the Roer river.

Above right: As the Allies advanced, many civilians sacrificed their homes which were requisitioned in battle or simply became uninhabitable after artillery fire. The best they could hope for was to rescue as many of their meagre possessions as possible.

Above left: Advancing over open ground, a lucky infantryman survived the shell that burst right next to him.

Middle: German troops surrender to US forces as the advance into Germany continues. It wasn't always this easy: the series of fierce battles fought between US and German forces in the Hürtgen Forest, which became the longest battle on German ground during World War II and the longest single battle the US Army has ever fought in its history, lasted for five months during an intensely cold winter.

Left: A platoon of Allied soldiers picks its way carefully through the narrow streets of a recently captured Belgian town. While they were more shielded than in open country, there was an ever-present risk from snipers or sudden attack by the enemy hiding in abandoned buildings.

Top: A B-17 Flying Fortress is photographed just after dropping its bombs on the Bettenhausen ordnance plant near Kassel in Germany on October 2. The target zone is outlined and smoke plumes from the burning installation.

Right: Under the nose of the biggest bomb lies the Friedberg marshalling yards.

Above: In late autumn, the pressure of Allied bombing over German industrial areas was overwhelming: on this occasion more than 1,000 B-17 and B-24s attacked vital railway marshalling yards near Osnabrück in Germany. Allied air forces now demonstrated total air supremacy in both bomber and fighter forces.

Warsaw uprising collapses

In August 1944, the Polish resistance movement launched their second uprising against the Nazi occupiers in Warsaw, intending to make their contribution to the advancing Russian liberators. The Russians arrived on the other side of the Vistula in September and made no move to liberate the city. The Polish resistance had no choice but to capitulate in October and when the Russians entered the city they found 85% of it in ruins. Around 200,000 citizens died in the uprising. Looking on from the West, it was suspected that Stalin deliberately watched the Polish position weaken in order to redefine Russian borders - something he had on his agenda since meeting with Churchill and Roosevelt at the Tehran Conference at the end of 1943.

Top: Warsaw's civilians, destitute, hungry, homeless, walk through the ruins of the city to a 'concentration point' chosen by the Germans. Hopeless, they face the future with despair.

Middle: Cologne inhabitants clearing a city street after Allied bombing raids. The German caption to the photo claimed it demonstrated German populations in high spirits.

Right: British troops dig-in near the River Maas in Holland at the end of November. The lowlands, interlined with canals and rivers, often flooded for defence by the Germans, made the advance difficult during the winter.

Italian partisans assist Allied armies

In Florence and all other cities of Tuscany, Italian patriots assisted the Allies by carrying out large-scale sabotage and guerrilla warfare. They played a decisive role in the liberation of the northern part of Florence, dealing with German snipers and suffering as many as 250 casualties a day in the liberation of their city. They were also of great assistance in pointing out to the advancing Allied armies where German mines had been laid. Many of the patriot bands had formed long before these events, during the Fascist regime, to keep alive the real traditions of Italy.

Left: Partisan gunners are shown with ten Spandaus captured from the Germans.

Below: British armour rumbles past a US post on its way to the front line.

Left: A US Ninth Air Force B-26 Marauder pictured on November 19 where it has just successfully bombed the Neuenberg rail crossing over the Rhine at the German border east of the Belfort Gap. The US 7th Army was advancing towards this point en route to Germany. The Ninth Air Force was based in France and was the main Allied tactical force, supporting troops from D-Day onwards.

Below: Bomber crews had their good days and many bad ones, casualties were high and flying conditions always uncomfortable and hazardous for the crew. The end could come suddenly as with this B-24 Liberator, which is breaking up in the air after being hit by flak over Germany. Fuel tanks were spread through the fuselage giving a tendency for the craft to catch fire or explode. The typical 10-man crew had little chance of survival.

Chapter Nine

Hitler's Last Stand

Although the Allies had made great strides through France and Belgium, Hitler would not accept the inevitability of defeat. A fresh offensive was planned in the Ardennes where the Allied line was weakest and his new 'wonder' weapons were ready to rain down a new terror upon London.

The German army launched its attack in the Ardennes in mid-December 1944. The plan was to split the Allied forces in two and create a corridor to the sea at Antwerp. The Allies managed to halt the advance on Antwerp, but not before it created a large bulge in the Allied line. The Wehrmacht found itself up against the might of the United States army and air force and by January the attack had waned. The attack only served to delay the Allied invasion of Germany temporarily and came at a cost of thousands of German lives.

Left: **The minutes following the devastating explosion of the V2 that fell on Smithfield Market, London.**

'Wonder weapons'

In addition to his offensive in the Ardennes, Hitler had placed his faith in a new generation of secret weapons that would, he believed, inflict devastating damage on Britain. The first of these was the V1, a pilotless flying bomb, which began falling on London and South East England from June 1944. They caused casualties and heavy damage, as well as a dip in morale since most people had thought that the dangers of the Blitz had passed. They also somewhat helped Hitler reverse his rapidly declining popularity at home. Many Germans wanted retribution for the relentless Allied bombing campaign and Hitler's new weapon offered just that; the letter V was short for 'Vergeltung' the German word for revenge. The threat from the V1 decreased as the Allied troops overran the launch sites in northern France. Between June and early September, it is thought that almost 7,000 were launched; over half were destroyed before reaching their intended targets.

Above: A flying bomb is successfully destroyed in the air after striking the cable of a barrage balloon. Other balloons are visible around the explosion.

Above right: An anti-aircraft gun shoots down Hitler's 'wonder weapons' over Belgium.

Right: An RAF Halifax bombs concrete structures identified as launch sites for V1 flying bombs in the Pas de Calais.

Top left: One of the many flying bomb sites captured during the British advance on the Pas de Calais. The site was destroyed by German engineers before they retreated. The photograph, dated early September 1944 shows the launch ramp aligned on South East England.

Top right: Canadian troops, clearing a captured V1 launch site near Zutphen in the Netherlands, inspect a flying bomb that misfired: it was the markings on the ground from the many misfires that betrayed many of the launch sites, as well as the development site at Peenemünde.

Above left: This V1 which failed to explode was displayed in an exhibition in Piccadilly at the end of October.

Above: A member of the French Resistance and Sgt H A Barnet of Montreal, Canada, examine the interior of a robot bomb which crashed near its launching site in the Pas de Calais area. The ball-like object is a fuel tank.

Left: Fragments of fallen V1s were carefully harvested for every piece of intelligence. Here is shown the dump where the Ministry stored the wreckage, tended by a female mechanic.

London Blitzed again

London came under attack from another German 'wonder' weapon, the V2, from September 1944 onwards. These, in contrast to the V1s, were long-range rockets and were fired from sites in places still controlled by the Nazis. The renewed threat from the skies revived the need to evacuate children from the threatened areas, and some 200,000 mothers and their children were forced to leave London. Nevertheless, Hitler's 'wonder weapons' were too little too late. Hitler had promised the German public great things from his 'wonder weapons', and when it became obvious that they would not alter the outcome of the war, the Nazis lost whatever public support they still had.

Above left: One of the Temple's historic buildings in Temple Place was also damaged after a direct hit on the building next door – the offices of the Cable and Wireless Company.

Above: Rescue workers at Old Jewry where a V2 fell, killing one person and injuring about 25 on October 6. This coincided with a crisis in public information. Home Security continued to withhold information about the rocket attacks and newspaper reporting was strictly limited. However, on the 6th, the New York Times broke the story. But it wasn't until November, after Germany made a specific announcement, that Churchill was forced to make a statement to the House, admitting that Britain had been under rocket bomb attack for several weeks. Until the formal announcement was made, Home Security tried to divert attention from the rocket attacks by finally making public details of the parachute mines that had been falling since 1940.

Below left: A dramatic rescue from the rubble of burning flats at the corner of Boundary Street and Calvert Street in Shoreditch, after a flying bomb fell on August 22.

Top: The Elizabethan timber-framed Staple Inn, Holborn, was completely destroyed by a flying bomb on the night of August 24, having been saved from the flames of the first Great Fire of London in 1666 by diarist John Evelyn.

Above: A hospital in the South of England was hit in August killing 2 patients and injuring 3 nurses.

Below left: Lewisham Hospital hit on July 26.

Antwerp bombarded

Information about the V2 had been kept under embargo by the censor though it was known to the military and the ARP in London – but not necessarily outside. Although the cause was not elaborated upon, the results of the V2 that fell on Old Jewry were widely reported and to divert public attention, the censor released material via the media on parachute mines that had been embargoed since 1940. This quelled the questions about what were called 'flying gas mains' by some, 'Big Bens' by others.

The continuing bombardment of Antwerp diverted V2s and V1s away from London but on November 25, 1944 London's worst V2 incident took place at New Cross, South London, destroying a packed Woolworths store and killing 160 and injuring 108. This terrible toll was overshadowed by the V2 that fell on the Rex Cinema in Antwerp in December killing 567 – of which 296 were Allied service personnel. Around 150 V2 bombs fell on Britain during November.

Top: The night of December 6, a V2 hit the Red Lion pub on the corner of Duke St and Barrett St close to Selfridges in London's West End. The blast seriously damaged the Base Transportation Office located across the road, which was the HQ controlling all service movements around the UK. The staff included many Americans, seven of whom were reported killed.

Above: Houses were completely obliterated in this V2 blast on October 9. The scene is one of total desolation.

Left: Street shelters stand intact in Islington after a flying bomb attack in September.

NOVEMBER 9, 1944

V2 Terror in London

Hour by hour last night Germany put out claims that V2 is causing widespread damage in London. Here, said radio spokesmen, was a long-range weapon more dangerous than V1. They said it had destroyed Euston Station, smashed a railway bridge, and devastated five named areas.

Goebbels seized on V2 as a morale builder to replace the anniversary celebrations of the Munich beer cellar putsch, abandoned this year for the first time.

The weapon - neutral sources have described it as a rocket-shell 'like a flying telegraph pole with a trail of flame behind it' - was said to have been in use for some weeks. But Berlin made no mention of it until yesterday.

First came a brief reference in the High Command's communiqué and then a spate of boosting radio reports and commentaries. Among all the claims there was one significant admission - that the launching of the 'deadly weapon' caused sacrifices 'among the crews.'

The Germans claimed to be in possession of full information of the damage caused by V2. 'The British Government,' said one radio spokesman, 'has so far concealed from its people that a more effective, more telling, and therefore more dangerous long-range weapon has been in action in addition to the so-called flying bomb, which everyone knows about now.

'The German Command possess exact reports on the success and the effect of V2. If they required further proof of its accuracy, official British reports have supplied it by announcing, after nights in which London was exclusively attacked with V2, that flying bombs had again been over the capital.

'For the time being nothing further can be made known about the technical details of this missile. According to reports from England, the characteristic feature of the new weapon is that it cannot be heard or seen before its extraordinarily heavy detonation.'

Reports from Sweden and other neutral countries have credited V2 with a range of between 200 and 300 miles and a warhead of something under a ton of high explosive. Bases in Germany, Holland, Denmark, and Norway have been claimed as feasible for attacks on Britain. A rocket, it is said, would have to rise some 50 miles into the sky to achieve any considerable range, and it would travel at well over 700 miles per hour.

Above: Bombs in the North. A rescue party searches for bodies. Many homes were damaged in the V bomb attack on Oldham, Lancashire. Rescue gangs are at work in Abbey Hills Road where a whole terrace was destroyed on Boxing Day.

Left: Sniffer dogs work with a rescue squad in the ruins of a hospital in early January 1945.

Below left: The night sky is lit up with tracer as AA opens up on an incoming flying bomb which can be seen plunging to earth in flames.

This page & opposite: **This extraordinary sequence of photographs captures the chaos in the minutes following the devastating explosion of the V2 that fell on Smithfield. In the picture sequence opposite right, traders and other civilians work with police and ARP to release a casualty but it's clear there was nothing that could be done for this unnamed victim. The images on this page top left show the ironwork forming the roof and facade of the handsome Victorian building twisted beyond recognition and tangled in the rubble causing complications for the heavy rescue squad, seen at work with a crane (this page left centre).**

Smithfield Market Destroyed

One of the worst V2 incidents of the Blitz was the devastation of Smithfield, London's historic meat and poultry market – an extensive enclosed indoor market at the corner of Farringdon Street and Charterhouse Street where the rocket landed. At 11.10 it was filled with buyers and sellers, while others were queuing outside to get in. The V2 fell out of the sky virtually destroying the crowded building, its blast making a crater that penetrated the railway tunnel and extensive sidings running below; the casualties, commodities and rubble mingled in a horrible melée. The decorative ironwork that formed the intricate facade collapsed in a tangle, making rescue work even more difficult. 110 people died immediately from the blast and many more were seriously injured.

Above left: As the Allies moved across Europe, they began to come across concentration camps where hundreds of thousands of prisoners had been murdered. This camp in Holland was now being used to house German prisoners.

Above: The tragic and harrowing result of an attack on a Belgian town on December 4, 1944. Although the Germans were withdrawing they were still capable of mounting attacks on liberated towns by using pilotless V2 rocket bombs.

Left: British troops hunting snipers in the streets of Blerick, a town on the River Maas, in December 1944. This marked the end of the German bridgehead on the western bank of the Maas.

Above left & above: **French and American Officers** discuss the truce, agreed to allow civilians to be transported from the encircled bastion of St Nazaire on the Atlantic coast, with Hauptmann D Müller who represented the town's Nazi commander; it was agreed that trains could come and go from the town twice a day for 5 days while an hour's ceasefire was observed. St Nazaire was a strategic base for Germany's Kriegsmarine and its submarine fleet. The port was severely disabled in a commando raid in 1943 but the garrison held out from September 1944 until several days after the Armistice in 1945.

Middle: **Women peep out of a train** which is being handed over to Allied troops. They are among 13,000 civilians evacuated from the town of St-Nazaire which, in January 1945, was still held by the Germans.

Below left: **German troops held out at Metz** in France until the end of 1944, when the last garrison was surrendered to US troops.

Battle of the Bulge

On December 16 the German army launched a counter-offensive that took Allied Command completely by surprise. Advances by the Allies on all fronts compressed the German armies on home ground, consolidating and concentrating their strength. Hitler came up with a plan to punch through the Ardennes to retake Antwerp, cut off the supply chain to the Allied armies and force them into a truce in the bitter winter conditions. The success of this 'Operation Rhine Watch' was totally dependent on speed and surprise. At the outset, German armoured infantry achieved some success with the intricately planned attack. As predicted, the poor weather deprived the Allies of vital air cover and the diversionary tactics deployed by the Germans concealed their true intent, aided by the absence of information from local resistance fighters or Ultra traffic. Furthermore, the Allied forces occupying the Ardennes region were thinly spread novice troops or recuperating veterans.

In the centre of the attack zone was the Belgian town of Bastogne, located on a strategic crossroads which the attacking Germans made an essential objective. Despite the element of surprise and the mixed quality of the US troops, their resistance to the surprise attack was determined and the fighting, during what became known as The Battle of the Bulge, was intense. American forces held onto Bastogne even after the town was enveloped by the German advance. Occupants of the town fled towards Allied lines.

Above: American troops move in to deal with the German counter-attack in Belgium in December 1944 as refugees head for the safety of the Allied lines.

Middle: On Christmas Eve 1944 specially modified Luftwaffe Heinkel H-111s carrying 45 V1 rockets launched them off the Lincolnshire coast. Half an hour later 31 buzz bombs found targets in the north of England, 15 of them on Greater Manchester. A total of 27 people died and 49 were seriously injured in this street alone.

Left: Besieging the forts of Metz had not cost the Aliies too dearly but it slowed up the advance on Germany and gave the Werhmacht time to gather itself for a major counter attack offensive.

Above: **Bastogne in Belgium is liberated following the German siege during the 'Battle of the Bulge' which left the town in ruins.**

Above right: **GIs huddle in their coats riding the truck towing an anti-tank gun into this Belgian town shrouded in snow. The intense cold of the winter during the weeks of the Battle of the Bulge meant troops had to carefully maintain their weaponry and attend to their vehicles, running the engines regularly to avoid the sump-oil and fuel lines freezing.**

Left: **An anti-aircraft artillery piece is brought to bear in close fighting during the Battle of the Bulge. The recent revolutionary new armament, the proximity fuse, was first used by field artillery in the Battle. After the fuses' startling success in anti-aircraft ordnance against V1 bombs, the Pentagon was desperate to avoid the mechanism falling into enemy hands and therefore resistant to its deployment in artillery; but Eisenhower insisted and the new technology vastly improved the efficiency of Allied bombardments because the shells exploded before they hit the ground but near to substantial military targets.**

Top: The 101st Airborne were one of the tenacious units holding Bastogne and fought off these unfortunate attackers whose bodies lie frozen in the snow. The Americans were in dire circumstances, down to 10 rounds of ammunition per gun per day, but fortunately the weather improved, allowing supplies to be dropped by parachute, relieving shortages of food, ammunition and medical supplies. A team of medics flew in by glider to attend to the many wounded. Eventually, elements of Patton's Third Army broke through to relieve Bastogne on December 26.

Top: Mounted French soldiers with German prisoners.

Middle: As the Allies ground away on the Western Front, the Russians were steadily moving towards Berlin in the east. Eisenhower decided to increase the pressure on the capital by a devastating bombing campaign early in 1945. Almost 1,000 B-17 bombers of the Eighth Air Force, protected by P-51 Mustangs attacked the Berlin railway system on February 3, having been informed that the German Sixth Panzer Army was moving through Berlin by train on its way to the Eastern Front. The raid killed between 2,500 and 3,000 people and made 120,000 homeless. Anhalter Station, pictured here, was destroyed.

Left inset: Part of a small infantry group of the US 82nd Airborne ambush a German patrol near Bra in Belgium.

Below: Mourners grieve at the funeral of 34 young Belgian men murdered on Christmas Eve in an atrocity by German soldiers. The men had been part of a forced labour group formed by the Germans when they re-took the town of Bande.

Opposite below left: The frozen corpse of a German soldier appears still to be in a firing position. The conditions of fighting during the Battle of the Bulge were dreadful and although both sides showed great determination, morale was hard to maintain. In the first day of fighting, German troops overran and captured around 9,000 US troops, while German advance guard dressed in US uniforms set about causing confusion and chaos. On the German side, planned tactical operations went astray when a parachute force was widely spread around a missed drop zone; ironically this gave the Allies an impression of a much larger attack.

Opposite below right: Troops of General Patton's Third Army trudge through the winter snow in January 1945 on their way to rendezvous with Montgomery's 21st Army Group at Houffalize, Belgium, effectively closing down the German offensive – which, having suffered serious losses, was running out of steam. Hitler finally allowed his battle-weary troops to retreat on January 7 and on January 25 the Battle of the Bulge was finally over – the most costly American military engagement to date in the war. But for Germany it was the final turning point, this gamble exhausted its military reserves and put the Luftwaffe beyond recovery.

Chapter 10

The Final Battles

Despite the ultimate defeat of the German Ardennes offensive, the Allies realised they were still facing a determined and resourceful enemy. Although Germany was being systematically destroyed by strategic bombing, the Allies could not calculate the remaining Wehrmacht strength as military intelligence coming out of Germany was very limited. However, the Battle of the Bulge had exhausted Germany's remaining reserves and almost finished off the Luftwaffe – although V1 and V2 rockets continued to be effective weapons and the latest Messerschmitt Me262 jet fighters continued to give an impression of strength.

As the winter weather cleared on the Western Front, the Allies pressed home their advantage and crossed the Rhine in March 1945, heading steadily for Berlin and taking many prisoners on their way. Gruesome discoveries were made by the advancing troops as they liberated prisoner of war camps and, worse, the Nazi death camps. In the east, the Russians hastened towards Berlin, meeting their western allies at Turgau on the River Elbe on April 24.

Japan fought on and after intense battles to secure the Pacific Islands of Okinawa and Iwo Jima the Allies prepared to invade the Japanese home Islands.

Left: **US marines attempt to flush Japanese soldiers out of a cave on Okinawa.**

Iwo Jima and Okinawa

Through 1944 into 1945, the Allies were successful in the Far East and Pacific regions, as the Japanese suffered increasingly severe losses both on land and at sea. British and American forces reopened the Burma Road after decimating Japanese forces in June. In the same month, the Battle of the Philippine Sea established Allied naval superiority. The American forces continued 'island hopping' through the Pacific towards Japan, reclaiming the Philippines and enduring some of the worst fighting of the war on Iwo Jima and the Ryukyu Islands, including Okinawa, where fighting was to last for months.

On February 19, 1945 the 3rd, 4th and 5th divisions of the United States Marine Corps staged an amphibious invasion of Iwo Jima, an island some 700 miles south of Tokyo. The fighting was among the fiercest in the Pacific theatre, costing almost 7,000 American lives, making it the deadliest battle in the history of the US Marine Corps. Countless more Japanese died as they defended the island to the death, first engaging the marines in the open and later resisting from hiding places in caves. The battle ended on March 26, by which time 27 American servicemen had performed acts of bravery that would later win them the Medal of Honor.

Top: Seaborne US invasion forces head for the beaches of Iwo Jima on the morning of February 19. The assault on Iwo Jima was a turning point in the Pacific war as Japanese sovereign territory was being invaded for the first time in the war. After capturing the Marianas in 1944, the US was ready to focus on Japan itself. Iwo Jima's three airfields made it a potent attack base for Japanese aircraft and would make it a perfect strategic airbase for assault on Japan. Over 70 days of aerial bombardment preceded the invasion and heavy naval guns pounded the Japanese positions for three days before. In the first wave, 30,000 US troops landed in the first day.

Left: Realising the strategic importance of the island to the advancing Allies, the Japanese increased the garrison to 18,000 and a defensive plan was initiated. The Japanese commander designed his fortifications to take advantage of the island's topography, especially the extinct volcano Mt Suribachi, where a network of tunnels and gun emplacements enabled the defenders to survive the pulverising American bombardment and to mount a strong defence against infantry attack.

Below: Marines of the 4th division storm the shores of Iwo Jima.

Iconic moment on Iwo Jima

This page: Five days after the invasion, US forces on Iwo Jima numbered 70,000 and on February 23 a platoon of marines scaled Mt Suribachi and raised the Stars and Stripes at its summit. This moment was captured by photographer Louis R Lowery and achieved iconic status for the American people in general and US forces in particular. The battle would last another month; the last assault by the Japanese being on March 25. Bitter fighting on both sides resulted in many casualties: of the total Japanese military of around 22,000 only a couple of hundred were captured alive - it is assumed the rest died. Of the final number of US troops engaged (110,000), 26,000 became casualties, 7,000 of them fatalities.

Three month battle for Okinawa

In mid-March as the Battle for Iwo Jima was drawing to a close, the US began the next offensive against the island of Okinawa. At just over 300 miles from Kyushu, the southernmost of Japan's four main islands, Okinawa was to be a springboard for the invasion of Japan proper. After a week long 'softening up' bombardment from the air, US troops of the Tenth Army came ashore largely unopposed. However, the Japanese were lying in wait at better-defended locations and the battle soon became a bloodbath. It took the US almost three months to wrestle control of the island and defeat the Japanese, who once again fought to the death. Unlike Iwo Jima, Okinawa had a large civilian population, which had been warned by Japanese propaganda not to expect any mercy from the Americans. Such scaremongering had terrible consequences; thousands of civilians committed suicide and thousands more died in the fighting. By the end of the battle, an estimated 100,000 Japanese and 12,000 American servicemen had lost their lives.

Top: This photograph show the horrific task the US troops faced on Okinawa, often taking out the Japanese positions one at a time, using explosives and facing suicidal counterattacks that might come without warning. Americans landed on the Island on April 1 and secured it on June 21. In addition to the loss of over 100,000 troops, the Japanese suffered horrific civilian casualties which have never been defined but were estimated between 40-150,000.

Middle: Three marines kneel to pray in their fox holes in a rare quiet moment during the Iwo Jima campaign.

Left: The capture of the Marianas Islands in 1944 enabled Admiral Nimitz to set up his HQ on Guam with harbour facilities for a third of the US Pacific Fleet. This was followed by the building of Isely Field on Saipan - the first of five airbases in the Marianas which would accommodate the B-29 Superfortresses whose bombs ended the Japanese military regime. Here, more material and machinery are unloaded through the bow doors of LSTs directly onto the quay.

Battle for the Philippines

The United States had shared a close relationship with the Philippines ever since the islands were ceded to Washington at the end of the Spanish-American War of 1898. Thousands of American troops were in the Philippines when the Japanese invaded within hours of the attack on Pearl Harbor. Many were captured and, together with Filipino POWs, they were forced to endure an infamous death march to their internment camp in Bataan. The battle to liberate the Philippines from Japanese rule began on October 20, 1944 when US troops under the command of General Douglas MacArthur landed on the island of Leyte. The Japanese attempted to obstruct the landings in what became the largest naval battle of the entire war. The US scored a decisive victory, neutralizing the Japanese navy and allowing US and Australian forces to steadily recapture the Philippines. The Battle for Manila began in February 1945 and ended up being the only major urban battle fought in the Pacific campaign. Fighting was fierce and it took American soldiers more than one month to secure the city. By the time it fell on March 3, thousands of civilians had been killed and the city was almost utterly destroyed.

Top: An aerial view of the devastation caused during the fight for Manila. It was to be the only major urban battle of the Pacific campaign.

Middle: Plumes of smoke rise above Manila during fierce fighting between US and Japanese forces in February 1945.

Right: Some of the most intense and ferocious fighting of the Pacific conflict took place as US and Filipino forces battled with the Japanese in the streets of Manila. Battle commenced on February 3 and, after much bloodshed, ended on March 3. The street fighting was reminiscent of Stalingrad and over 100,000 civilians died, either as collateral damage or resulting from deliberate Japanese action. Much of Manila's unique ancient heritage was destroyed as the Japanese defenders used the Intramuros as their bastion. In this picture a wounded GI is carried by stretcher to a dressing station in City Hall.

Soviet advances in the East

In January the Red Army broke out from captured Warsaw and began a series of offensives that would culminate in the capture of Berlin in April. In the so-called Oder-Vistula offensive, the Soviets outnumbered Germans 5-1. Not only did they have superiority in numbers, their vast quantity of armour enabled them to move with a speed equivalent to the German Blitzkrieg. However casualties were high – in the 23 days the Russians suffered 194,000 casualties and lost 1,267 tanks and assault guns.

Above: Not everyone was as happy to see the Red Army liberators as these citizens of Rostov when the city was recaptured from the Nazis in 1943. The end of the German terrorizing of the Slavic *untermenschen* was some cause for celebration, although the advancing Soviet troops brought their own terror to the civilian populations.

Middle: The Red Army on the offensive in northern Russia.

Far left: Anti-aircraft gunners take up a position in Kharkov after liberating the city for a second time in August 1944.

Left: Soviet troops install an anti-aircraft gun in Kharkov after its first liberation in February 1944. The Germans recaptured the city the following month.

Yalta Conference

In February 1945, the historic meeting of Allied leaders took place in Yalta in the Black Sea area of the Russian Crimea. Winston Churchill, Franklin D Roosevelt and Josef Stalin decided the final fate of Germany: it was to be divided into four zones of influence supervised by each of the main Allied powers, including France. Despite the bonhomie, Churchill deeply distrusted Stalin; Roosevelt was more trusting and supportive of Stalin. Once again, Churchill's instincts were suppressed by the judgement of others. History proved him right once more.

Below: British Prime Minister Winston Churchill shakes hands with the Soviet Union's Marshal Stalin, while US President Roosevelt looks on from his chair at a meeting of the three main Allied powers at Yalta in the Crimea. At this meeting in February 1945, plans were made to divide Germany into four zones, controlled by Britain, Russia, America and France and to establish post-war 'zones of influence'. More immediate plans were drawn up for the invasion of the Japanese mainland.

Bottom: Stalin and Roosevelt discuss the post-war settlement in Europe at the Yalta Conference in February 1945.

FEBRUARY 13, 1945

Big Three Lay Down Framework for Peace of the World

The shape of the new Europe after the defeat, occupation, and all-time demilitarisation of Germany is outlined in a communiqué issued last night at the end of the Three Power Conference in the Crimean port of Yalta. It is the fullest and most dramatic declaration to emerge from any of the meetings of the leaders of the United Nations during this war.

The declaration indicates clearly that as they sat round the Conference Table, Marshal Stalin, President Roosevelt, and Mr. Churchill were so confident of an early victory over Germany that they concerned themselves mainly with the problems of peace.

The Conference was held in the Livadia Palace at Yalta, on the southern coast of the Crimea, a district of great scenic beauty where the hillsides are covered with vineyards and thick woodlands.

It lasted eight days - twice as long as the Teheran Conference of more than a year ago. At Marshal Stalin's suggestion, it is to go down to history as the Crimea Conference.

The main points of the declaration are:

1. Nazi Germany is doomed, and the German people are warned that the cost of their defeat will be heavier if they continue to resist.
2. The demand for Germany's unconditional surrender is reiterated, and it is stated that the terms have been prepared, but will not be made known until the final defeat of Germany.
3. Germany is to make good "in kind to the greatest extent possible" all damage she has caused to Allied nations, this to be controlled by a commission operating in Moscow.
4. The declaration says that it is not the purpose of the Conference to destroy the people of Germany, but only when Nazis and militarism have been extirpated will there be any hope of a decent life for the Germans. To achieve this end the following programme is laid down:
   All German armed forces to be disbanded.
   The German General Staff to be broken up for all time, and all German military equipment to be removed or destroyed.
   All German industry used for military production to be eliminated or controlled. Justice and swift punishment for all war criminals.
   Nazi Party to be wiped out, and all Nazi laws, organisations, and institutions eliminated, until there is no Nazi influence remaining in Germany.
   Any other measure necessary to ensure the future peace and safety of the world.
5. Each of the Three Powers will occupy separate zones of Germany under a Central Control Commission consisting of the Supreme Commanders of the Three Powers, with headquarters in Berlin. France will be invited to take a zone of occupation and participate in the work of the Control Commission.
6. The close working partnership among the three Staffs, attained at the Conference to shorten the war, will continue, as and when meetings are necessary in the future.
   Other points of the Declaration include:
   Establishment at the earliest possible moment of an international organisation to maintain peace and security in the world, based on the foundations laid at the Dumbarton Oaks Conference.
   Agreement to hold a conference of the United Nations at San Francisco on April 25 next to prepare the Charter of such an organisation.
   Declaration providing for the co-ordination of the policies of the Three Powers for the assistance of the liberated countries of Europe in their pressing political and economic problems.

Top: Advancing from Belgium. British and Dutch infantry man a defensive perimeter around this bridge in Belgium as a Sherman M4 tank surges forward into attack.

Above: Although there were heavy snows, RAF bomber crews continued to operate from Belgium to support the Allied drive and weaken German resistance.

Left: The British Second Army on patrol in tanks in the Dutch town of Susteren.

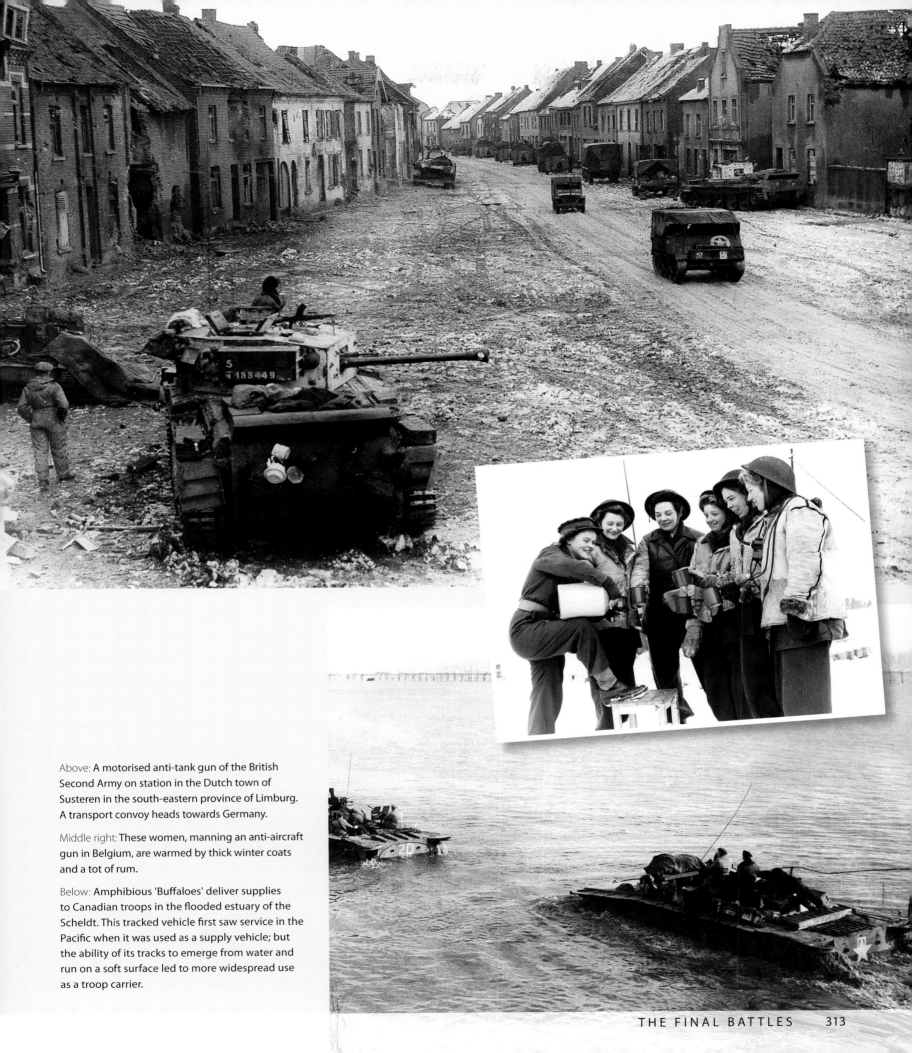

Above: A motorised anti-tank gun of the British Second Army on station in the Dutch town of Susteren in the south-eastern province of Limburg. A transport convoy heads towards Germany.

Middle right: These women, manning an anti-aircraft gun in Belgium, are warmed by thick winter coats and a tot of rum.

Below: Amphibious 'Buffaloes' deliver supplies to Canadian troops in the flooded estuary of the Scheldt. This tracked vehicle first saw service in the Pacific when it was used as a supply vehicle; but the ability of its tracks to emerge from water and run on a soft surface led to more widespread use as a troop carrier.

MARCH 5, 1945

'Dresden a City of the Past'

"Dresden was completely wiped out by the massive Allied air blows on February 14 and 15," said the German Overseas News Agency last night.

"Not a single building remains, and tens of thousands of people are buried under the ruins," added the agency's war correspondent. "The raids caused the greatest destruction a big urban area has ever suffered.

"The Dresden catastrophe is without precedent. In the inner town no a single block of buildings, not a single detached building, remains intact or even capable of reconstruction. "The town area is devoid of human life. A great city has been wiped from the map of Europe.

"What happened on that evening of February 15? There were 1,000,000 people in Dresden at the time, including 600,000 bombed out, evacuees, and refugees from the east. "The raging fires which spread irresistibly in the narrow streets killed a great many from sheer lack of oxygen. "Tens of thousands who succeeded in getting out, none knows how, fled to the green belt surrounding the city.

"Then at midnight another British bomber fleet appeared on the blood-red horizon and caused further destruction. "Twelve hours later - the siren system had long since ceased to function - a third wave spread further devastation.

"To-day we can only speak of what was once Dresden in the past tense."

Above: Bombs dropped by this USAAF B-17 erupt as they land on Berlin, casting a huge pall of smoke and dust over the city. The German capital became a focus for bombing as Allied troops drew nearer; it was feared that the city would be fiercely defended so Allied High Command was determined to crush all opposition.

Left: Flying Fortresses in formation over Germany. Every day that weather conditions permitted, as many as 1,500 bombers and fighter escorts would fly bombing missions over Germany.

Above: On March 23, 1945 General Montgomery set in motion Operation Plunder, the much-awaited crossing of the Rhine into Germany's heartland. In the preceding weeks the landing area designated for the bridgehead had been bombarded, virtually destroying the towns of Wesel and Rees. Gordon Highlanders, elements of 21st Army Group, patrol through the ruins of Rees which was secured by fierce house-to-house fighting.

Left: The carefully planned Rhine crossing offensive was successful and within four days the Allied bridgehead was 35 miles wide and 20 miles deep.

Right: British infantrymen cooking a hasty meal outside Udem with a rifleman on the lookout. Following the capture of Udem on February 27, British and Canadian troops fought their way southeastward between the Maas and the Rhine, advancing to Kervenheim, three miles south of Udem. Other British troops struck eastward to the Hochwald where fighting was very heavy.

Below: The ruins of the German town of Jülich, west of the Rhine, were shown to Winston Churchill when he visited the troops in Germany at the beginning of March, pictured here leading senior Allied officers with US Ninth Army commander General William H Simpson.

Left: General Eisenhower and Field Marshal Montgomery had established their headquarters in Jülich. Winston Churchill is pictured with Monty and Major General Alvin Gillian of the US Army 13th Corps outside the citidel.

Above: A rifle section of the 44th American Brigade in action in the French Alps, in March, 1944. Since the Riviera invasion, the 44th American Brigade and other units held the most remote Allied front in Europe – in the Alps, between France and Italy. Rarely mentioned in war reports, the less-spectacular job done by the packhorse artillery of this Alpine force had been carried out through the bitter winter under arduous conditions, often in the clouds, sometimes above them, and always surrounded by snow and ice. Guns, ammunition and heavy supplies had to be moved by mule train; when this became impossible the men raised a funicular line between the mountain tops to get their 75mm howitzers into new positions. With the coming of spring, their fight against the Germans and the Italians on Kesselring's right flank proceeded in sunshine and clear weather, with firm, dry emplacements for the gunners and the infantrymen.

Middle: Members of the various armed forces enjoy some rest and relaxation at the 21 Club in Brussels. With the city liberated, it became an important base for the Allies in Europe.

Left: For the first time in United States military history, a whole Division was cited when General Eisenhower presented a Presidential Unit Citation for 'extraordinary heroism and gallantry in defence of the key communications centre of Bastogne' to the 101st Airborne Division. The ceremony took place 'somewhere in France'. General Eisenhower, accompanied in a Jeep by General Maxwell D Taylor, reviews the 101st Airborne Division during the presentation ceremony on March 16, 1945.

Allies cross into Germany

With numerous crossing points secured, the Allies poured men across the Rhine in vast numbers in March 1945.

Operation Plunder started at 1800 hours on March 23 with a barrage of 5,500 guns along the 22 mile front and a bombing raid on the city of Wesel. The 51st (Highland) Division led the river crossing at 2300 hours with the Canadians crossing later 4 miles south of Rees, then the 1st Commando Brigade, a mile north of Wesel. The assault craft were guided across the river by searchlights and tracer fire from machine guns. General Patton had earlier put the US 5th Infantry Division across the Ludendorff railway bridge at Remagen – a day earlier than planned – thus drawing off German reinforcements and reducing the opposition to the main landings.

Top: British troops traverse the floodbank of the Rhine as they prepare to cross the river.

Above: An amphibious vehicle makes a crossing of the Rhine

Left: US engineers had this pontoon bridge over the Rhine operational during the first day of the crossing. The 972-feet-long bridge was created in record time and was one of three that the Allied forces deployed early in Operation Plunder.

The Rhine Crossed

We've done it. Early this morning strong infantry forces of General Hodge's American First Army are streaming across the Rhine into our newly won bridgehead on the east bank of the river. The final drive to meet the Russian armies in the heart of Germany - the last heave to end the war - has begun.

You can throw your hats in the air to-day. The success of our lightning stroke undoubtedly shortens the war by months. We are massing substantial forces in our rapidly expanding bridgehead 290 miles from Berlin.

This historic moment in the war came at 4.30 p.m. on Wednesday, when a spearhead task force of the First Army crossed the river in a sudden thrust which took the Germans completely by surprise. The crossing was made between Bonn and Coblenz. Opposition was light. Once on the other side the Americans spread out to get elbow-room. Then our main forces poured over. Before their tremendous onslaught the German defences cracked - then collapsed like a pack of cards.

More and more men swarmed across the river, and swiftly, efficiently, the bridgehead was built up. I crossed with a wave of American infantry. There was little enemy fire during the first 24 hours after we crossed, showing the complete confusion of the Germans as they fled from the river. Our casualties have been light.

'We're Doing Fine'

The Rhine in this area is nearly half a mile wide. The shore on the Remagen side is flat, but across the river it rises to cliffs south of the small town of Erpel. A railway bridge, which also carries a path for foot passengers, crosses the Rhine to Erpel. In an almost direct line from our bridgehead to Berlin lie the big cities of Cassel and Magdeburg.

When the full story of our crossing can be told it will be revealed as one of the most fantastic of the whole war. We made a pounce - and it came off. I have just had a word with the commanding officer of the bridgehead. He gave me this heartening message: "You can say we are doing fine. We have a well-armed force across, and we are all in good spirits, ready to close with anything the enemy like to throw at us."

We have already captured a number of prisoners. They are a poor lot of troops, with no real fight in them.

Top: With the Allied forces crossing the Rhine in overwhelming numbers and using the bridges to move heavy armour into place, German opposition varied but there was much fierce fighting and deadly machine gun defence. Here infantry of US 7th Army provide covering fire from the west bank of the Rhine as their fellow soldiers cross.

Above: Field artillery units stand by their guns ready to give support to the next phase of Operation Plunder.

Above: The retreating German forces operated a scorched earth policy, destroying roads and bridges as they went. As a result, Allied engineers established several crossing points on the Rhine; this floating pontoon bridge was one of them.

Left: Earlier in the month Winston Churchill, on his visit to the Command HQ at Julich, walked over a Bailey bridge across the Roer, announcing, 'After the magnificent job your troops did getting across, it will be an honour to walk its length.'

MARCH 9, 1945

United States First Army, Won The Race

As our troops pushed outwards, rapidly widening their hold on the eastern bank, a message from General Eisenhower to all ranks of the First Army was circulated among the troops. It said: The whole Allied Force is delighted to cheer the United States First Army, whose speed and boldness have won the race to establish a bridgehead over the Rhine.

A young American officer was first to cross the river. His name will go down in history. It was the extra resource and dash of that officer and his buddies that helped the crossing to get off to a flying start. Immediately after our crossing, the American troops seized high ground overlooking the bridgehead, thus denying the enemy observation and hampering his artillery.

Evening mists quickly enveloped us, adding to our cover. This morning, the weather is still misty. Low-lying, grey clouds make it difficult for the Germans to pin-point us.

We are engaged in exploiting our bridgehead. As I write, smiling keen-eyed troops are swarming up the Rhine banks, heading rapidly for the interior of Germany. I am unable to go into detail, but I can assure you that, so far as supplies are concerned, we have not much to worry about. The actual crossing didn't cost us a single man.

Above: Paratroopers of the First Airborne Division drop on the eastern banks of the Rhine from C-47 transport carriers.

Left inset: Views of the vast air armada above Germany.

Left: Gliders being towed across the Rhine.

Opposite above: Allied troops gathering up supplies parachuted in from the air during Operation Plunder on March 26.

Opposite middle: Churchill visited the front line on numerous occasions to make a personal appraisal of the tactical situation and to encourage his forces. On March 25 he arrived at Montgomery's HQ; with Monty and a number of senior US officers he crossed the Rhine by boat to an area still controlled by German forces; targeted by artillery the party swiftly withdrew.

Opposite below: Awestruck civilians watch several waves of transport planes passing overhead. The fleet of thousands of aircraft stretched for 500 miles.

The airborne fleet

Soon after the main assault began on the Rhine, US and British airborne troops parachuted into forward positions to disrupt German defence and occupy strategic positions. After the Market Garden fiasco, Montgomery could not afford another failure at this critical point in the war. Operation Varsity on March 24 was the biggest single airborne operation of all time when 16,000 troops jumped into German territory.

RAF's New Ten Ton Bombs Blast The Ruhr

Gigantic ten-ton bombs are now being used by R.A.F. heavy bombers in their all-out offensive to blast a path for the Allied armies waiting to spring over the Rhine for the last battles deep in the heart of Germany.

News of this explosive monster - 25ft. 5in. long and 3ft. 10in. in diameter - was released by the Air Ministry last night soon after a great force of Lancasters had unloaded ten-tonners over rail targets in the fourth daylight raid on the Ruhr area in four days.

The world's biggest bomb is four tons heavier than the 12,000-pounder which has been the R.A.F.'s No. 1 missile until now. Never before has such a jump in bomb weight been achieved. Designed by "Back-room Boy" Mr. B. Neville Wallis, creator of the 12,000lb. block-buster, the new super-bomb combines great power of penetration with terrific blast force.

It completely dwarfs the type which sank the Tirpitz, penetrated the 15ft. thick concrete roofs of U-boat shelters, and made craters more than 100ft. across the Saumur Tunnel when the Germans held France. A crew of six is needed to load it on to the Lancaster, and the operation takes half an hour. To deal with it, a new design of bomb trolley and special handling tackle had to be made.

So that the new bomb could be delivered in Germany in large numbers, Messrs A. V. Roe and Co. undertook to modify the Lancaster. This bomber began its career with an all-up weight of 60,000lb., and the fact that it can now operate at a vastly increased weight is an indication of its high quality and perfection of design.

This Is What It Can Do

In yesterday's attack on the big Bielefeld viaduct north-east of the Ruhr six to eight spans were knocked out.

A flight engineer who returned from the raid said: "When our ten-tonner hit the target there was a colossal fountain of debris. "The blast made the six-tonner's explosion look like a 50-pounder's."

Squadron Leader C. C. Calder, D.S.O., D.F.C., of Forres, near Inverness, said: "I thought the new bomb would have a surprising effect, and I wasn't wrong. "As it burst, it felt as though someone had hit me severely in the back. I didn't expect the kick quite so soon. The force of the explosion caused a pain in my spine which lasted more than a minute. "As soon as the bomb was released I ran the stick forward but, even so, we were lifted well over 500ft."

MARCH 9, 1945

Heading For Berlin

Now, the enemy has started shelling the bridgehead. We get a certain amount of rifle and machine-gun fire. But so far the Germans have not launched a counter-attack either with infantry or tanks.

Considering the momentous importance of our crossing, it is astonishing what little the enemy is doing about it. Our plans must be cloaked in secrecy, but the general idea is obvious.

Having crossed the Rhine, we now head in massed force for Berlin to link with the Russians.

Our crossing was so swift and unexpected we caught some Germans in barges still moving up and down the Rhine, thinking that Hodge's men had not even reached the west bank, let alone the east. As soon as they saw our infantry going across they stood up gesticulating in the barges, and waved white flags.

On the other bank, we have found no evidence of fortifications, nothing that could be called organised resistance. It is possible the enemy will rush up some of his best divisions, but so far things are reasonably quiet.

The moment we set foot on the east bank, hundreds of "slave" foreign workers rose in neighbouring villages, begging us to get them to the other side of the Rhine in boats, away from the Germans.

We have taken so many prisoners in the action approaching the point of crossing, and since the crossing, that we are incapable of handling them all. The Germans are being told simply to make their way back behind our lines in their own way as best they can.

Everything we have seen of the German forces for days has given us a clear impression that the whole Wehrmacht is utterly demoralised. The ease with which we have made this flying crossing suggests something more than demoralisation. It suggests that the Germans are going completely to pieces.

Top: Eisenhower's 'Broad Front' assault and attack over the Rhine enabled overwhelming land forces to break into Germany from the west – a crushing blow to German morale – and local commanders quickly realised their position was untenable.

Above: British infantry advance into Germany on foot after crossing the Rhine.

Top: Amid the ruins of Wesel, British commandos operate machine guns while waiting to be relieved by reinforcements after they spearheaded the crossing of the Rhine in assault boats on the night of March 23.

Above: A transport convoy crosses a Bailey pontoon bridge. A seemingly endless stream of supplies was brought across the Rhine to support the Allies as they pushed eastwards.

Left: Rhona Churchill, war correspondent with the *Daily Mail*, was the first woman to cross the Rhine. She is accompanied by Winston Churchill and Field Marshal Montgomery on March 25, 1945. Montgomery had crossed the Rhine at midnight on the 24 in amphibious craft, backed by air attack, a 2,000-gun bombardment and two airborne paratroop divisions. Earlier in the day, further south at Remagen, a platoon of American soldiers had spotted a rail bridge left intact by the Germans and managed to cross it and hold it until relieved by reinforcements.

Hitler's final rally as Germans ready to surrender

On March 30, in a final and desperate attempt to rally both civilians and troops, Hitler issued the statement: 'Fanatic determination can guarantee the success of the coming fight. Then the battle before Berlin must and will end with a decisive defensive victory'. However, many German soldiers were by now ready to surrender, and they did so in their thousands.

Left: Around 20,000 German prisoners of war wait for marching orders in the grounds of a German military academy near the Rhine.

Below: Hitler tried to rally his troops with a message encouraging 'fanatic determination' to defend Berlin and achieve victory. Whether anybody believed his words, many Germans fought on - especially on the Eastern Front where the Russian advance was ruthless. Here, Patton's forces escort German prisoners to holding camps.

Top left: Any German soldiers making a determined defence knew that their cause was lost; furthermore they knew that if there was a choice between being captured by Americans or Russians, they would sooner give themselves up to US or British forces. Thousands of German prisoners were taken as the Allies advanced.

Top right: One of the youngest German prisoners taken by the Allies. This boy, not yet 15, was captured in March as Allied troops attacked the Siegfried Line.

Above left: Young German soldiers under guard.

Above right: As the 15th Scottish Division move up towards the front line, they pass a line of captured Germans headed for captivity in what had become Allied territory.

Germans surrender Italy

In Italy, 1945 the Eighth Army continued to push forward in preparation for the spring offensive. It was launched in April, and proved to be the decisive action in clearing the Germans from the country. By the end of the month Spezia, Genoa and Venice had been liberated. Senior German officers, who had been engaged in secret negotiations with the Allies to end the war in Italy since February, signed a document of unconditional surrender without reference to Berlin. This was to take effect from 2nd May. The cease-fire took place as agreed, just as the Allies were reaching Trieste.

Above: **A captured werewolf. German guerilla units, known as 'werewolves', began to appear behind Allied lines in the closing weeks of the war. However, their numbers were small and by this time it was too late for them to mount an effective resistance.**

Right: **Men of the Seaforth Highlanders sweep through the Dutch town of Uelzen clearing houses of enemy snipers.**

Top left: Civilians in the German city of Rheydt, birthplace of Joseph Goebbels, emerge with white flags as the Allies approach, apparently unsure of how they will be treated.

Top right: Germans surrender in the city of Trier.

Above: German civilians stand amid rubble following the capture of their town by Allied troops.

Left: As the US Third Army entered Bitburg they found fewer than 100 inhabitants remaining.

Russians advance in the East

Towards the end of March 1945 several vital crossings had been established across the Rhine. Amongst the most important of these was at Remagen, where the US First Army was able to secure a railway bridge intact. In the East the Russian advance on Germany was also gaining momentum, and Eisenhower ordered the Allies to press on towards Berlin with the aim of meeting up with the Red Army.

Right: Russian soldiers advance across open fields in Germany.

Below: Citizens of Saarbrucken congregate with their few possessions in the centre of the destroyed city. Most of its population of 135,000 fled in the face of the Allied aerial onslaught and ground attack in March 1945.

Victory in sight

By the spring of 1945, with victory in sight, the Allied forces pressed home their advantage, mobilising troops into Germany along a huge front, with assaults towards Hamburg in the north, the Elbe in the centre, and in the south through Bavaria, Czechoslovakia and Austria, where they would ultimately be joined by Italian forces. By April 14 the Red Army had reached as far as Vienna in the south, and General Zuhkov's armies, advancing further north, had reached the Oder. It was his men who would lead the attack on Berlin, unleashing perhaps the largest artillery barrage in history on April 15, when over a million shells were fired against German positions. Ten days later, Russian troops made contact with General Bradley's forces at Torgau, and by now the Russians had encircled Berlin, and began to move into the city.

Top: The Allies controlled a significant area of Germany by April 1945 and had to establish a workable government under military jurisdiction. A German policeman accepts weapons handed in by civilians under American supervision in the town of Bad Godesberg which was the first major town to surrender to the Allies without armed resistance. It was also the location of a historic meeting between Chamberlain and Hitler in 1938 when they met to discuss the Sudetenland crisis.

Above: RAF Liberators of Strategic Air Force Eastern Air Command attack bridges on the Siam railway.

Left: The broken rail bridge at Kalunpe with the road ferry point nearby. The central span of the steel bridge is lying in the river.

Top & left: An American Liberator bomber plunges towards the ground over Italy. Its wing is severely damaged by anti-aircraft fire.

Above: A cocktail mixture of high explosive and incendiary bombs descends on Gladbeck in the industrial Ruhr region of Germany. Gladbeck's railway marshalling yards were vital to the distribution of coal from the town's mines. 1,250 B-17s and B-24s of the Eighth USAAF carried out the raid on March 23 escorted by 350 P-51 Mustang fighter aircraft.

Liberating POWs

As the Allies were establishing POW camps in Germany, they were liberating their own troops from others. Some of the prisoners that were rescued had been held captive since the outbreak of war. Germany and Italy generally treated prisoners from the British Commonwealth, France, the US and other Western allies in accordance with the Geneva Convention, which had been signed by these countries. In German camps, when soldiers of lower rank were made to work, they were compensated, and many officers were not required to work. The main complaints of British, British Commonwealth, US and French prisoners of war in German Army POW camps—especially during the last two years of the war—concerned the bare bones menu provided, a fate German soldiers and civilians were also suffering due to the blockade conditions.

Left: British soldiers from a camp near Brunswick cheer their release. Most of the men here were captured in the blitzkreig of 1940 when Germany swept through western Europe, pushing the British Expeditionary Force back to the beaches at Dunkirk.

Below: An American soldier, machine gun trained on the compound below, keeps a watchful eye as he guards German detainees.

Right and Below: **Russian POWs pour out of the unlocked gates of their prison camp to greet their liberators in April 1945. This camp held 9,000 prisoners but the death toll had been terrible as starvation and typhus were rampant. Some accounts suggest that 30,000 Russians died in Stalags XIB and XID alone.**

Top: Some of the 18,000 POWs at the Altengrabow Camp waiting for their release.

Above: Liberated British prisoners at Stalag 11B read the newspapers, anxious for news from home.

Right: British POWs suffering from malnutrition are pictured here at Stalag 11B just south of Fallingbostel. It was the first POW camp housing British prisoners to be liberated.

Above: A close up of some of the Nazis who were captured and caged with the barbed wire of their own concentration camp by the 50th Division of the United States Army.

Left: British and Commonwealth soldiers held prisoner in Oflag 79 near Brunswick, liberated by the US army after being detained for five years.

The Holocaust

The Nazi regime subscribed to the belief that the German people sat atop of a global racial hierarchy and that other races – particularly Jews, but also Gypsies and Slavs – were inferior and a threat to German racial purity. After they came to power in 1933, the Nazis began an incremental process of government-sponsored persecution against the country's Jewish population. They passed laws to deny Jews of their citizenship, to forbid them from marrying Aryans and to force them out of their jobs and businesses. The night of November 9, 1938, 'Kristallnacht', witnessed the first coordinated nationwide attack against Jews; many of Germany's synagogues were damaged and people were rounded up and sent to concentration camps. The following year, the war intervened and Germany's treatment of the Jews took an even deadlier turn.

Above: Allied troops advancing through Germany began their discovery of the gruesome Nazi death camps; the POW camps were bad enough, but the dawning realisation of the scale of the Nazi extermination programme horrified the world. Josef Kramer, nicknamed the Beast of Belsen, was captured at Bergen-Belsen. He was tried for war crimes, convicted and hanged in December 1945.

Left: The German military authorities understood how the Allies would view the death camps and some efforts were made to conceal them. In the last months of the war, concentration camps in the East of Germany and Poland were evacuated, their occupants forced to march deep into Germany under terrible conditions that killed many thousands. Here a mass grave is uncovered – the last resting place of prisoners on their way to Bergen-Belsen who died in transit. They were buried by their surviving inmates, who in turn were shot and then added to the burial.

The Final Solution

From October 1939, as the Nazis consolidated their control of Poland, the country's large Jewish population was forced to live in walled-off ghettos where thousands of people died of starvation and disease. After the invasion of the Soviet Union in June 1941, the Nazis began directly killing Jews using mobile killing units called 'Einsatzgruppen', which murdered more than one million men, women and children behind the German lines. In late 1941 the Nazis began constructing death camps and by early 1942 they had decided upon a 'Final Solution': the extermination of all the Jews of Europe. Millions of people were sent to death camps such as Auschwitz, Treblinka, Sobibor and Belzec, where they were murdered in specially designed gas chambers. The 'lucky ones' were sent to work camps, where they faced gruelling labour and death from disease, hunger and maltreatment. By 1945, as Allied soldiers closed in on the camps, thousands of inmates were moved by train or on forced 'death marches' to prevent them from being liberated and to prolong their suffering. By the time the war was over, more than six million Jews had lost their lives, which is an estimated two thirds of Europe's pre-war Jewish population.

In addition, the Nazis dehumanized, detained and murdered hundreds of thousands of other people deemed to be racially undesirable or politically unsound. These groups included gypsies, homosexuals and Communists, as well as people with physical or mental illnesses who were also subjected to forcible sterilization as part of a campaign of so-called 'racial hygiene'.

Above: **Photographs like this helped people understand the scale and horror of the death camps: the personal possessions of the murdered inmates, such as these shoes, were stock-piled in storage in their tens of thousands.**

Middle: **British soldiers liberated Belsen concentration camp on April 15. Thousands of people were found still alive but threatened by typhus, typhoid and dysentery, which were running rampant in the camp.**

Right: **The liberation of the Nazi prison camps presented a huge challenge to the Allies; the prisoners were in terrible physical condition and continued to die in large numbers after being liberated. Of those that survived, most were vast distances from their home, which very probably had been destroyed, along with the relatives, neighbours or other possible support for these shattered people. Repatriating Allied POWs was relatively straightforward, but the civilians generally continued to live in camps, moving from the concentration camps into displaced persons centres, while the Red Cross and other organisations supported their search for lost relatives and a way to return home.**

The Fall of Munich: Crowds intermingled with freed prisoners, watch tanks and troops pass through Dachauerstrasse to occupy the city.

Left: The airfield on the German island of Dune disappears under a cloud of smoke and debris caused by a concentrated bombardment of nearly 1,000 RAF bombers. Heligoland, a group of rocky islands, originally fortified by the British, acted as a strategic base for Germany in World War II. In particular protecting the approach to the Kiel Canal and German North Sea ports, while giving a valuable striking base for targets in the North Sea and northern Britain. The islands were heavily garrisoned and equipped with artillery and anti-aircraft guns. Submarines and motor torpedo boats were based there. After the raids on April 18 and 19, the fortifications were virtually destroyed and the islands were uninhabitable for many years.

Below: In northern Germany, close to the River Elbe, mechanised troops of the 15th Scottish Division enveloped then cleared the town of Uelzen on April 19. Uelzen hosted a concentration camp and was strategically placed on the Mittelland Canal.

19 APRIL, 1945

RAF's major attack on Heligoland

On 18 April, 45 nearly a thousand aircrafts pounded devastated Heligoland. This rocky island is an important outpost guarding the ports and naval bases of northwest Germany and lies 31 miles from the mainland, some 50 miles north of Wilhelmshaven. Well garrisoned, it has very strong defences, including super-heavy coastal batteries, and many anti-aircraft guns. These are shelters for E and R-boats and submarines. The island of Dune, three quarters of a mile from Heligoland has an airfield and this was also heavily bombed. In all there were three aiming points, two on Heligoland and the Dune airfield. The attacks lasted for more than an hour.

The Battle of Berlin

The Battle of Berlin lasted from late April 20, 1945 until the morning of May 2 and was one of the bloodiest battles in history.

The first defensive preparations at the outskirts of Berlin were on March 20, when the newly appointed German commander correctly anticipated that the main Soviet thrust would be made over the Oder River. Before the main battle in Berlin commenced, the Soviets managed to encircle the city as a result of the smaller Battles of the Seelow Heights and Halbe. During April 20, 1945, the 1st Belorussian Front started shelling Berlin's city centre, while the 1st Ukrainian Front had pushed north. The German defences consisted of several depleted, badly equipped, and disorganised SS divisions, as well as Hitler Youth members. Over the days that followed, the Soviets rapidly advanced through the city reaching the city centre to capture the Reichstag on April 30 after fierce fighting.

Before the battle was over, German Führer Adolf Hitler and many of his followers committed suicide. The city's defenders finally surrendered on May 2, 1945. However, fighting continued to the north-west, west and south-west of the city until the end of the war in Europe on May 8 (May 9 in the Soviet Union) as German units fought westward so that they could surrender to the Western Allies rather than to the Soviets.

Above: On April 25 US and Soviet troops linked up at the town of Torgau on the River Elbe. This photograph, staged for the press had great symbolism for the Allied world: the handshake of infantry on the demolished bridge showed that a shattered Europe could be restored.

Left: Russian and US officers talk animatedly to Ann Stringer, Universal Press's front line correspondent. Ordered back to Paris on April 25 she instead managed to requisition a military intelligence plane that flew her to Torgau where she tracked down the meeting point of the two armies. She then hitched a ride on a C-47 back to Paris, scooping the story for the world press. The return to Paris would give her mixed feelings as her husband William, a Reuter's correspondent, was killed there during the city's liberation.

Victory in Europe

By mid-April 1945, Russian troops were fighting their way through Berlin street by street, heading towards the Reichstag. Hitler had ordered 'fanatic determination' from all Germans in the defence of Berlin. However, he retreated to his underground bunker on April 16 and began to lose his grip on reality. On April 30, after nominating Admiral Karl Doenitz as his successor and blaming the Jews for the war, Hitler and his new wife Eva Braun committed suicide. On the same day, above ground, the battle for Berlin was won and the Soviet flag fluttered atop the ruins of the Reichstag building. The following day Hitler's propaganda minister Joseph Goebbels and his wife supervised the deaths of their six children before killing themselves. The remains of the German armies now began to surrender and, on May 7, General Eisenhower formally accepted the unconditional surrender of Germany. VE Day was celebrated across the world the following day, but the world was not yet at peace.

MAY 3, 1945

Goebbels Is Dead - Official

Hitler and Goebbels committed suicide. Hans Fritzsche, director of Nazi radio propaganda, gave this dramatic news to the Russians, it was announced in Marshal Stalin's communiqué early to-day.

Fritzsche was taken prisoner with a number of other German military and political chiefs when Berlin was captured, said the communiqué. Fritzsche was described as "first deputy of Goebbels for propaganda and Press." The communiqué went on: "Fritzsche, when interrogated, stated that Hitler, Goebbels, and the newly appointed Chief of the General Staff, Infantry General Krebs, have committed suicide."

No further details of the suicides were contained in Stalin's communiqué, but it is presumed the Soviet authorities will do everything possible to find the bodies and obtain complete proof of Fritzsche's statement.

Last news of Goebbels - who was in charge of Berlin's defence - was on April 22, when he was stated to have declared: "I and my colleagues are of course remaining in Berlin. My wife and children are also here and will remain."

Fritzsche's statement, if true, completely repudiates that made by Admiral Doenitz on Tuesday that Hitler had died at his post "fighting in defence of Berlin."

Top: Troops from the Third US Army move through the Czechoslovakian town of Asch in search of enemy snipers.

Middle right: German civilians turn over weapons to GIs in Usla. Several also hand over Nazi flags.

Right: An American Corporal, assigned to a military police platoon in Germany, holds an inspection of female prisoners at a camp in Magdeburg May 1945. Over 200 women who had been part of the German forces were held there.

Middle inset: The Allies begin to exert powers of civil control, establishing a Military Government in British occupied Germany. The first trials held by the Allies in Germany related to civilians crossing into Holland without authority. This man, Josef Gielen, was sentenced to six months imprisonment for the offence.

Italy, Austria, And Berlin Fall With 1,000,000 Prisoners

The Wehrmacht has collapsed. Berlin has fallen. Hitler and Goebbels are now reported to have killed themselves in the dying capital.

The German armies - 1,000,000 men - in Northern Italy and Western Austria have surrendered unconditionally. The Southern Redoubt has been torn to pieces. And, according to San Francisco reports, surrender in Holland, Denmark and Norway is expected at any hour.

These are the highlights of the war news this morning as Germany totters to complete defeat. Surrender of the shattered remnants of Berlin's garrison was announced in an Order of the Day by Marshal Stalin to Marshals Zhukov and Koniev. The end came at three o'clock yesterday afternoon. By nine o'clock 70,000 German prisoners had been counted.

It was left to General Webling, an obscure artillery commander, to give up the keys of Berlin to the Russians after 11 days' fighting. Stalin's Order described Hitler's former capital as "the centre of German aggression and cradle of German imperialism."

Surrender of the German armies in Italy and Western Austria was announced by Mr. Churchill to a cheering House of Commons. President Truman, giving the news in Washington, said: "Only folly and chaos can now delay the general capitulation of the everywhere-defeated German armies."

In Northern Germany the whole pocket covering the North Sea ports and Denmark is swiftly collapsing. Germans running blindly from the Russians are being swamped. Denmark is cut off. British troops have raced 50 miles across its southern approaches, captured Lübeck, and swept beyond to another Baltic port -Wismar.

Montgomery's British and American forces are storming forward on a 40-miles front to meet Rokossovsky's army. The Russians are less than 28 miles away after seizing Rostock, on the Baltic, and a number of other towns to the south.

Civilians In Chaos

Roads leading from the Lübeck area towards Denmark are an inferno of destruction. British planes, swooping on the fleeing Germans, have smashed more than 1,000 lorries. For miles the highways are cluttered with burning German transport mingled with frantic civilian refugees.

An hour before announcing the fall of Rostock last night, Marshal Stalin reported that the big German pocket south-east of Berlin has crumbled. The Russians captured more than 120,000 Germans.

In the doomed Southern Redoubt, Patton's tanks are closing on the ruins of Hitler's Berchtesgaden "fortress." Swarming into Austria, other Third Army forces are 16 miles from Lina - about 70 miles from the Russians beyond Vienna.

News of the military position in Western Holland is obscure. But food is now pouring in to the hungry Dutch by land and air with full German agreement.

They quibble to the end.

Above: A Russian Red Army infantryman pictured in Berlin after a bitter battle which left more than 100,000 Germans dead and the city a smoking mass of ruins. In the last three weeks in April the Allies took over a million German soldiers prisoner. On the last day of April and with the Russians closing in on the Chancellery, Hitler committed suicide, as a final acknowledgement of Germany's defeat.

Below right: The Allies in Berlin on April 21, 1945. during the battle for the city. Before the main fighting commenced the city was encircled.

Below left: The ruins of the Reichstag, the building which housed the German Parliament, in June 1945.

Chapter Eleven

Defeat of the Axis

Churchill's VE Day speech reminded the world of the urgent task of defeating Japan; the steady advance of Allied forces in the Pacific – on the mainland through Burma and across the ocean through the Philippines and other islands – kept its impetus, despite determined and often suicidal defence by the Japanese. The taking of the island of Iwo Jima in March 1945 had signalled the final phase of the Pacific war, but there was no sign that the Japanese resolve was weakening: on Iwo Jima almost the entire Japanese garrison perished in its defence, a scenario repeated on other islands. At sea, Allied naval ships were subject to continuous Kamikaze raids but these could not deter the advance to Japan which, in spring 1945, was subject to heavy strategic bombing.

On June 21, the island of Okinawa fell, surrendering territory that was Japanese homeland. But the bitter fighting continued. Allied leaders met up on July 17 for the famous Potsdam Conference outside Berlin: Harry S Truman, who had stepped into the presidential role following the unexpected death of Roosevelt in April 1944, met Stalin for the first time and enraged the Russian leader by holding back information on the top-secret Manhattan project that was building the nuclear bomb. The Potsdam Declaration gave an ultimatum to Japan to surrender or be destroyed; together, Truman and Churchill had decided that the atomic bomb would be dropped on Japan if it did not comply. This British commitment stood even though Churchill had to step down during the Conference to be replaced by Clement Attlee, the new British Prime Minister.

The Japanese simply ignored the Potsdam Declaration: they interpreted the terms of the Declaration as taking away their Imperial powers and submitting their leaders to be tried for War Crimes. The die was cast and on August 6 the world changed forever when the first nuclear device was dropped on Hiroshima killing tens of thousands, flattening the city and creating national confusion – but no surrender. The bombing of Nagasaki followed three days later. With some further delaying tactics, the Emperor announced to his people that Japan would surrender, because to do otherwise would result in total annihilation. On August 15, Japan capitulated: finally the world could begin a recovery process that would take years and generations. On VJ Day, jubilant crowds in the Allies' cities around the world began celebrations that would continue in some form or another for over a year, ranging from street parties to Victory parades.

Left: **VE Day in New York. Thousands of people pour into Times Square in celebration of Germany's unconditional surrender.**

Left: Eager soldiers pulling copies of *Stars and Stripes* from the press of the London *Times* at 9pm on May 7, 1945, when an extra edition was put out to announce the news of Germany's surrender. The headline reads 'Germany quits.'

Below: The crowds in Trafalgar Square stand silently listening to the words of King George VI that were relayed from Buckingham Palace to a tannoy system. Ecstatic crowds in the Mall cheered the Royal Family who waved from the Palace balcony.

VE Day - it's all over

London, dead from six until nine, suddenly broke into victory life last night. Suddenly, spontaneously, deliriously. The people of London, denied VE-Day officially, held their own jubilation. 'VE-Day may be tomorrow,' they said, 'but the war is over to-night.' Bonfires blazed from Piccadilly to Wapping.

The sky once lit by the glare of the blitz shone red with the Victory glow. The last trains departed from the West End unregarded. The pent-up spirits of the throng, the polyglot throng that is London in war-time, burst out, and by 11 o'clock the capital was ablaze with enthusiasm.

Processions formed up out of nowhere, disintegrating for no reason, to re-form somewhere else. Waving flags, marching in step, with linked arms or half-embraced, the people strode down the great thoroughfares - Piccadilly, Regent-street, the Mall, to the portals of Buckingham Palace.

They marched and counter-marched so as not to get too far from the centre. And from them, in harmony and discord, rose song. The songs of the last war, the songs of a century ago. The songs of the beginning of this war - 'Roll out the Barrel' and 'Tipperary'; 'Ilkla Moor' and 'Loch Lomond'; 'Bless 'em All' and 'Pack Up Your Troubles.'

Right: Winston Churchill made his historic broadcast to the nation from the Cabinet Room, 10 Downing Street on May 8 announcing Victory in Europe. The King gave a speech from Buckingham Palace to thousands assembled in the Mall and in Trafalgar Square. Churchill and members of his Cabinet then appeared on the balcony of the Ministry of Health to greet the crowds in Whitehall. Ever focused, Churchill addressed the task ahead - to subdue treacherous Japan.

Below : A British sergeant, with his wife and son, is greeted by locals upon his return to a Devon villiage from a German POW camp.

Submerged In Humanity

Rockets - found no-one knows where, set-off by no-one knows whom - streaked into the sky, exploding not in death but a burst of scarlet fire. A pile of straw filled with thunder-flashes salvaged from some military dump spurted and exploded near Leicester-square.

Every car that challenged the milling, moiling throng was submerged in humanity. They climbed on the running-boards, on the bonnet, on the roof. They hammered on the panels. They shouted and sang.

Against the drumming on metal came the clash of symbols, improvised out of dustbin lids. The dustbin itself was a football for an impromptu Rugger scrum. Bubbling, exploding with gaiety, the people "mafficked." Headlights silhouetted couples kissing, couples cheering, couples waving flags.

Every cornice, every lamp-post was scaled. Americans marched with A.T.S., girls in civvies, fresh from their work benches, ran by the side of battle-dressed soldiers. A handful of French sailors lent a touch of Cosmopolis to the scene. Wherever one went, song was in the air.

Half-way up Regent-street the shouts of Piccadilly smote on the ear like a ceaseless machine-gun fire of sound.

Over Buckingham Palace soared aircraft, their navigation lights like coloured stars, while a throng, convinced the Royal Family would not appear, still chanted monotonously and happily, "We want the King."

The police in their wisdom took no steps to check the gaiety the people had earned. Only here and there did a kindly hand fall on an obstreperous shoulder and shift somebody on. The American M.P.s - "Snowdrops" - stood about grinning humorously, good-humouredly, and . . . helplessly.

Flashes of Press cameras stabbed the lurid sky. The whirr of rattles - once to warn us against gas, the single terror weapon not used - confounded the confusion.

And yet - and yet, what a good-humoured crowd! No violence, no stampede, no rough stuff. A kindly crowd, a little drunk, but incredibly more intoxicated with victory than alcohol, cheered and laughed and broke into dance.

Ships in the river sounded their sirens continuously. It went on for two hours.

Wherever there was a piece of derelict land, there was a bonfire.

Main Picture: Spirits ran high in London with the announcement by Winston Churchill on June 8 that the war in Europe was at an end. Westminster and the West End of London filled with jubilant people; forming a human pyramid on a truck held no fear for those who survived the Blitz!

Right: VE Day, May 8, 1945, and people dance in Fleet Street amid the paper thrown from the offices of the major British newspapers.

Below: Crowds gather in the Mall outside Buckingham Palace to cheer the King and Queen and the two princesses on VE Day. After Hitler's death, it was a week before General Jodl signed Germany's unconditional surrender.

Bottom: In streets up and down Britain the flags came out and the people partied.

Right: Winston Churchill in the grounds of Buckingham Palace with King George VI. Churchill would later make several appearances on the royal balcony.

Below inset: In Salisbury Square a family party celebrates with V for Victory signs, flags and streamers made from the tickertape that fed the news to newspaper offices in Fleet Street.

Bottom: Piccadilly Circus at the heart of London, jammed with crowds awaiting the official announcement of VE Day.

Left: As the celebrations gather momentum, the Australian flag is carried. Although fighting continued in the Pacific, VE Day was a time of joy for all the Allied nations.

Middle left: ATS and American soldiers cheer from one of the plinths in Trafalgar Square.

Below: May 8, 1945 was a warm sunny day, reflecting the mood of the nation, and this group was one of many to paddle in the Trafalgar Square fountains.

Top: The King, Queen, Winston Churchill and the Princesses Elizabeth and Margaret appeared on the royal balcony eight times to acknowledge the crowds. Later on in the evening, the princesses left the Palace to join the revellers in the streets.

Above: Churchill, members of the Cabinet and the Chiefs of Staff with the King at Buckingham Palace, which became the centre for much of the celebrations during the daylight hours.

Left: In Piccadilly Circus, adventurous revellers climb the protective shell around the statue of Eros.

Street Parties

While the entire civilian population of Britain celebrated VE day with formal events and neighbourhood street parties, the untold damage of the war needed attention at home and abroad; the work of Allied troops was not over in Europe: the armies of occupation supervised German prisoners, protected civilian populations and aided the restoration of the transport infrastructure and other essential services.

Left: A children's VE Day party in Brockley, South London.

Below: With flags strung between the houses and a 'V' for victory chalked on the cobbles, the residents of this street in Leeds prepare for a VE Day street party.

Above left: Crowds in Oslo turned out to greet the British Military Mission assigned to conduct the surrender of German occupying forces. The night before on May 7, German commander, General Böhme broadcast that his soldiers would obey their capitulation orders and there followed an astonishing turn of events where German troops arrested their SS colleagues as well as prominent Norwegian Nazis; here they are on street duty in Oslo's main square.

Left: The Tricolour of the Netherlands flies again in free Rotterdam, and citizens rejoice after five years under Nazi rule; they crowd onto a Canadian armoured car leading a convoy bringing food to the long-suffering and hungry Dutch.

Below: Wild with delight, the people of Rotterdam run to meet a Canadian column entering the city with supplies, on the day of liberation, victory and relief from five years of German domination.

Left: The streets at the heart of Berlin lie wrecked. Most of the damage was caused by RAF and USAAF bombing raids mounted to destroy defensive positions and offer protection to the ground troops who entered the city in April.

Below: Searchlights which once scanned for enemy aircraft now light up the skies in celebration over the Russian capital, Moscow, as thousands of citizens flock to Red Square on VE Day.

Bottom left: The Soviet Union holds its official victory parade in Red Square, Moscow, on June 24.

Bottom right: Mr. Churchill makes a tour of his Essex constituency. He gives his famous V-sign at Loughton, while Mrs. Churchill shelters under an umbrella.

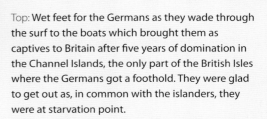

Top: Wet feet for the Germans as they wade through the surf to the boats which brought them as captives to Britain after five years of domination in the Channel Islands, the only part of the British Isles where the Germans got a foothold. They were glad to get out as, in common with the islanders, they were at starvation point.

Above: The U-776 surrendered German U-boat was brought up the Thames to Westminster Bridge yesterday – the first U-boat of the war to be put on view for Londoners.

Above left: Victory crowds celebrating in the streets of Utrecht, Holland, were fired on by Nazi fanatics hiding in a building overlooking the parade. After a sharp skirmish the Germans were captured by Dutch patriots, and the celebrations were resumed. A middle-aged civilian, who was hiding in the building from which the shots were fired, is arrested by men of the Dutch Liberation Forces who left the victory parade and dealt with the incident.

Left middle: Liberation of Copenhagen. The Prinz Eugen German heavy cruiser seen in the docks at Copenhagen. A Danish sentry is on duty in the foreground. The terms of the surrender stated that all German ships should be handed over but in some cases this was delayed.

Left: Liverpool dockers watch the German long-range U-boat 532, first of its type to fall into Allied hands, sail into Gladstone dock after her surrender in the Atlantic. Aboard her were 140 tons of vital war materials, brought from Japan, which the crew began to unload.

Victory in Japan

While victory was being celebrated in Europe, the war against Japan was still raging, but here too the Allies were pushing steadily forward. British forces finally liberated Burma from Japanese control on August 2, 1945, and the American push through the Pacific was bringing US troops gradually closer to Japan.

Roosevelt had died suddenly on April 12 and the new President, Harry Truman, was confronted with the challenging task of winning the war in the Far East. In July 1945, America successfully tested the first nuclear device and it was up to Truman to decide whether this potentially devastating piece of military technology should be used in the Pacific theatre. Truman realized how costly an invasion of the Japanese mainland would be; he had been given a foretaste when an estimated 12,000 Americans died taking Okinawa Island in March. He was also aware that the Allies were exhausted and that many people had lost focus on the Pacific campaign amid the jubilation of the victory in Europe. In addition, the Soviet Union was preparing to declare war on Japan and Truman was keen to stem Stalin's influence in the region. All these considerations encouraged Truman to take the momentous decision to use the bomb.

Top: The scene as troops of the Australian Seventh Division landed east of the Japanese–held Borneo port of Balikpapan, a great oil centre, supported by American ships and aircraft.

Above: Australian forces begin their seaborne landings on the island of Tarakan, Borneo on May 1, 1945. The invasion was well-executed, though there were problems in landing; the Allies had overwhelming numbers by comparison with the Japanese garrison because fierce resistance was expected. Tarakan's oilfields were strategically important and the Allies hoped to make good use of the island's airfield. This picture shows the effectiveness of the modified landing craft that were equipped with rockets; these LCMRs could deliver devastating barrages with lightning speed, just before attacking infantry landed. Pockets of Japanese soldiers held out until June 21.

Above inset: A Japanese tank trap on the beach at Tarakan Island, off the East Coast of Borneo, snares an Australian light tank. Aussie engineers of the Ninth Australian Imperial Forces division try to free it with another tank. A landing craft in the background is made ready to disgorge its valuable cargo.

Left and bottom: Irrawaddy rail-head town, Prome, was liberated after a sharp encounter with a few straggling Japanese who held on while the bulk of their troops in the district were wandering aimlessly and defeated around the wild country south of the town. Allied armoured vehicles on the road to Prome were held up by a river crossing.

Above: Fort Drum, nicknamed the Concrete Battleship, was a defensive installation built on a tiny island in Manila Bay to cover its approaches and the US garrison of Corregidor. The heavily fortified installation bristled with guns and fought hard to resist the Japanese who took it in 1942. When Allied forces recaptured Corregidor in February 1945, Fort Drum remained in the control of the Japanese until April 13 when US forces approached, avoided its heavy guns and landed. A landing craft tanker was called into use and several thousand gallons of an inflammable mixture were poured into the ventilation system and TNT charges set, creating an explosive inferno that wrecked the fort and killed its garrison. In this remarkable photograph, taken by Acme War Pool Correspondent, Stanley Troutman, the LCM can be seen in the foreground while infantry cover the engineers who are feeding the fuel into the vents and setting their charges.

Middle left: While conflict subsided in the European and Mediterranean theatres of war, the Allies remained engaged in fierce and deadly combat with Japan in the Far East. Australian troops were fighting in the jungle of New Guinea under the most difficult conditions resulting in many casualties.

Middle right: Ready for emergency a Bren-gunner takes cover alongside the track of the Western Railway at Labuan Island, Borneo to cover the advance of the 9th Division Infantry.

Far left: A feature of the naval operations off the Sakashima Islands in support of the Okinawa landings was the Japanese suicide aircraft attack. Here, firefighters are busy on board one of H.M. carriers of the British Pacific Fleet after a Japanese suicide plane had crash landed on the flight deck.

Left: Australian soldiers pass the corpse of a dead Japanese soldier killed in the gateway leading to a plantation property on Labuan Island, Borneo.

Ultimate weapon unleashed on Japan

An outcome of the Potsdam Agreement was the Potsdam Declaration which set out the terms for Japan's unconditional surrender. These were sent to the Japanese government by Truman, Churchill and China's President Chiang Kai-shek on July 26. The Japanese government adopted a policy of ignoring the ultimatum because it took away all Japanese sovereignty and reduced its territories as well as threatening the prosecution of war crimes. The response was delivered indirectly by the Japanese Prime Minister in a press conference. The ultimatum was uncompromising in guaranteeing the total devastation of Japan if it did not surrender, but the Imperial forces had no knowledge of the atomic bomb and had already withstood strategic bombing that had destroyed vast areas of some of its cities; the military would rather fight to the death than surrender and leave the Emperor at the mercy of foreign powers.

Above left: The Allied powers called time on the Japanese and sent three B 29 bombers, one of them the Enola Gay, equipped with the 'Little Boy' nuclear device to bomb Hiroshima on August 6, followed by 'Fat Man' dropped on Nagasaki on August 9. The world suddenly became acquainted with the awesome weapon that would dominate military and political reality for generations to come, symbolised in the terrifying mushroom cloud, photographed here over Nagasaki.

Above: The casing of an atomic bomb of the same type as 'Fat Man', on display in the USA.

Left inset: Directly under the Hiroshima hypocentre was a modern ferro-concrete building which was one of the few that remained standing after the blast. A dazed survivor wanders the scorched streets of Hiroshima. In the months and years to come the survivors continued to die, many of them from terrible burns and horrible radiation sickness.

Left: Nagasaki razed to the ground.

City of 300,000 vanishes

Hiroshima, Japanese city of 300,000 people, ceased to exist at 9.15 on Monday morning. While going about its business in the sunshine of a hot summer day, it vanished in a huge ball of fire and a cloud of boiling smoke - obliterated by the first atom bomb to be used in the history of world warfare.

Such is the electrifying report of the American crew of the Super-Fortress which dropped the bomb as a cataclysmic warning to the Japs to get out of the war or be destroyed. Hiroshima, the whole crew agreed, was blotted out by a flash more brilliant than the sun.

They told their astonishing story here at Guam to-day. The explosion, they said, was tremendous and awe-inspiring. The words 'Oh my God' burst from every man as they watched a whole city blasted into rubble. Although they were ten miles away from the catastrophe, they felt the concussion like a close explosion of A.A. fire.

The men had been told to expect a blinding flash. They wore special black goggles. Only three of them knew what type of bomb was being dropped. 'It was hard to believe what we saw.' That was how Col. Paul W. Tibbits, pilot of the Super-Fort, described the explosion.

He said: 'We dropped the bomb at exactly 9.15 a.m. and got out of the target area as quickly as possible to avoid the full effect of the explosion. We stayed in the target area two minutes. The smoke rose to a height of 40,000ft.

'Only Captain Parsons, the observer; Major Ferebee, the bombardier; and myself knew what was dropped. All the others knew was that it was a special weapon. We knew at once we had got to get the hell out of there. I made a sharp turn in less than half a minute to get broadside to the target.

'All of us in the plane felt the heat from the brilliant flash and the concussion from the blast. 'Nothing was visible where only minutes before there was the outline of a city, with its streets and buildings and piers clearly to be seen. 'Soon fires sprang up on the edge of the city, but the city itself was entirely obscured.'

Top: The trio of planes flying towards Hiroshima on August 6 was picked up by Japanese radar and judged to be a reconnaissance flight so no defensive measures were taken. At around 8.15 am, the Little Boy nuclear device exploded about 2,000 feet above the target area in central Hiroshima creating a blaze of light and a shock wave that killed an estimated 70,000 citizens instantly and demolished all of the traditionally constructed buildings in range. In the Enola Gay, co-pilot Robert Lewis asked the question that would be repeated around the world: 'My God, what have we done?'

Above: Both Hiroshima and Nagasaki, though they were important cities for military reasons, were relatively untouched by strategic bombing, which enabled the Manhattan Project's researches to continue in 'real' conditions. Tokyo, pictured, was not so unscathed - fire-bombing had already destroyed vast areas of the capital. The Allies avoided fire-bombing Kyoto but many other Japanese cities such as Nagoya were also devastated, fire-bombs destroying the many wooden buildings, rich with Japan's cultural and religious heritage.

Above inset: A selection of newspapers from across the United States during the week of the bombings.

Right: The devastated city of Tokyo is pictured from the heavily-defended US embassy in September 1945.

The big three
at Potsdam

The Potsdam Conference was held at Cecilienhof,
the home of Crown Prince Wilhelm Hohenzollern,
in Potsdam, occupied Germany, from 17 July to 2
August 1945. Participants were the Soviet Union,
the United Kingdom, and the United States. The
three nations were represented by Communist
Party General Secretary Joseph Stalin, Winston
Churchill and US President Harry S. Truman. They
gathered to decide how to administer punishment
to the defeated Nazi Germany, which had agreed to
unconditional surrender nine weeks earlier, on May
8, 1944. The goals of the conference also included
the establishment of post-war order, peace treaties
issues, and countering the effects of war.

VJ Day Celebrations

Victory in Japan was made official on August 15 and London came to a standstill as celebrations began in earnest. By coincidence, it was also the State Opening of Parliament and the King and Queen's horse-drawn carriage ride to Westminster turned into an impromptu victory parade. In Trafalgar Square a fountain became part of the victory parade!

Left: A London policeman is held aloft by military men from the US and New Zealand in celebration of VJ Day.

Below: This was the scene in Piccadilly at three o'clock in the morning. Celebrations for VJ Day were, if anything, even more unrestrained than those for VE Day. It was the end to a war which for people in Britain had lasted just twenty days short of six years.

Below inset: Service men and women celebrate in Piccadilly.

Top: The Royal Family on the balcony at Buckingham Palace.

Above left: The crowds gathered in Trafalgar Square on VJ Day - everyone had their own way of celebrating!

Above: Eisenhower returns to a hero's welcome as crowds throng Broadway in New York City in the hope of seeing the general.

Left: People throng London streets on August 11 as news of the defeat, if not surrender, of Japan filters through.

Peace

On July 17, 1945 the Allied leaders met at Potsdam near Berlin. Churchill and Stalin met with the new US President, Harry Truman, and during the conference, Churchill was replaced with Clement Attlee, the new British Prime Minister. He had defeated Churchill in a General Election on July 5 with the promise of nationalizing major industries and introducing a welfare state. At Potsdam, the Allied leaders agreed that Germany would be disarmed, 'de-nazified' and divided into four zones of occupation, controlled by Britain, the United States, the Soviet Union and France.

'Iron Curtain'

A final peace agreement was never signed and the Second World War soon gave way to the Cold War. The erstwhile Allies could not agree on the post-war make-up of Europe because of the ideological gulf between them. In southern and western Europe, Britain and America promoted democracy, free trade and anti-Communism, while in Eastern Europe, the Soviet Union imposed centrally planned economies and Communist governments. According to Winston Churchill an 'iron curtain' had descended across Europe. A final resolution to the Second World War in Europe would elude the world until after the fall of the Berlin Wall and the collapse of Communism at the end of the 1980s.

In the Pacific theatre a peace treaty was more forthcoming. Japan was placed under American military occupation from 1945 until 1952. In the early 1950s, the United States had to turn its attention to the war in Korea and sought a peace treaty with Japan. The Treaty of San Francisco was signed in September 1951, officially ending the War in the Pacific when it came into effect the following April.

Top: **Japan signs its official surrender to the British in Burma on September 12, 1945.**

Middle: **Churchill met British military commanders at Berlin airport when he arrived for the Potsdam conference** which started on July 15. The conference continued until the end of the month but by that time Churchill was no longer British Prime Minister. Immediately after the victory against Germany, the coalition government he had led since 1940 was dissolved and a new election called. Churchill's Conservative party suffered a shock defeat as Labour won a landslide victory in a country eager for change. The Labour Prime Minister, Clement Attlee, replaced Churchill at Potsdam.

Right: **In July 1945, the three major Allied powers met again at Potsdam in an attempt to sort out the fine details of the peace process in Europe. The handshake here is the first meeting of Prime Minister Churchill with Harry S. Truman, the new American President.** Tragically, President Roosevelt had died unexpectedly on April 12, 1945, less than a month before Germany's unconditional surrender and as Vice-President, Truman was sworn in.

Above: On a visit to Berlin Churchill rests in a chair that was said to have been in the bunker in which Hitler committed suicide.

Right inset: When the Japanese signed the Allied surrender terms aboard the USS Missouri in Tokyo Bay, HMS Duke of York, flagship of Admiral Sir Bruce Fraser, Commander-in-Chief of the British Pacific Fleet, was alongside. Here, the Japanese interpreter who accompanied the pilot is searched upon his arrival aboard H.M.S. Duke of York.

YOU ARE ENTITLED TO

1 SUIT.   1 TIE.
1 RAINCOAT. 1 HAT.
1 SHIRT.   1 Pr SHOES.
2 COLLARS.   2 Prs SOCKS.

YOU WILL SERVE
YOURSELF.

CIVILIAN EXPERTS ARE
E TO ASSIST YOU.

Top left: Private H. Salter, being measured here, is the first man to claim a 'non-austerity discharge suit'. Austerity Regulations had come into effect in March 1942. Clothing styles which used valuable materials merely for show were not permitted; so double-breasted jackets, turn-ups on trousers and decorative buttons were banned. By the time Private Salter was ready for discharge in October 1944, the war was going well enough for the regulations to be relaxed.

Top right: A happy Private Salter with his complete 'demob' outfit.

Left: Being measured for a 'demob' suit. Many men had been in service for the duration of the war and had not acquired any new civilian clothing for years. Their clothing entitlement was outlined in a poster in the demobilisation centre.

Middle and above: Scenes like this were repeated for the thousands of service personnel returning to 'civvy street.'

Demobilising the armed forces

Nine million American men and women had enlisted in the United States Armed forces during World War II. Following the Axis surrenders, troops were deployed to Japan and Germany to occupy the two defeated nations. Two years after World War II, the Army Air Forces separated from the Army to become the United States Air Force.

At the start of the Second World War the British Army Strength stood at 897,000 men including reserves. By the end of 1939, the strength of the British Army stood at 1.1 million men, and further increased to 1.65 million men during June 1940. By the end of the war and the final demobilisations in 1946, over 3.5 million men had been enlisted in the British Army.

Right: **Sgt Arthur Freund receives his Honourable Discharge, which gave him the thanks of a grateful nation, a substantial cash payment, a service badge for his jacket and his discharge papers. A grand total of 11 million service personnel would follow in his footsteps.**

Below: **Axis POWs are put to work by British forces running feeding centres.**

Below inset: **German prisoners of war who have been attending divine service at Somerton Parish Church near Bury St. Edmunds, photographed at choir practise. They sing their hymns from pencilled carbon copies from a German book.**

Right inset: The smiles of these recently demobilised men speak louder than words.

Living in peace

The end of the war brought enormous relief to the many that survived in its shadow but left millions displaced, bereaved, wounded, scarred psychologically or awaiting release from prison - or the serving of a sentence in the courts of justice assembled by the victors. Some German prisoners had been transported across the Atlantic to labour for the war effort; many of them were content to stay in the countries that had imprisoned them, knowing the deprivations in their native land.

The rubble of Berlin had to be cleared and the civilians of the city set about creating some order, but there was much suffering as the German economy was shattered, the people dazed and afraid of the occupying troops. Food was scarce in Germany and the typical ration for German civilians left many close to starving. However, those that were willing to work, particularly those involved in heavier duties such as construction, fared much better and were paid well enough to supplement their rations, while aiding the reconstruction of their cities.

Above and below: **Berliners, mainly women, work in chain gangs to clear rubble from bomb-sites.**

Left: On traffic duty at the Brandenburg Gate is a 22-year-old Russian woman soldier, Feodora Bondenko, who had marched from Kiev with Marshal Zhukov's forces.

Middle: At a bend in the Kurfürstendamm, in front of the Kaiserin Augusta Gedächtniskirche scarred by Allied bombing, two Berlin women pass by a Russian signpost.

Bottom: A crowd of Berliners wait for a bus in a street just off Potsdamer Platz. Buses were one of the few ways for citizens to get around the city but the service was severely curtailed. Life for the defeated citizens was harsh. They had to set about trying to clear up the wreckage, as much rubble and a damaged vehicles still littered the street. Food, clean water and shelter were all in short supply.

Left: A huge portrait of Josef Stalin hangs outside the Adlon Hotel on Unter den Linden. By the time this photograph was taken in July 1945 it was known that Russia was to occupy almost half of Germany and a sector of Berlin.

Below inset: A citizen of Leipzig reads the *Hessische Post*, a publication produced under direction of the US 12th Army Group.

Bottom: Civilians in Berlin begin to clear the streets of rubble in the Soviet sector under direction from Russian troops.

Right: A series of Victory Parades was held in Berlin: the first was a late celebration of VE Day on July 6, the second, pictured here, was a British celebration that paid homage to Winston Churchill and celebrated the endurance of British troops, such as the Desert Rats who saw action in 1940 and had marched from the Western Desert to Berlin. Churchill attended the event on July 21 with Field Marshalls Montgomery and Brooke, first inspecting the troops then viewing a parade that drove down the crowded Charlottenburger Chaussee. Here the distinctive Sexton armoured vehicles sporting their 25-pounder howitzer guns, are immaculately cleaned and painted for the parade. The last of the Victory Parades involved all the Allied forces in a massive march-past on September 7.

Below: The American Embassy (on the right) and the Brandenburg Gate in Berlin, both bearing the scars of battle.

The Nuremberg trials

Once the war was over, there was widespread agreement that the Nazi leaders should be brought to trial as war criminals. Some of them had escaped in the confusion of the final days of the war, and others, like Goebbels and Hitler himself, had avoided retribution for their actions by committing suicide. Those who had been captured were brought before an International War Crimes Court. This met at Nuremberg in November 1945 and sat for several months, during which time it considered enormous amounts of evidence and heard very many witnesses. Of the twenty-one defendants, three were acquitted, seven received prison sentences ranging from ten years to life and the remainder were sentenced to death. The most notable among those to be executed were Field Marshal Göring and Joachim von Ribbentrop, the German Foreign Minister. Hours before he was due to be hung, Göring committed suicide by swallowing a cyanide capsule which he had managed to keep hidden, but on October 16, 1946 the executions of the others took place. Their bodies, together with that of Göring, were taken to Munich to be cremated and, according to the official announcement, their ashes were 'scattered in a river somewhere in Germany'.

Top: **The defendants listen to the summing-up.**

Left: **Rudolf Hess (left) and Joachim von Ribbentrop during a mealtime at the Nuremberg courthouse.**

Below: **Prisoners in the dock during the Nuremberg trials. Göring is on the far left.**

Top: The verdicts are read out on October 1, 1946.

Left: An armoured car stands guard outside the Palace of Justice on the day before sentencing.

Above: In a very different court scene, thirteen priests and one civilian appeared in a Paris court on July 31 at the opening of a trial in which they were accused of hiding collaborators in French convents.

VE Parade '46

On June 8, 1946 there was an opportunity for formal celebrations in London to give thanks to everyone who contributed to the war effort. A 21,000 strong parade of British and Allied forces as well as civilian workers stretched for twenty miles. King George VI with Queen Elizabeth standing next to him, seen pictured on the page opposite, took the salute at the march-past.

Left: Crowds pack Oxford Street pavements as the parade makes its way from Marble Arch. This view, showing a half-mile of Victory Parade and sightseers, was taken from the roof of the Columbia Hotel.

Below: Troops from India march in the parade. There were representatives from all the nations who fought with the Allies, as well as men and women who gave their efforts to defend the Home Front.

Top right: Side by side on the Royal saluting dais on Victory Day, June 8, 1946, are Prime Minister Clement Attlee (left), alongside Winston Churchill, the man who had led Britain through five years of war. Commonwealth leaders also attended: Mackenzie King, Prime Minister of Canada sits to Churchill's right, with Field Marshal Smuts, the South African Prime Minister, next to him.

Above: The King and Queen taking the salute.

Left: Contingents of military from the Commonwealth march along Whitehall in the Victory Day parade.

Top: On June 16, 1948 a ceremony took place in Cardiff as the remains of over 4,000 American soldiers, most killed during the D-Day landings, were carried onboard the USS Lawrence Victory bound for New York.

Above: The King and Queen, with Queen Mary, Princess Margaret and Princess Elizabeth (behind the King), watch a fly-past by 300 RAF aircraft on Victory Day.

Middle and right: Montgomery at the head of the vehicles in the Victory Day parade is welcomed in the East End among people living in an area which continues to bear the scars of German bombing. Many people were in temporary housing a year into the peace and many would never return, settling instead in the areas to which they had been evacuated.

The World's Biggest Conflict

When the largest conflict the world had ever known finally came to an end, it had claimed the lives of an estimated 55 million people, the majority of whom were civilians. Some 20 million Russians, 10 million Chinese and 6 million European Jews, who were never part of the 100 million mobilised to fight, are believed to have perished. Modern warfare had been characterised by the employment of advanced technologies, which had led to the deaths of civilians across the globe, and had culminated in the use of the atomic bomb, the threat from which continues to overshadow our existence to this day.

Below: Celebratory fireworks make a spectacular display in the night sky over the River Thames giving a suitable climax to Victory Day.

Index

Acknowledgements

The photographs in this book are from the archives of the *Daily Mail*. Particular thanks to Alan Pinnock, Steve Torrington, Dave Sheppard and Brian Jackson.

Thanks also to Sarah Rickayzen, Cliff Salter and John Dunne.

Many Allied service personnel lay buried close to where they fell, killed in action. Few sights are more stirring and sad than the serried ranks of headstones in these haunting places that mark the heroism of those who gave their lives in the face of inhuman conflict. Here on Iwo Jima, in the US Cemetery of the Fifth Marine Division, lie nearly 7,000 American servicemen who died in the capture of this tiny island that became so symbolic to the world.